Group Work
and
Outreach Plans
for
College Counselors

edited by
Trey Fitch and Jennifer L. Marshall

American Counseling Association
5999 Stevenson Avenue • Alexandria, VA 22304
www.counseling.org

Group Work
and
Outreach Plans
for
College Counselors

10   9   8   7   6   5   4   3   2   1

American Counseling Association
5999 Stevenson Avenue • Alexandria, VA 22304

Director of Publications • Carolyn C. Baker

Production Manager • Bonny E. Gaston

Editorial Assistant • Catherine A. Brumley

Copy Editor • Beth Ciha

Cover and text design by Bonny E. Gaston.

Library of Congress Cataloging-in-Publication Data
Group work and outreach plans for college counselors/Trey Fitch and Jennifer L. Marshall, Editors.
    p. cm.
Includes bibliographical references.
ISBN 978-1-55620-311-4 (alk. paper)
    1. Counseling in higher education—United States.   2. Group guidance in education—United States.   I. Fitch, Trey   II. Marshall, Jennifer L.
    LB2343.G67 2011
    378.1´94—dc22
                                      2010048587

This book is dedicated to our first group leaders, Jeri, Jim, and Lynda.

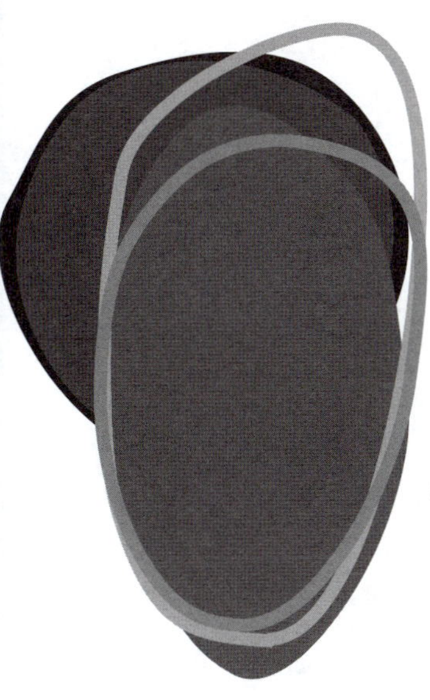

Table of Contents

vi

Part III
Outreach Activities for College Settings

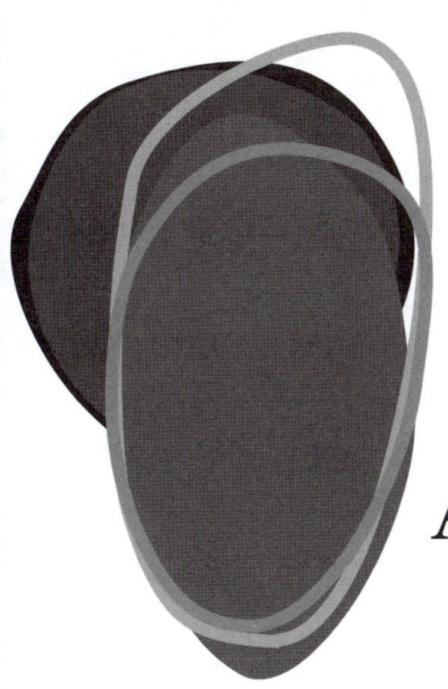

About the Editors

Trey Fitch, EdD, NCC, LPC, is an associate professor of counseling and psychology at Troy University–Panama City. He received a BS in psychology from Troy University, Troy, Alabama; an MEd in counseling from Auburn University, Auburn, Alabama; and an EdD in counseling from Texas A&M University–Commerce, Commerce, Texas. Dr. Fitch has taught counseling and psychology for 12 years and has counseling experience in college and school settings. He has published more than 20 journal articles and book chapters. He coauthored "Group Work Theory" in *The ACA Encyclopedia of Counseling* and "Acting Out: Dramatic Life-Skills Activities" in *The Group Therapist's Notebook: Homework, Handouts, and Activities for Use in Psychotherapy*, edited by Dawn Viers. Dr. Fitch has been an officer of the Association for Specialists in Group Work and is an editorial reviewer for *Counselor Education and Supervision.*

• • •

Jennifer L. Marshall, EdD, LPCC, PCC, NCC, is an associate professor of counseling and psychology at Troy University–Panama City. She received a BA in psychology from Miami University, Oxford, Ohio; an MA in counseling from Heidelberg University, Tiffin, Ohio; and an EdD in counseling from Texas A&M University–Commerce, Commerce, Texas. She was previously director of counseling and psychological services at Berea College, where she led numerous counseling groups. She has authored or coauthored numerous articles on the topics of group and college counseling. Her research interests include online groups dealing with eating issues and self-injury. She is also active with various committees of the Association for Specialists in Group Work and teaches the Group Counseling class at Troy University–Panama City.

About the Contributors

Deepti Athalye, MA, University at Buffalo, The State University of New York

Susan R. Barclay, MS, The University of Mississippi

Rebecca Bartuska, MA, The College of New Jersey

Mary A. Belknap, MS, University of Wisconsin–Stout

Burt Bertram, EdD, Private Practice

Jason Braun, PsyD, Slippery Rock University

Michael D. Brubaker, PhD, University of Cincinnati

Juleen K. Buser, PhD, Rider University

Trevor J. Buser, PhD, Rider University

Jamie S. Carney, PhD, Auburn University

Courtney Clippert, MA, Western Kentucky University

Catherine Cook-Cottone, PhD, University at Buffalo, The State University of New York

Charles R. Crews, PhD, Texas Tech University

Debra Crisp, PhD, Western Kentucky University

Janice DeLucia-Waack, PhD, University at Buffalo, The State University of New York

Richard Driscoll, PhD, American Test Anxiety Association

Suzanne L. Dunn, MS, Argosy University–Atlanta

Trey Fitch, EdD, Troy University–Panama City

Kelly Floyd, MA, University at Buffalo, The State University of New York

Perry Francis, EdD, Eastern Michigan University

Janet Froeschle, PhD, Texas Tech University

Michael Tlanusta Garrett, PhD, Eastern Band of the Cherokee Nation, Counselor and Private Consultant

Kevin Gaw, PhD, Georgia State University

S. Lenoir Gillam, PhD, Columbus State University

Stephen Giunta, PhD, Troy University–Tampa

Dennis E. Gregory, PhD, Old Dominion University

Dana Griffin, PhD, The University of North Carolina at Chapel Hill

Shamika Y. L. Hall, PhD, Western Michigan University

Paul F. Hard, PhD, Auburn University–Montgomery

Miranda Hellenbrand, PsyD, Minnesota State University, Mankato

Whitney A. Hendricks, EdS, University of Florida

Mandy Howard, MEd, University at Buffalo, The State University of New York

Carolyn W. Kern, PhD, University of North Texas

John L. Klem, PhD, University of Wisconsin–Stout

Donald E. Knight, MA, Western Michigan University

Sarah Kuszczak, University at Buffalo, The State University of New York

Eric Manley, PhD, Western Kentucky University

Leslie Markowitz, PsyM, Wright State University

Jennifer L. Marshall, EdD, Troy University–Panama City

Rodney Martin, MA, Western Kentucky University

Kelly A. McDonnell, PhD, Western Michigan University

Kari Much, PhD, Minnesota State University, Mankato

Amy Nitza, PhD, Indiana University–Purdue University Fort Wayne

Perry Peace, EdS, University of Florida

Elaine L. Phillips, PhD, Western Michigan University

Gayle L. Reed, DMin, Private Consultant

Mary Kate Reese, PhD, Argosy University Atlanta

Linda Riccobono, MA, The College of New Jersey

Sherri L. Rings, PhD, The City College of New York

Edil Torres Rivera, PhD, University of Florida

Chester Robinson, PhD, Texas A&M University–Commerce

Dan Rose, PsyD, Columbus State University

Ron Rountree, MDiv, Westminster Baptist Church, Bowling Green, Kentucky

Qi Shi, MS, George Washington University

Allison Smith, PhD, Antioch University New England

Stacy Smyk, MS, Georgia State University

Sheila Soslow, MEd, University of North Texas

Mark W. St. Martin, PhD, Western Michigan University

Sam Steen, PhD, George Washington University

Kevin B. Stoltz, PhD, The University of Mississippi

M. Carolyn Thomas, PhD, Auburn University–Montgomery

Amanda M. Thomas-Evans, PhD, University of Wisconsin–Stout

Brian Van Brunt, EdD, Western Kentucky University

Mara Washburn, PhD, The City College of New York

Martyn Whittingham, PhD, Wright State University

Cyrus R. Williams, PhD, Regent University

Lori A. Wolff, PhD, The University of Mississippi

Mark Woodford, PhD, The College of New Jersey

Ana L. Zevallos, PhD, The City College of New York

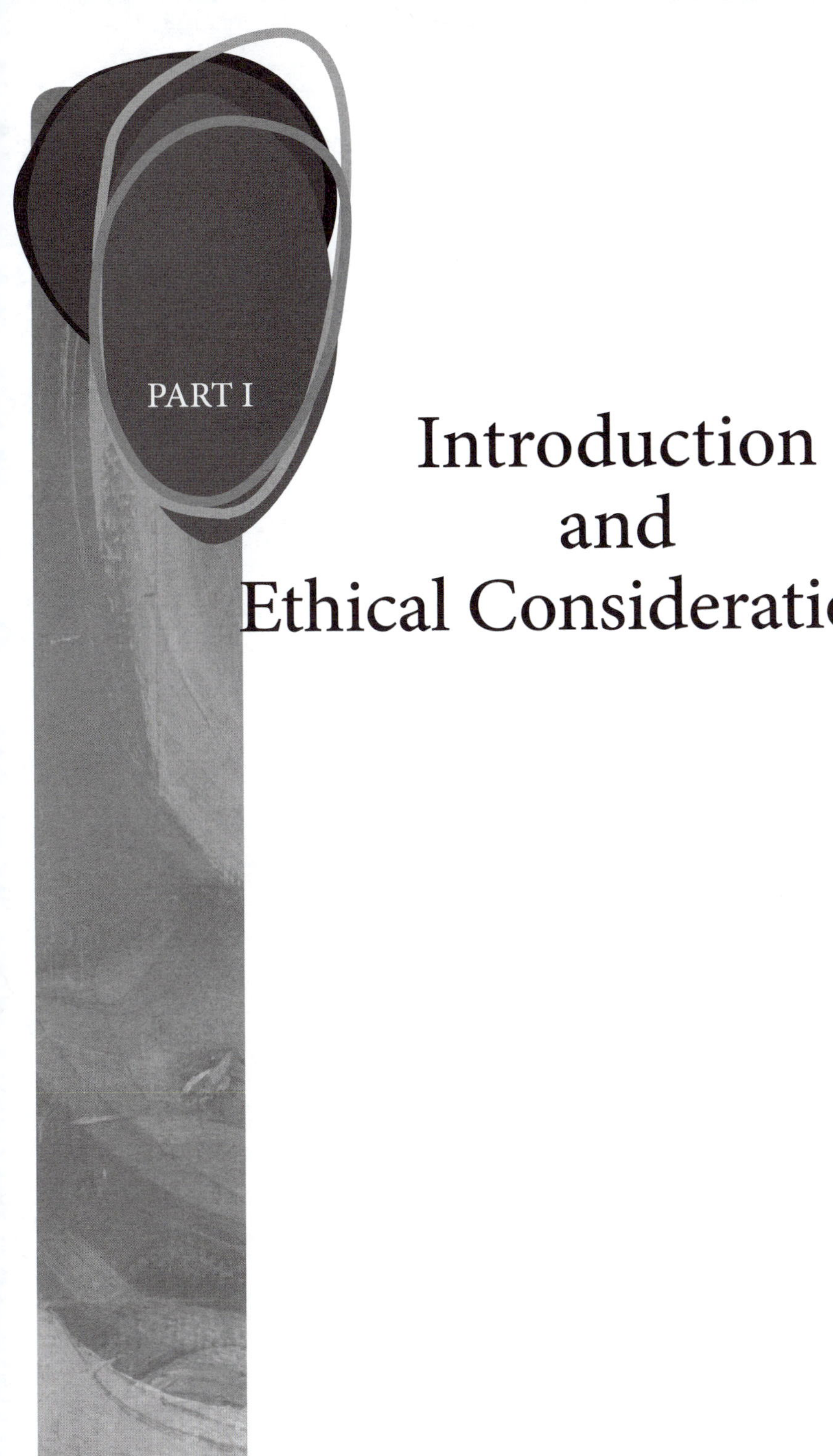

Introduction
and
Ethical Considerations

Introduction

Trey Fitch and Jennifer L. Marshall

College Student Development and Counseling

College can be an inherently stressful time, and college counselors work to help students manage and overcome social, emotional, and academic challenges. Common sources of stress identified by students include social changes and conflict, course workload, poor grades, sleeping and eating problems, financial difficulties, and even vacations (Ross, Niebling, & Heckert, 1999). These challenges, along with more extreme problems such as mood disorders and substance abuse, can impair a student's academic and psychosocial development. The Center for the Study of Collegiate Mental Health (2009) surveyed students using college counseling services; 14% reported that they had used psychiatric medication after starting college, and 6% reported that they had seriously considered suicide after starting college. Daily hassles and these more serious problems not only cause distress but also impede academic achievement. Indicators of mental health problems are related to academic distress, which has been connected to lower grade point averages. Group counseling can be an especially appropriate intervention for addressing these issues with college students (Archer & Cooper, 1998). In this book, a variety of group interventions are proposed to assist students in managing both day-to-day stressors and more severe challenges. Group work is highly effective (e.g., Clarke et al., 2001; Garcia, 2004; Mallinckrodt, 1989) and reaches a broad spectrum of students.

According to developmental models, there are common stressors and developmental tasks for college students. Chickering and Reisser's (1993) developmental model includes seven vectors that outline tasks specific to college-age students. Although this model focuses on traditional-age students, the concepts apply well to all students. Group work is an excellent approach for promoting these areas with college students. The seven vectors are outlined here with examples of how group work can facilitate these tasks.

1. *Developing Confidence: developing intellectual, physical/manual, and interpersonal confidence.* Group work allows students to practice and master novel social interactions, and it produces confidence in interpersonal skills.
2. *Managing Emotions: recognizing, accepting, appropriately expressing, and controlling emotion.* Students can normalize affective responses in groups, leading to greater acceptance. Group members learn from others the best reactions for expressing and regulating emotions.
3. *Moving Through Autonomy Toward Interdependence: increasing emotional independence, self-direction, and problem-solving abilities, as well as recognizing and accepting interdependence.* Group work highlights interdependence in a safe setting, and problem solving is enhanced when multiple perspectives are expressed.
4. *Developing Mature Interpersonal Relationships: developing the capacity for healthy intimate relationships that contribute to a sense of self while accepting and appreciating differences.* Group work teaches students to gain trust and work toward establishing intimate relationships with diverse populations.
5. *Establishing Identity: establishing identity based on feedback from significant others; developing comfort with one's self (physically and emotionally), lifestyle, gender, sexuality, and cultural heritage.* Students get to explore new ideas, perspectives, and people from different lifestyles and cultures in group work. This exploration promotes identity development.
6. *Developing Purpose: developing clear vocational goals and committing to personal interests and activities.* Group work helps students clarify goals and seek deeper meaning in activities and choices. Social interaction allows students to discuss values and plan how to place those values into action.
7. *Developing Integrity: moving from rigid, moralistic thinking to a more humanized personalized value system; acknowledging and accepting the beliefs of others.* Group work exposes students to many perspectives, ones that are often different from their own. Being part of an interdependent group can create more accepting and open attitudes.

Chickering and Reisser's (1993) vectors provide an excellent theoretical framework for group work in a college setting. The social, cognitive, and existential components to group work foster development across all domains of this holistic model. The group plans outlined in this book are designed to address concerns in all of these areas and provide a comprehensive approach to group programming for college counseling centers. In addition to theoretical support, group work in college settings has much empirical support. Throughout this book the authors highlight research that supports the use of group work in a given area. Consequently, this book is meant to be a guide for comprehensive program management for group counseling and outreach on campus settings. Although the group plans are useful individually, they are best used balanced to provide comprehensive services in all domains (e.g., social, emotional, and cognitive).

College Campus Outreach

College counseling centers offer outreach programs to assist in the development of students (Archer & Cooper, 1998). Counselors often provide these important programs to groups such as classes, fraternities and sororities, and student clubs (Marks & McLaughlin, 2005). Outreach programs are typically psychoeducational in nature and often meet for one session; however, they can also meet for multiple sessions. Obviously, providing more sessions can increase the impact of the program. The size and focus of the group distinguish outreach from counseling groups. An outreach group can have as many as 20–40 members (Gladding, 2003), and its goals are based in skills and knowledge. Outreach services are offered to a broad base of students, including those who would not normally use counseling services (Marks & McLaughlin, 2005). Examples of outreach topics include general coping skills (Steinhardt & Dolbier, 2008), test anxiety (Schenk, 1998), and grief and bereavement (Vickio & Clark, 1998).

The psychoeducational model often used with outreach can be preventive/growth oriented or remedial (Gladding, 2003). For example, in this book the outreach program for career development is growth oriented and is applicable to a wide array of students. The eating issues and wellness outreach targets a more defined audience and may seek to help individuals who already have problematic behaviors and attitudes. It is common to use subgroups of 12 students or fewer for skills training (Gladding, 2003). Effective outreach programs use experiential activities and avoid lecture-only formats. At the conclusion of the program, participants should have an opportunity to evaluate the program so that improvements can be made.

Diversity and Group Work in College Settings

The Association for Specialists in Group Work (1999) delineated competencies for understanding how diversity influences group work. These competencies reflect attitude, knowledge, and skills for awareness of self, awareness of group members' worldviews, and understanding of appropriate interventions. These competencies are supported by the substantial demographic changes taking place in colleges. For example, enrollment rates for minority students increased from 2 million in 1980 to more than 4 million in 2000–2001 (American Council on Education, 2003). In the area of self-awareness, the Association for Specialists in Group Work encourages group workers to understand their own cultural influences related to ethnicity, socioeconomic status, gender, sexual orientation, abilities, religion, and spirituality and how these affect the group process. In the area of awareness of group members' worldviews, group workers need to be aware of how these factors in group members affect the group process. For example, how does the racial or gender configuration of the group affect participation? Finally, group workers need to alter their facilitation style and recognize ways to remove cultural barriers to the group process.

In conclusion, group work can help college students develop in many areas. This book is designed as a resource for college counselors offering group work to a variety of students from many different perspectives. The group plans provide comprehensive guidance for the entire process, and the outreach programs described are supported nationwide. The book is meant to provide structure and expert guidance for conducting college counseling groups while recognizing that such guidance does not replace the importance of group facilitation skills and the group process. When planning programs for the year, counselors are encouraged to take a comprehensive view and coordinate all groups and outreach programs in relation to program goals.

References

American Council on Education. (2003, October). *Minority college enrollment surges over the past two decades; students of color still lag behind Whites in college participation*. Retrieved from http://www.acenet.edu/AM/Template.cfm?Section=Home&CONTENTID=3719&TEMPLATE=/CM/ContentDisplay.cfm

Archer, J., Jr., & Cooper, S. (1998). *Counseling and mental health services on campus: A handbook of contemporary practices and challenges*. San Francisco, CA: Jossey-Bass.

Association for Specialists in Group Work. (1999). Principles for diversity competent group workers. *Journal for Specialists in Group Work, 24,* 7–14.

Center for the Study of Collegiate Mental Health. (2009). *Pilot study: Executive summary*. Retrieved from http://ccmh.squarespace.com/storage/2009-CSCMH-Pilot-Report.pdf

Chickering, A. W., & Reisser, L. (1993). *Education and identity* (2nd ed.). San Francisco, CA: Jossey-Bass.

Clarke, G., Hornbrook, M., Lynch, F., Polen, M., Gale, J., Beardslee, W., . . . Seeley, J. (2001). A randomized trial of a group cognitive intervention for preventing depression in adolescent offspring of depressed parents. *Archives of General Psychiatry, 58,* 1127–1134.

Garcia, M. (2004). Effectiveness of cognitive behavioral group therapy in patients with anxiety disorder. *Psychology in Spain, 8,* 89–97.

Gladding, S. T. (2003). *Group work: A counseling specialty*. Upper Saddle River, NJ: Merrill.

Mallinckrodt, B. (1989). Social support and the effectiveness of group therapy. *Journal of Counseling Psychology, 36,* 170–175.

Marks, L., & McLaughlin, R. (2005). Outreach by college counselors: Increasing student attendance at presentations. *Journal of College Counseling, 8,* 86–97.

Ross, S. E., Niebling, B. C., & Heckert, T. M. (1999). Sources of stress among college students. *College Student Journal, 33,* 312–317.

Schenk, L. (1998). *C³: The curriculum for test mastery* (ERIC Document Reproduction Service No. ED423475). Retrieved from http://www.eric.ed.gov/PDFS/ED423475.pdf

Steinhardt, M., & Dolbier, C. (2008). Evaluation of a resilience intervention to enhance coping strategies and protective factors and decrease symptomatology. *Journal of American College Health, 56,* 445–453.

Vickio, C., & Clark, C. (1998). Growing through grief: A psychoeducational workshop series for bereaved students. *Journal of College Student Development, 39,* 621–623.

Chapter 2

Ethics and Legal Issues for Group Work

Burt Bertram

Ethical professional behavior is the foundation upon which good clinical practice is built. This is never truer than when one is serving college students. As noted in Chapter 1, the developmental tasks of traditional college-age students (Chickering & Reisser, 1993) demand that professional counselors and psychologists model the developmental characteristics that college students are striving to attain. Confidence, emotional self-management, appropriate autonomy, mature interpersonal relationships, personal and professional identity development, meaningful purpose, and personal integrity are all integral to the ethical and competent professional counselor. These developmental tasks, combined with the array of adjustment and mental health issues within any traditional college-age population, can create a stew of challenges for group workers. This chapter reviews the typical ethical issues associated with group work and gives special emphasis to the unique ethical challenges and risks of leading groups with college students. However, it does not include an exhaustive discussion of counselor ethics. For a comprehensive discussion of the legal and ethical issues associated with the practice of counseling, including group work, readers are referred to professional association ethics codes (including the *ACA Code of Ethics* [American Counseling Association, 2005]) as well as a number of excellent texts, including Corey, Corey, and Callanan (2011), Herlihy and Corey (2006), Remley and Herlihy (2010), and Wheeler and Bertram (2008).

Standard of Care

Most professional liability lawsuits and licensure board complaints are based on an accusation of failure to practice to the standard of care. Failure to practice to the standard not only places the practitioner at risk but also creates the distinct possibility of harm to the client. What exactly is this standard? The standard is a constantly evolving body of knowledge and experience that increases what is minimally expected of professional counselors. Like a river, the standard of care is fed by many smaller streams of influence, including

1. professional association ethics codes,
2. professional association training standards (e.g., the Association for Specialists in Group Work, 2000),
3. state counseling licensing laws,
4. state statutes (privileged communication, abuse-reporting requirements, mental health and substance abuse services, and many others),
5. federal statutes (e.g., the Health Insurance Portability and Accountability Act of 1996 [HIPAA]; Title 42 Public Health, Part 2, Confidentiality of Alcohol and Drug Abuse Patient Records; the Americans With Disabilities Act of 1990; the Family Educational Rights and Privacy Act of 1974),
6. professional association ethics committee guidance and determinations,
7. research-informed best practices (e.g., the Association for Specialists in Group Work, 2007),
8. case law (e.g., *Tarasoff v. Regents of the University of California*, 1976; and other such landmark cases),
9. insurance and third-party payer influences, and
10. institutional policy (school, agency, or organization).

Of course, in school and college counseling settings the standard of care has also been dramatically affected by the tragic events at Virginia Tech and Columbine High School, as well as the more than 40 other school shootings in which one or more students or faculty have been murdered ("Report of the Virginia Tech Review Panel," 2010).

When clients initiate a complaint to an ethics committee, licensing board, or college administration, the substance of the complaint often rests on the assertion that the practitioner failed to meet the standard of care. One of the first questions that will be asked following a complaint is whether the practitioner was practicing beyond the limits of his or her competence. Too often, counselors are pressured or required (by their employer) to lead groups for which they lack the necessary education, training, experience, and/or supervision. Some of this occurs because group work is sometimes considered to be a secondary activity, somehow less important than individual therapy. This can result in the counselor not being provided the time, or failing to take the time, to properly design and execute the group experience. When counselors do not know how to design or conduct a group, do not take the time to learn, or simply fail to do the required due diligence, ethical and sometimes legal risks are predictable.

The nature of counselor-led group work on a college campus can make it difficult to apply the expected ethical procedures to every group experience. Traditional counseling or psychotherapy groups afford the opportunity of group member screening and a thorough informed consent. However, this can change when (a) the purpose or focus of the group is centered on academic issues, campus adjustment, or psychoeducation; (b) the organization of the group is casual; or (c) the duration of the group is shorter. Under these circumstances, ethical challenges can mount. Difficult though these ethical challenges may be, they are not an excuse for failing to make a good faith effort to apply ethical practices to every group experience. Group leaders are encouraged to think, "What can I do to make the group I'm planning conform to ethical practice?" rather than giving themselves a pass on ethics because the purpose, structure, or format of the group makes some aspects of ethical practice difficult.

Essential Ethical Practices for Groups

Ethical practice is required at all times. However, certain types of groups challenge the group worker's ability to actualize every ethical ideal. Counseling and psychotherapy groups as well as psychoeducational and psychosocial groups should rarely present challenges. These groups can be intentionally designed, members screened (more so for psychotherapy and counseling groups, less so for psychoeducational and psychosocial groups), proper informed consent executed, confidentiality concerns regularly emphasized, and the group worker ready to act on any clinical or ethical dilemma that may surface. These standard ethical procedures become more difficult to implement with groups in which "treatment" is not the stated intention. Orientation and outreach groups, as well as other one-time or drop-in groups, are examples of groups that can present ethical challenges to group workers. Readers are encouraged to consider how they can infuse the following essential ethical principles into the design and execution of every group.

Group Design

Successful groups require planning. One of the primary purposes of this book is to offer an array of options from which group workers can design the group experience that best fits the needs of the students and a group that delivers the desired outcome. The ethical group worker determines the need (e.g., stress management, career exploration, support, counseling, college adjustment) and then designs a group experience that is intentional. When groups are well planned and thoughtfully executed, the group worker is better prepared to proactively address the many ethical challenges that can arise. Therefore, the standard of care will likely be met. Design is not the same for every group and does not necessarily require the creation of a curriculum. For example, growth groups are designed to have minimum content so that the emphasis can be on experiencing the here-and-now interpersonal moment. Most other groups involve more content structure, from just a little to a tight agenda. The ethical group worker can explain the design of the group and how the group will meet the needs of the clients and deliver the desired outcome.

Member Screening

Ideally, all potential members for every group should be screened to ensure that they are appropriate for the group as it has been designed. "Not everyone will benefit from a group experience, and some people may be psychologically harmed by certain group experiences" (Corey et al., 2011, p. 489). For this reason, screening is essential for counseling and psychotherapy groups or for any other group in which it is likely that clients will become emotionally activated. The more potential there is for emotional activation, the more critical the need for prescreening. Group members who are unable to contain their emotional reactivity can create an unsafe and unwelcoming place for other members and may have experiences in the group that they are not ready to understand or process. When prescreening is not possible, group workers should remain ever vigilant to determine whether any members of the group are demonstrating emotional activation and/or interacting inappropriately with other members. Of course there is always a tension in making this determination. Some emotional activation is necessary for learning, and some level of interpersonal tension is an essential element of the group process. Knowledgeable group workers would argue that most such situations are best addressed within the group, for it is in that context that significant learning and growth can occur. However, the ethical group worker is constantly monitoring these variables in the context of the purpose and design of the group to ensure that members do not cross a threshold that can lead to harm to themselves or others. If such concerns arise, group workers must take some action by facilitating the necessary group process, meeting alone with the affected member(s), or, if necessary, removing a member from group.

Informed Consent

The informed consent is the foundation of ethical and legal practice. The informed consent should help the client understand what to expect from the group experience so that he or she can make an informed decision—give informed consent to membership in the group. The *ACA Code of Ethics* (American Counseling Association, 2005) states counselor and psychologist licensing laws, and many institutional policies, require clients to sign an Informed Consent for Treatment. This document confirms that clients consent to participate in treatment and that they understand what to expect from the experience; what is expected of them; the ground rules and exceptions of confidentiality, privacy, and privilege; and any other essential element of the experience (e.g., fees, if applicable). For some college counseling group experiences, the consent process can be somewhat challenging. To be sure, many groups offered by college counseling group workers are not "treatment." So the question arises: Is an informed consent necessary for psychoeducational, psychosocial, orientation, and other information or support groups?

It is probably best to establish a policy within the college counseling center regarding groups that are not traditional treatment groups. The policy might involve providing group members with a written brochure that outlines expectations and defines the limits and exceptions of confidentiality, privacy, and privilege. The policy might also require group members to make an announcement at the beginning of each group that outlines such issues and makes clear that participation in the group is voluntary.

Rarely is there a problem . . . until, of course, there's a problem. Once a problem has surfaced it is certain that a lawyer can be found who will argue that a duty was owed to provide the client with an informed consent. Of course, a defense attorney will argue that an informed consent was not needed for the kind of group in question. Why not resolve this up front? Depending on the purpose and structure of the group, provide participants with a written informed consent or, at the minimum, a verbal explanation. Finally, remember that when policy and procedures are established, they must be followed. The fastest way to exposure is not to follow institutional policies and procedures.

Confidentiality, Privacy, and Privilege

Groups must be safe. Emotional or interpersonal tension is a necessary aspect of group work, but ultimately group workers must do all they can to help create and maintain an environment that is safe enough for members to risk speaking and being known. The promise of confidentiality is a critical element in the creation of a safe environment. When a group is confidential, the group worker will not disclose information gained through the counseling relationship without the permission of the client. Yet absolute confidentiality is difficult to guarantee in a group. Although the group worker can commit to honoring his or her ethical or legal duty to maintain confidentiality, he or she cannot prevent disclosure by other members of the group. It is, however, the group worker's responsibility to discuss the importance of confidentiality, to directly address the issue, and to ask (orally and/or in writing) that members agree to hold in confidence disclosures made by their fellow group members. Group workers are strongly urged to discuss the topic of gossip. One of the developmental challenges of the college-age person is recognizing appropriate boundaries. Group members will likely need assistance in understanding how easy it is to breach confidentiality and the harm that may well be caused to the individual and to the group by doing so. In addition, it is recommended that group workers explain to everyone how some members might want to tell a friend or loved one outside of the group about something they learned about themselves in the group and how this can be done without identifying other group members directly or providing identifying information about them. Group workers must also be ready to readdress issues of confidentiality whenever important disclosures have been made and/or if ever there is even a hint of a breach of confidentiality.

Privileged communication is another important aspect that must be addressed. *Privilege* involves the protection of confidential information between the counselor and the client in the context of a judicial (legal) setting. In other words, clients have the privilege of determining whether the counselor may provide information (records, deposition, testimony, etc.) to the court. It is the client's privilege to *claim* privilege (i.e., the counselor is not authorized to provide information) or *waive* privilege (i.e., the counselor has permission to speak or provide information). Information gained in a group setting can confound privilege. Group workers are to assume that privilege remains absolute unless or until they receive a ruling from a judge (order of the court) that requires them to disclose information. This ruling may come about as a result of a motion filed by the client's attorney, or under certain circumstances the counselor himself or herself may need to retain counsel to file the motion. The receipt of a subpoena is not sufficient to waive privilege communication. In any situation in which the group worker is unsure of his or her legal responsibilities, consultation with an attorney is strongly recommended.

Privacy is a basic right having to do with a person having control over information that is shared about him or her. This concept has gained prominence as HIPAA guidelines have come to define the interaction of patients with health care and mental health professionals. College counseling centers are typically not covered entities under HIPAA. HIPAA compliance issues should be addressed by policy through the college or university legal department. Group workers are encouraged to discuss specific HIPAA compliance responsibilities with the counseling center director and/or student services administrator.

Ethically Challenging Situations

"The primary responsibility of counselors is to respect the dignity and to promote the welfare of clients" (American Counseling Association, 2005, A.1.a., p. 4). The foundational principles of *nonmaleficence* (the avoiding of doing harm) and *beneficence* (doing good for others) compel counselors to remain ever vigilant to create and manage group experiences that reduce the possibility of harm occurring to a member and that maximize the likelihood that members will profit from the experience. Groups present many interesting and challenging situations that require group workers to carefully balance legal and ethical requirements, individual psychological dynamics, and the overall functioning of the group. One of the most important characteristics of an ethical practitioner is his or her willingness to recognize when an outside perspective is needed. Seeking colleague consultation and/or clinical supervision is an essential risk management activity. When difficult or challenging clinical, ethical, legal, or moral issues present, consult, consult, consult!

Breach of Confidentiality

Nothing can derail group cohesion like a breach of confidentiality . . . and it is so easy for group members to breach confidentiality. Group workers must actively protect the sanctity of the interpersonal trust that is the foundation of healthy group process. Confidentiality breaches occur so casually that the offending member may not remember doing it. As mentioned earlier, emotional self-management, mature interpersonal relationships, and personal integrity are but a few of the developmental tasks that might give rise to a thoughtless breach of confidentiality. Combine these developmental tasks with a banquet of possible opportunities for contact outside of the group, sometimes involving alcohol or drugs, and it is not hard to imagine how easy it would be for two group members to gossip about another group member or for one member to make comments about a group member to a mutual friend or acquaintance. If those traditional dynamics weren't challenging enough, now the ubiquitous presence of social media must be factored in. The potential ways in which confidentiality can be breached and the scope of the breach are nearly limitless. Social networking sites, including Facebook, MySpace, Twitter, and the anonymous gossip website collegeabc.com (to name just a few), are factors that must be addressed by group workers proactively during the informed consent process and as part of the norm-setting discussion. Breaches of confidentiality using social media are rarely innocent and can be intentionally malicious. This new ethical challenge must be addressed vigorously because containing and rectifying the damage done through a malicious status update or tweeting of confidential information is likely not possible.

Danger to Self or Others

The impact of a breach of confidentiality, although potentially serious for the client and ethically challenging for the group worker, pales in comparison to the life-and-death consequences of self-harming behaviors, suicide threats and attempts, and threats of homicide. In the wake of the Virginia Tech shooting and other tragic campus events, college counseling will never be the same. A new level of vigilance has become the norm. What does this mean for group workers in the context of leading groups on a college campus?

Ethics, law, and the literature are unambiguous and extensive when it comes to the responsibilities of mental health professionals when they become alert to the possibility of client harm to self or others. When clients make comments during the group or in any other setting that suggest that they are contemplating harming themselves or others, mental health professionals must take action. When danger-to-self comments are made during the group, the group worker must decide to what extent this can or should be addressed by the group or whether it is best addressed privately. The legal and ethical imperative is that danger-to-self-or-others threats must be competently assessed, appropriate action taken, and fully documented. These actions are easier when the group is an ongoing counseling or psychotherapy group and less easy when the group is part of outreach or some other preventive, support, psychoeducational, or psychosocial group. Group leaders should remain ever watchful for behaviors and comments made by group members that might signal a concern. Requesting an immediate private meeting with the student is generally necessary.

Clients who are a danger to others (i.e., by stalking others, threatening others, engaging in domestic violence or homicidal ideations/intentions) must be immediately assessed and addressed. Every college counseling center and student services division should have in place a protocol for intervening when a student makes comments or engages in behaviors that are threatening or potentially threatening to others. Group workers have a vital responsibility, especially in their outreach activities, to help identify and intervene with students who have the potential to become violent.

Summary

Like every professional activity provided by mental health professionals, group work is filled with ethically challenging situations. Group workers have a responsibility to design and implement groups that address real needs and that are intentionally constructed to deliver desired outcomes. In addition, group workers should not allow groups to become ethical stepchildren. Groups deserve the same level of thoughtful preparation, supervision, consultation, and ethical practice as practitioners reserve for individual psychotherapy. In group work this includes prescreening, informed consent, and the creation of group norms that invite respect and safety. In the day-to-day conduct of the group, events will occur that require the group worker to take action. Managing confidentiality, privilege, and privacy in a group can be tricky. Group workers should at all times be mindful of client behaviors that may signal the potential for harm to self or others.

References

American Counseling Association. (2005). *ACA code of ethics*. Alexandria, VA: Author.

Americans With Disabilities Act of 1990, 42 U.S.C.A. § 12101 *et seq.*

Association for Specialists in Group Work. (2000, January 22). *Professional standards for training group workers*. Retrieved from http://www.asgw.org

Association for Specialists in Group Work. (2007, March 23). *Best practice guidelines*. Retrieved from http://www.asgw.org

Chickering, A. W., & Reisser, L. (1993). *Education and identity* (2nd ed.). San Francisco, CA: Jossey-Bass.

Corey, G., Corey, M., & Callanan, P. (2011). *Issues and ethics in the helping professions* (8th ed.). Belmont, CA: Brooks/Cole.

Family Educational Rights and Privacy Act of 1974, 20 U.S.C. § 1232g (2006).

Health Insurance Portability and Accountability Act of 1996, Pub. L. No. 104-191, 42 U.S.C. §§ 201 *et seq.*

Herlihy, B., & Corey, G. (2006). *ACA ethical standards casebook* (6th ed.). Alexandria, VA: American Counseling Association.

Public Health Service Act, 42 U.S.C.A. § 290dd-2 (2007).

Remley, T. P., & Herlihy, B. (2010). *Ethical, legal, and professional issues in counseling* (3rd ed.). Upper Saddle River, NJ: Merrill Prentice Hall.

Report of the Virginia Tech Review Panel. (2010). Retrieved from http://www.governor.virginia.gov/TempContent/techPanelReport.cfm

Tarasoff v. Regents of the University of California, 551 P.2d 334 (Cal. 1976).

Wheeler, A. M., & Bertram, B. G. (2008). *The counselor and the law: A guide to legal and ethical practice* (5th ed.). Alexandria, VA: American Counseling Association.

Group Activities
for
College Settings

Transitions: Connecting and Succeeding on Campus

Amy Nitza, Martyn Whittingham, and Leslie Markowitz

Student retention is a vital issue among colleges and universities across the country, with dropout rates in the first year of college averaging up to 30% and 40% for many types of 4-year institutions (ACT, 2010). Consequently, much effort has gone into identifying the factors that contribute to student engagement and persistence through the first year of college. Although a great deal of emphasis has been on the role of academic factors, a number of nonacademic factors contribute to student persistence throughout the first year of college as well.

Well-known student development theories have articulated a role for nonacademic factors as contributors to student retention. Astin (1996) argued that student involvement with peers as well as with academics and faculty contributes to student engagement and retention. Similarly, Tinto (1993) argued that students' social integration along with their academic integration contributes to persistence and retention. These theories are now increasingly supported by a large body of empirical research. A meta-analysis showed that alongside the established role of academic factors such as goals and prior scholastic performance, social support and social involvement are also key variables in college retention (ACT, 2004). As the ACT Policy Research advisory panel stated, "Students who master course content but fail to develop adequate academic self-confidence, academic goals, *institutional commitment, and social support and involvement* may still be at risk of dropping out" (p. vii, emphasis added). Therefore, in order to improve student retention, colleges and universities must target first-year students' need for social support and involvement alongside their efforts to improve academic success.

The psychoeducational group described here is designed to supplement and expand on student retention programs by addressing the social and interpersonal skills underlying successful engagement with the college experience. It is designed to offer an initial connection to the institution and to provide a sense of social support while helping students develop and practice the interpersonal skills necessary for continued success. Students will explore their own interpersonal style and learn or enhance the skills necessary to work through interpersonal problems or barriers that may hinder their college experience. Specifically, the goals of the group are to

- facilitate the development of self-awareness of members' own interpersonal style and skills,
- identify and explore how members' interpersonal style and skills may impact their experience on campus,
- facilitate the development of new skills necessary to increase members' potential for success on campus,
- facilitate the development of a social support network within the group itself to increase members' initial sense of connectedness to campus, and
- facilitate the identification of other sources of academic and social support to be called on when needed.

Group Outline

This group is structured so that the sessions that introduce new content (Sessions 2–5) each has a self-assessment for group members to complete at the beginning of the session. There is no scoring or interpretation for these assessments; they are simply prompts that are intended to help members begin to reflect on their own interpersonal styles, patterns, and preferences. The ideas raised in each assessment are then expanded on in the rest of that session. Some sessions also make use of handouts to deliver specific information. All self-assessments and handouts are provided at the end of the chapter.

Group Plan

Session 1: Introduction
- Introductions activity
- *What to expect:* Brief explanation of the goals and structure of the group
- Development of ground rules
- Cohesion-building activity (see DeLucia-Waack, Bridbord, Kleiner, & Nitza, 2006, for possible activities to be used here)
- Facilitate a discussion of members' perceptions of what it will take to be successful in college and what they perceive as potential barriers to success.

- Introduce the importance of social support and engagement as well as the importance of having the interpersonal skills to persevere through the many interpersonal challenges that will come their way.
- *Closing:* What is one thing you would like to get out of this group or one barrier you perceive for yourself that you might like to explore?

Session 2: Reaching Out: Initiating New Relationships

- Opening check-in
- Have members complete Handout 3.1.
- *Review members' responses:* This can be done using a version of a "vote with your feet" activity in which students move to different spots in the room based on their responses to the self-assessment. For each question, the leader designates a spot in the room that represents each possible response. Members move to the spot that best represents them. They can then be invited to verbally explain or elaborate on their responses if they so choose. Suggested questions follow; many others are possible.
- Do you generally consider yourself
  - shy?
  - outgoing?
- Do you generally prefer
  - seeking out people who are very similar to you because it is more comfortable?
  - seeking out people who are different from you because it is energizing?
  - waiting for other people to seek you out?
- Are you most comfortable with other people in
  - one-on-one situations?
  - small groups of two or three?
  - large groups?
  - none—you are most comfortable alone
- Processing the activity
  - Based on your responses, what kinds of situations are going to be the best for you to make connections with new people on campus?
  - What situations are going to be the most challenging?
  - What makes it easy for you to reach out to someone?
  - What makes it hard?
  - What about adults or people in authority (professors, advisors, etc.)? What makes it easy or hard to reach out to them? When would you know you needed to seek them out even if you were nervous about it?
- Making changes
  - Based on the discussion today, are there any changes you would like to make or skills you would like to develop in order to successfully connect with others on campus?
  - Encourage members to share ideas, skills, and experiences with one another.

- *Closing:* What is one new thing you learned about yourself today, or what is one thing you would like to do differently based on the discussion today?

Session 3: Maintaining and Deepening Relationships

- Opening check-in
- Facilitate a brief opening discussion around the following ideas: Going away to college often means leaving behind close friendships while also trying to form new ones. Many of the old relationships were developed over a long period of time. Developing new close relationships on campus will also take time. Sometimes students would prefer to stay connected to their old network of friends and do not work too hard to make connections on campus. Other students are excited to have the opportunity to develop a new set of friends. Often, the way people go about trying to make new friends is based on their past experiences in close relationships.
- Have members complete Handout 3.2.
- Review members' responses.
    - What did you learn about yourself or become aware of in answering these questions?
    - Where do you stand currently in terms of *wanting to* and/or *trying to* forge new relationships on campus?
    - Do you see any barriers to making close friendships on campus?
- *Practice:* Autobiography activity
    - *Directions:* Take 5 minutes to get to know the person sitting next to you. Think about what you want to share about yourself from your life story. This might include where you come from and grew up, major interests, or unique life events. Try and find things that are interesting about you. Also, try to reveal something about yourself that is *slightly* more than you might normally reveal.
- Process what members experienced in the activity.
- *Closing:* What is one new idea you could take away from the day's session that might be helpful to you?

Session 4: Support: Giving and Receiving

- Opening check-in
- Have members complete Handout 3.3.
- Review members' responses.
    - What did you learn about yourself by considering these questions?
    - Did you notice any patterns?
    - Was there anything that surprised you?
- Taking a closer look
    - Distribute Handout 3.4 and ask each member to find which category best fits their own perception of themselves for both giving and receiving.
- Process members' responses.

- How and to what extent do cultural norms influence your style?
- How and to what extent do family norms influence your style?
- Explore how members' styles interact with one another in the group and how this might also apply to their relationships outside the group.
- In what ways or in what circumstances is your style a strength?
- In what ways or in what circumstances does your style get in your way?
- Effective interpersonal styles require both balance and flexibility depending on the circumstance. What if anything would you like to change? Who in the group might you be able to learn from?
- Making changes
  - In terms of receiving support, are you content with your current style, or would you consider it too little or too much? Is there anything you would like to change?
  - In terms of giving support, are you content with your current style, or would you consider it too little or too much? Is there anything you would like to change?
  - If you do want to make any changes, who in the group might you be able to learn something from? What about outside the group?
- *Closing:* What is one thing you are taking away from the group today that might apply to your life this week?

Session 5: Managing Conflict

- Opening check-in
- Have members complete Handout 3.5.
- Review members' responses.
  - What did you notice about yourself in answering the questions?
  - How would you generally describe your approach to handling conflict and/or confrontation?
  - How do you think you might have developed this style?
  - Are there times when your style is a strength? A barrier?
  - What, if anything, would you like to change about your style?
- *Situations for practice:* How would you address the following situations:
  - Asking a professor for extra time to complete a paper
  - Not allowing a roommate to play loud music at night when you have an exam the next day
  - A friend asking you to help him or her cheat on an assignment
  - Leaders can ask for other examples to use as practice or facilitate a role play that allows members to think through and practice the application of the skills to the situation. See "Note to Leaders" below.
- *Closing:* What is one new idea you are walking away with today that you could apply to your life between now and next week? What is one new skill or idea about dealing with conflict that you learned from someone else in this session?

Note to Leaders: This session is intended to provide an opportunity to practice applying conflict management skills. As with any of the sessions in the group, members who indicate a need for further work on a specific personal issue should be referred to a university counseling center.

Session 6: Tying It All Together

- Facilitate a brief review of the topics covered in the group and the major points of interest that have arisen for members over the past five sessions.
- Sticky situations activity
  - Provide all members with a slip of paper and ask them to write down a situation they have found difficult to manage or for which they would like some feedback and ideas. This can be done anonymously. Collect all responses and put them in a container in the center of the group.
  - Have members take turns drawing a situation from the container and reading it aloud.
  - Facilitate a discussion of possible options for dealing with each situation using the material covered in the group as well as the members' own experiences.
- *Closing:* What are the most helpful ideas from the past weeks that you need to keep with you this year after the group has come to a close?

Note to Leaders: As described for Session 5, leaders must provide enough structure and guidance in this session to allow for meaningful discussion that allows members to connect personally with the ideas without delving too deeply into personal issues or allowing any one individual's situation to monopolize the session.

Session 7: Termination

- Ask members to reflect on the most beneficial aspects of the group experience for them.
  - What did you learn?
  - How did you learn it?
  - How can you apply what you have learned as you continue through your first year of college and beyond?
- Encourage members to share feedback with one another.
  - What growth or progress did you see other members make?
  - How have they impacted you personally?
  - What wishes do you have for them as they continue through their first year of college?
- *Planning for the future:* What sources of support will you use or seek out now that the group has ended?

Note to Leaders: Many activities can be used to facilitate the goals of this final session. See Delucia-Waack et al. (2006) for several examples.

References

ACT. (2004). *The role of academic and non-academic factors in improving college retention.* Retrieved from http://www.act.org/research/policy-makers/pdf/college_retention.pdf

ACT. (2010). *College student retention and graduation rates from 2000 through 2009.* Retrieved from http://www.act.org/research/policymak-ers/pdf/09retain_trends.pdf

Astin, A. W. (1996). Involvement in learning revisited: Lessons we have learned. *Journal of College Student Development, 37,* 123–133.

DeLucia-Waack, J. L., Bridbord, K. H., Kleiner, J. S., & Nitza, A. (2006). *Group work experts share their favorite activities: A guide to choosing, planning, conducing and processing* (Rev. ed.). Alexandria, VA: Association for Specialists in Group Work.

Tinto, V. (1993). *Leaving college: Rethinking the causes and curses of student attrition* (2nd ed.). Chicago, IL: University of Chicago Press.

Handout 3.1

Initiating New Relationships

Mark each statement below as being more *true* (T) or more *false* (F) for you.

☐ T ☐ F 1. My past friendships have begun mostly because of my efforts.

☐ T ☐ F 2. It is highly anxiety-provoking for me to initiate a conversation with a stranger.

☐ T ☐ F 3. I tend to isolate myself from others.

☐ T ☐ F 4. I am too shy to begin a conversation with someone unless I know them very well.

☐ T ☐ F 5. I prefer to meet people one-on-one rather than in big groups.

☐ T ☐ F 6. Many of my past friendships developed because I put myself in a situation where I could meet new people.

☐ T ☐ F 7. If I feel lonely I usually seek out opportunities to connect with others.

☐ T ☐ F 8. After meeting someone, it is easy for me to build a friendship.

☐ T ☐ F 9. I am not used to making contact with people from backgrounds different from my own.

☐ T ☐ F 10. I would like to get to know people from backgrounds different from my own.

Handout 3.2

Maintaining and Deepening Relationships

Mark each statement below as being more *true* (T) or more *false* (F) for you.

☐ T ☐ F 1. I have no difficulty building and keeping friends.

☐ T ☐ F 2. My friendships are mostly casual and rarely move beyond a superficial level.

☐ T ☐ F 3. I trust my friends and believe that they will not betray me.

☐ T ☐ F 4. In past relationships, I have felt valued and understood.

☐ T ☐ F 5. My friends rarely ever see the "real" me.

☐ T ☐ F 6. I would describe my current friendships as deep and meaningful.

☐ T ☐ F 7. My friendships tend to be long lasting.

☐ T ☐ F 8. I would like to make deeper connections with people from different backgrounds.

☐ T ☐ F 9. Sometimes I think superficial first impressions get in the way of getting to know people properly.

☐ T ☐ F 10. I often keep people at a distance.

Handout 3.3

Support: Giving and Receiving

Mark each statement below as being more *true* (T) or more *false* (F) for you.

☐ T ☐ F 1. When I am struggling with something in some part of my life, I prefer to handle it on my own rather than ask others for help.

☐ T ☐ F 2. When I need support, I am confident that my friends will be there for me.

☐ T ☐ F 3. I am someone people turn to when they are in trouble or struggling in life.

☐ T ☐ F 4. Sometimes I have spent too much time trying to help others and have had a hard time setting limits with them.

☐ T ☐ F 5. Sometimes I wish it were safer to open up to people.

☐ T ☐ F 6. I would like to be able to help others but don't always know what to say or do.

☐ T ☐ F 7. I would like to understand the struggles of people from backgrounds different from my own.

☐ T ☐ F 8. I often wish people understood my struggles better.

☐ T ☐ F 9. I don't always know when I need help or support.

☐ T ☐ F 10. I would like to get help from others when I need it but have a hard time asking.

Handout 3.4

Support: Giving and Receiving

	*Independent?**	*Mixed?**	*Interdependent?**
Give	People should keep their issues to themselves and not bother me	I can be there for friends as needed but I can also look after myself in the process	If a friend had a minor problem I would stay up all night to listen, even if I had an important exam the next day
Receive	I would never confide in a friend, even if my suffering was unbearable and affecting my daily life in major ways	I can reach out for help when I need it but I don't overwhelm friends with my problems	I would call a friend at 3 a.m. with a minor problem, even if they had an important exam the next day

*Note. These are moderated by the effects of culture and should not be taken as right or wrong for everyone. Every culture has a distinct style of giving and receiving support, and this should be taken into account in this exercise. Please fill this out with respect to the norms of your cultural background (i.e., what you grew up believing to be true). You may then wish to compare your answers against the norms of other group members to see where your learned style connects and disconnects. Please remember, no one cultural style is better than another—this table is only *one* representation of what is appropriate in certain situations in certain cultural settings. Please also note that context and situations are *all important*—what is "normal" in one situation is unusual or different in another.

Handout 3.5

Managing Conflict

Mark each statement below as being more *true* (T) or more *false* (F) for you.

☐ T ☐ F   1. Sometimes it is important to avoid a conflict.
☐ T ☐ F   2. When I have a conflict it is always loud and heated.
☐ T ☐ F   3. When in a conflict I try and keep my cool.
☐ T ☐ F   4. I am uncomfortable trying to deal directly with conflict.
☐ T ☐ F   5. In the past I have had relationships end because of an unresolved conflict.
☐ T ☐ F   6. The only thing that matters in a conflict is winning.
☐ T ☐ F   7. It is more important that I get my point across than listen to the other person.
☐ T ☐ F   8. I would like to understand how people from backgrounds different from my own can experience and see the same event differently.
☐ T ☐ F   9. Growing up, I learned to always confront people directly about issues.
☐ T ☐ F 10. Growing up, I learned to never confront people about issues.

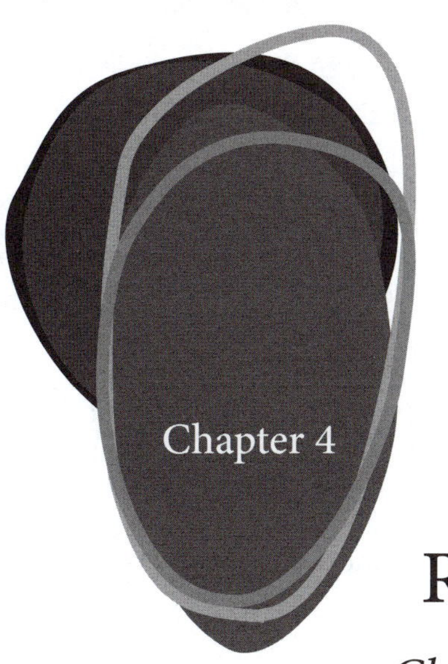

The Test Anxiety Reduction Program

Charles R. Crews, Janet Froeschle,
and Richard Driscoll

"Time is up! Drop your pencil and close your test booklet. Do not open your test booklet for any reason. A test administrator will circulate around the room and pick up your materials. Once your booklet has been gathered, please remain in your seat until you are dismissed."

"Thank goodness it's over. I couldn't remember anything, even though I studied so hard. I really thought I was having a heart attack during the test; my heart was beating so quickly, my palms were sweating, and I couldn't catch my breath! Maybe I do have test anxiety."

• • •

Test anxiety is a reaction to test taking that may have dramatic effects on a person's ability to prepare for a test or examination, take the test, and earn a given score (Cizek & Burg, 2006). Research on the treatment of test anxiety focuses on anxiety reduction in order to improve stress management. One effective approach to the treatment of test anxiety is psychoeducational group work. This chapter discusses the Test Anxiety Reduction Program, a 6-week multimethod psychoeducational group for the management of test anxiety in college students.

Tests have been used for many years to help track student ability. Excessive test anxiety reduces the ability of a test taker to perform well on a test even though he or she is capable of earning an adequate score. Test anxiety continues to warrant attention in the educational setting (Cizek & Burg, 2006). Because test anxiety is a stress response to being in a testing situation, the physical response is similar to a fight–flight choice. Well-documented research shows that test anxiety takes a serious toll mentally and physically on the body. Zettle and Raines (2000) wrote that women report higher levels of test anxiety than men. Thus, attention should be paid to both gender and individual differences in test anxiety.

Although one ordinarily thinks of anxiety as physiological overarousal combined with worry and dread, it is the performance impairment aspect that is especially troublesome for students and educators alike. In the group described here, students use the Westside Test Anxiety Scale (Driscoll, 2004) to measure their level of anxiety. The Westside scale is primarily an impairment measure meant to screen students for anxiety-impaired performance. The scale items cover self-assessed anxiety impairment and maladaptive cognitions, which can impair performance, but not physiological overarousal, which is only modestly related to impairment. Similar to other more familiar scales, the scale identifies about 16%–20% of students as test anxious. After anxiety reduction treatment, improved (lower) scores on the scale have been found to correlate with improved academic performance, with changes in Westside scale scores accounting for as much as 20% of the change in scores on various objective tests. The 10-item scale is brief, is easily scored, and is available to the public for no charge. It is thus a highly suitable instrument for identifying anxiety-impaired students who could benefit from intervention (see http://TestAnxietyControl.com/research for further information and ongoing research).

Group Plan

Session 1: Introduction

- *Overview.* To introduce the group and disclose group process. To complete Handout 4.1.
- *Goals.* Participants will identify attitudes and behaviors that lead to test anxiety.
- *Supplies.* Members will need chart paper, folders, pens/pencils, and a baseline anxiety scale. Ask participants to bring a three-hole puncher and a three-ring binder to keep handouts for the group organized.
- Introduce yourself and describe the purpose, time, and location of the group. Have group members introduce themselves, establish ground rules, and discuss the limits of confidentiality pertaining to various state and national standards.
- Explain the process of the group, introduce the topic of test anxiety, and challenge participants to think about the effect of test anxiety on themselves and their test scores.
- Initiate discussion on what participants expect to learn or offer to the group. Ask volunteers to illustrate their test anxiety by describing how they react physically to test anxiety, how the anxiety affects their test-taking skills, and what changes, if any, could be made.
- Encourage participants to think about how to improve their study environment in terms of location and distractions.
- Give participants a baseline anxiety scale (Handout 4.1) to determine their current anxiety levels. Discuss the results with the group. Ask

questions such as the following: (a) Tell me about your experience taking this scale. (b) What do you think of your score? Is it accurate? (c) What was your anxiety level taking this scale? (d) What score would you like to see as a result of participating in this group?

- For homework, have participants investigate an upcoming exam in terms of the number and types of questions and time limits. The results of this homework will be shared with the group.

Session 2: Exploring Catastrophizing and Expectations

- *Overview.* To identify catastrophic thoughts and learn to substitute rational expectations.
- *Goals.* Participants will learn how to identify and avoid catastrophic thoughts and optimize performance and test-taking expectations.
- *Supplies.* Members will need blank paper and colored markers or pencils.
- Review the homework assignment from the previous week and discuss the nature of catastrophizing.
- Review details gleaned from participants' research on anxiety-producing examinations.
- Define *catastrophizing.* Help participants learn to optimize performance and test-taking skills by eliminating catastrophic thinking.
- Have participants study and discuss strategies for decatastrophizing and embrace tools to reduce anxiousness.
- Have participants talk about their biggest fears associated with taking the test.
- Observe participants' irrational beliefs, and process the beliefs in the group.

Session 3: Identifying Emotional and Physical Responses Related to Test Anxiety

- *Overview.* To explore causes of test anxiety as well as the emotional and physical responses triggered by anxiety. To practice various anxiety reduction techniques.
- *Goals.* Students will learn to recognize the emotional and physical responses triggered by test anxiety and will learn methods for controlling these responses.
- *Supplies.* The group will need paper, pencils, and a whiteboard or chalkboard.
- Review the following ideas using Handout 4.2:
  - Some anxiety is good for the production of complex cognitive tasks, but too much is detrimental (Hopko, Hunt, & Armento, 2005). The two main causes of test anxiety are unfamiliarity with the test and a feeling of nonmastery of the material (Educational Testing Service, n.d.).
  - Negative thinking, mythical beliefs about testing, physical manifestations of anxiety, physical and emotional tension, the testing environment, and a wandering mind contribute to test anxiety.

- Have the participants share knowledge of the test they are taking or ones that cause them the most anxiety.
- Have group members practice techniques to reduce test anxiety: relaxation techniques, long-term relaxation techniques, self-talk, and thought-stopping techniques.

Session 4: Preparing for Testing and Enhancing Performance

- *Overview.* To learn general test preparation skills, which include tools for successful test-taking preparation, anticipating test content, tips for better test taking, and emergency test preparation.
- *Goals.* Participants will learn test preparation skills to reduce anxiety and enhance performance.
- Have participants review and discuss how to relax for tests (see http://www.helpguide.org/mental/stress_relief_meditation_yoga_relaxation.htm) and discuss a tool for emergency test preparation (Handout 4.3).
- Have students share successful tools they have used to prepare for an exam, such as using study checklists; identifying all of the material they will be tested on; breaking up the studying into organized, manageable chunks; using summary notes, "maps" recording notes, and significant portions of text on audio; and creating flashcards for memorizing definitions, formulas, and so on.
- Have group members practice exercises to use when anxiety arises while preparing for a test.
- Have each participant share how he or she will prepare for the next test in order to enhance his or her performance.

Session 5: Creating Personal Plans for Testing With Reflection on Process

- *Overview.* To identify steps for handling stress when the warning signs of test anxiety are noticed.
- *Goals.* Participants will develop a personal, systematic approach to test taking. Participants will discuss how they currently prepare for an exam. They will then identify at which point in the process they feel the most anxiety. Finally, the participants will identify the signs of test anxiety in order to enact coping strategies learned in this group.
- Review the signs of test anxiety and techniques to reduce test anxiety (see http://www.helpguide.org/mental/stress_relief_meditation_yoga_relaxation.htm).
- Have participants identify the warning signs they feel when experiencing test anxiety. Then have them select three activities to do when they recognize the signs of text anxiety.
- Begin the Personal Test Anxiety Reduction Plan while attaining feedback from the group.
- For homework, have participants complete a Personal Test Anxiety Reduction Plan and bring a nutritional snack to share with the group that helps reduce physical symptoms of anxiety.

Session 6: Coping With Future Test Anxiety Issues, Closing the Group, and Preparing for Follow-Up

- *Overview.* To learn to distinguish between rational and irrational test anxiety. To improve personal perspective of the test-taking experience. To gain knowledge of basic biological, emotional, and social needs.
- *Goals.* The participants will review their personal plans for dealing with future test anxiety.
- Generally speaking, everyone experiences some level of nervousness or tension before tests or other important events in their lives. A little nervousness can actually help motivate people; however, too much of it can become a problem—especially if it interferes with a person's ability to prepare for and perform on tests.
  - Share My Plan of Action to Reduce My Test Anxiety (Handout 4.4).
  - Share nutritional snacks.
  - Complete the posttest anxiety scale (Handout 4.1).
  - Review the results of the posttest.
- Have participants commit to making a change as evidenced by their Personal Test Anxiety Reduction Plan.

References

Cizek, G. J., & Burg, S. S. (2006). *Addressing test anxiety in a high-stakes environment.* Thousand Oaks, CA: Corwin Press.

Driscoll, R. (2004). *Westside Test Anxiety Scale.* Retrieved from http://www.amtaa.org/scalewest.html

Educational Testing Service. (n.d.). *Reducing test anxiety.* Retrieved from http://www.ets.org/Media/Tests/PRAXIS/pdf/01361anxiety.pdf

Hopko, D., Hunt, M., & Armento, M. (2005). Attentional task aptitude and performance anxiety. *International Journal of Stress Management, 12,* 389–408.

Zettle, R., & Raines, S. (2000). The relationship of trait and test anxiety with mathematics anxiety. *College Student Journal, 34,* 246–258.

Handout 4.1

Westside Test Anxiety Scale

Rate how true each of the following is of you from *extremely or always true* to *not at all or never true*. Use the following 5-point scale:

5 = *extremely or always true*   4 = *highly or usually true*   3 = *moderately or sometimes true*
2 = *slightly or seldom true*   1 = *not at all or never true*

_______ 1. The closer I am to a major exam, the harder it is for me to concentrate on the material.

_______ 2. When I study, I worry that I will not remember the material on the exam.

_______ 3. During important exams, I think that I am doing awful or that I may fail.

_______ 4. I lose focus on important exams, and I cannot remember material that I knew before the exam.

_______ 5. I finally remember the answer to exam questions after the exam is already over.

_______ 6. I worry so much before a major exam that I am too worn out to do my best on the exam.

_______ 7. I feel out of sorts or not really myself when I take important exams.

_______ 8. I find that my mind sometimes wanders when I am taking important exams.

_______ 9. After an exam, I worry about whether I did well enough.

_______ 10. I struggle with writing assignments, or avoid them as long as I can feel that whatever I do will not be good enough.

Scoring

_______ Sum of the 10 questions

_______ Divide the sum by 10. This is your Test Anxiety score.

What does your test anxiety score mean?

1.0–1.9	Comfortably low test anxiety
2.0–2.5	Normal or average test anxiety
2.5–2.9	High normal test anxiety
3.0–3.4	Moderately high (some items rated 4 = *high*)
3.5–3.9	High test anxiety (half or more of the items rated 4 = *high*)
4.0–5.0	Extremely high anxiety (items rated 4 = *high* and 5 = *extreme*)

Handout 4.2

Yerkes-Dodson Law

The Yerkes-Dodson Law (Yerkes & Dodson, 1908) predicts an inverted U shape as a function between arousal and performance (see chart below). As arousal increases, performance increases, but in the absence of arousal, performance decreases. Thus, if there is too little arousal (anxiety) or too much arousal, a person's ideal performance is reduced. Sometimes too much arousal can actually prevent someone from studying, and the person may become cognitively paralyzed. Have participants discuss and list on the whiteboard some physical and mental signs that may indicate that a person has test anxiety (Crews, 2006).

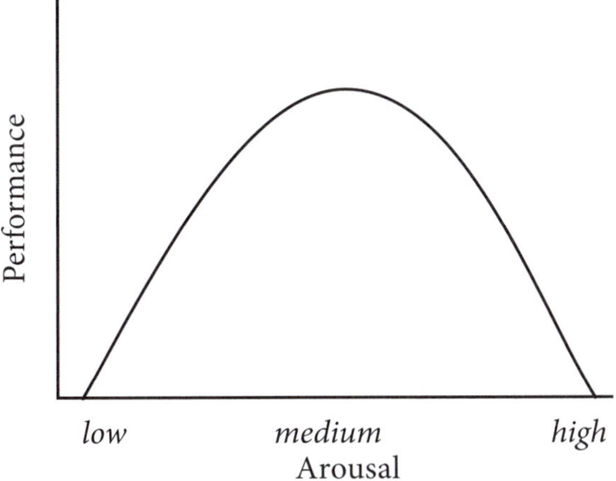

References

Crews, C. R. (2006). The relationship between personal strain and special education teacher perceptions of collective teacher self-efficacy: Implications for counselors. *Dissertation Abstracts International, 67*(12), 4463. (UMI No. 3245227)

Yerkes, R. M., & Dodson, J. D. (1908). The relationship of strength of stimulus to rapidity of habit formation. *Journal of Comparative Neurology and Psychology, 18,* 459–482.

Handout 4.3

A Planned Method of Cramming

Prioritize

- Quickly review each chapter and decide what the most important themes and key points are (testtakingtips.com, 2010).

Organize

- Write down the main points on a flashcard or notebook paper. Limit the main points to about five to nine, because this is how many you will most likely be able to memorize for each list you organize (Miller, 1956).
- Define and explain each concept, and then rank order them in importance.

Learn/Memorize

- For each main concept, write down your own explanation and definition without using the book or your notes. Do this in order of importance.
- Compare your responses to the ones from the book and your notes, checking for accuracy.
- Redo any answers that were incomplete or inaccurate until you understand the main concepts.
- Repeat this method with the lists of key concepts for each main concept.

References

Miller, G. A. (1956). The magical number seven, plus or minus two: Some limits on our capacity for processing information. *Psychological Review, 101,* 343–352.

Testtakingtips.com. (2010). *Cramming tips.* Retrieved from http://www. testtakingtips.com/

Handout 4.4

My Plan of Action to Reduce My Test Anxiety

1. A list of my personal stressors with my emotional and physical reactions to them.

   ____

   ____

2. Which stressors can I change?

   ____

   ____

3. The methods I can use to diminish the intensity of my stressors over a period of time rather than on a daily or weekly basis.

   ____

   ____

4. I will take the following actions whenever I feel stressed:

   ____

   ____

5. What strategies will I use to make a positive change?

   ____

   ____

6. When I do the following, my emotional reactions to stress will be decreased:

   ____

   ____

7. A list of measures I will use to diminish my physical reactions to stress.

   ____

   ____

8. I will do the following to increase my physical resources:

   ____

   ____

9. I will preserve my emotional assets when I do the following:

   ____

   ____

10. After I finish my next exam I will reward myself with the following:

    ____

    ____

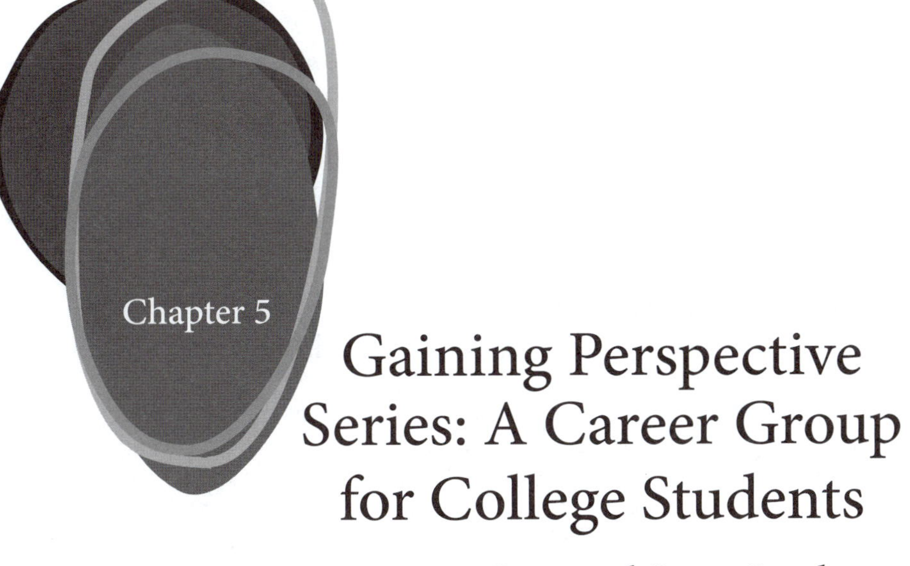

Gaining Perspective Series: A Career Group for College Students

Kevin Gaw and Stacy Smyk

The Gaining Perspective Series (GPS) was developed based on key career, group, and student development theories. Several of Yalom's therapeutic factors (Yalom & Leszcz, 2005) leverage the small-group environment for career development and personal growth over the classroom setting. First, past GPS participant feedback has suggested that the installation of hope is highly valued by participants, as it influences the degree of student optimism about career goal achievement, which increases by the termination of the series. Second, because personal results from activities and assessments are voluntarily disclosed and discussed in the group, interpersonal sharing and learning, as well as trust building, occurs in each session. Finally, self-understanding and universality are evident in that participants articulate insights into their personalities and experience validation from the shared experience with other students in the group (Yalom & Leszcz, 2005). For these group dynamic reasons, the career group is an extremely viable format.

Chickering and Reisser's (1993) psychosocial theory of college student development details vectors relating to identity formation in the college environment. Anticipating student need in the GPS group, leaders should be especially familiar with the fifth and sixth vectors of Establishing Identity and Developing Purpose. Awareness of one's self-concept, values, and lifestyle affects the development of one's career identity. Therefore, it is essential to create content that helps a student explore his or her personality, interests, values, and skills as a foundation of identity leading to the sixth vector of purpose in terms of career choice (Chickering & Reisser, 1993).

Super's theory of vocational stages across the life span sheds additional light on the student participants' frame of career mindedness and development (Zunker, 1994). Not only are students in an exploratory stage, but many are between crystallization (developing and planning a tentative career goal) and specification (firming up the chosen career goal). Overall, students are working toward a sophisticated vocational self-concept, and the GPS group is designed to increase knowledge of the self and of the work world so that career identity can become clearer and more solidified.

Group Plan

Session 1: Introduction

- Review expectations, attendance, confidentiality.
- Agenda summary with homework due dates.
- In the first session, students are given a blank piece of paper with the outline of a shirt. Students are invited to draw pictures and write words that describe personal characteristics, hobbies, and goals. Completed shirts are shared individually within the group.
- Discover the college majors of several celebrities, and have students guess which celebrity matches which major.
- For homework, have students complete the Self-Directed Search (Holland, 1994) at the college counseling or career center.

Session 2: Self-Knowledge

- Review the results of each member's Self-Directed Search and explain Holland's (1992) six-factor typology: Realistic, Investigative, Artistic, Social, Enterprising, and Conventional.
- Have group members complete Handout 5.1.
- After the group members complete Handout 5.1, have them choose 5–7 different career-related values, such as variety and time with family. Have the members write these values on index cards and then walk around the room and attempt to trade and bargain with other students for desired value cards. As group leader, you may also hold several popular value cards until the end and trade each one to the student who raises his or her hand the fastest.
- Discuss the results of the values card activity and the implications for career choice.
- Make the connection between career interest results and values, and discuss the importance of considering both factors with career choice.
- For homework, have students complete the Myers-Briggs Type Indicator (Myers & Myers, 2004) at the career center and bring the results to the next meeting.

Session 3: Self-Knowledge

- Complete Handout 5.2 on the work environment and discuss the results.
- Have each member review the results of his or her Myers-Briggs Type Indicator and the implications for his or her career choice.

- Discuss the strengths and weaknesses of members' profiles with regard to different careers.
- For homework, have students complete the Strong Interest Inventory (Donnay, Morris, Schaubhut, & Thompson, 2004; Grutter, Hammer, & Prince, 2004) and bring the report to the next meeting.

Session 4: Assessment Interpretation

- Review the results of the Strong Interest Inventory and compare and contrast them with previous assessments (Myers-Briggs Type Indicator, Self-Directed Search).
- Discuss the results of the Strong Interest Inventory with regard to career choice.

Session 5: Information Gathering

- Review career research tools at the career center, including SIGI (System of Integrated Guidance and Information, n.d.) and the *Occupational Outlook Handbook* (Bureau of Labor Statistics, 2010).
- Have group members research 3–5 careers of interest using the *Occupational Outlook Handbook* and present what they learned about requirements, pay, and job outlook.
- For homework, have students interview one person who works in a career of interest and be prepared to discuss what they learn in the next group meeting.

Session 6: Evaluation and Decision Making

- Process the results of the informational interviews.
- Create an action plan worksheet that includes goals, objectives, and deadlines for further career exploration (e.g., classes to take, possible internships, and an outline of new skills needed for certain careers).
- Review resources from the career center and academic advising.
- Ask group members to review their plans with the group, and conclude the group by asking students to discuss what they have learned during the entire group process.

References

Bureau of Labor Statistics. (2010). *Occupational outlook handbook, 2010–11*. Retrieved from http://www.bls.gov/oco/

Chickering, A. W., & Reisser, L. (1993). *Education and identity* (2nd ed.). San Francisco, CA: Jossey-Bass.

Donnay, D. A. C., Morris, M. L., Schaubhut, N. A., & Thompson, R. C. (2004). *Strong Interest Inventory* manual: Research, development, and strategies for interpretation*. Mountain View, CA: Consulting Psychologists Press.

Grutter, J., Hammer, A. L., & Prince, J. P. (2004). *Strong Interest Inventory* and Myers-Briggs Type Indicator* career report with Strong profile and Strong college profile*. Mountain View, CA: Consulting Psychologists Press.

Holland, J. L. (1992). *Making vocational choices: A theory of vocational personalities and work environments* (2nd ed.). Odessa, FL: Psychological Assessment Resources.

Holland, J. L. (1994). *Self-Directed Search.* Lutz, FL: Psychological Assessment Resources.

Myers, P. B., & Myers, K. D. (2004). *Myers-Briggs Type Indicator: Profile form M.* Mountain View, CA: Consulting Psychologists Press.

System of Integrated Guidance and Information (SIGI^3) (n.d.). [Computer software]. Tucson, AZ: Valpar International.

Yalom, I., & Leszcz, M. (2005). *The theory and practice of group psychotherapy* (5th ed.). New York, NY: Basic Books.

Zunker, V. G. (1994). *Career counseling: Applied concepts of life planning* (4th ed.). Pacific Grove, CA: Brooks/Cole.

Handout 5.1

Values Ranking

Please rank your top 5 values, with 1 representing your most important value.

__________	Make lots of money
__________	Job security
__________	Autonomy/independence
__________	Work with people you like
__________	Convenient location
__________	Health and financial benefits
__________	Interesting and engaging work
__________	Make a contribution to society
__________	Innovation and creativity
__________	Opportunities for advancement and professional development
__________	Recognition and achievement
__________	Challenge
__________	Power/influence
__________	Flexibility
__________	Work–life balance
__________	Variety of tasks
__________	Leadership role
__________	Meaning and fulfillment in work
__________	Prestigious organization or job title

Handout 5.2

Work Environment

How would you describe your preference?

Slow to medium to fast pace

____

Teamwork vs. independent tasks

____

Mobility (inside office vs. other settings)

____

Structure and procedure vs. creativity (completing assignments)

____

Internal vs. external client interaction

____

Variety vs. predictability (daily workflow)

____

Relocate vs. stay local

____

What else would be present in your ideal work environment?

____

Chapter 6

Career Development Through Career Construction Counseling: A Group Method

Susan R. Barclay, Kevin B. Stoltz, and Lori A. Wolff

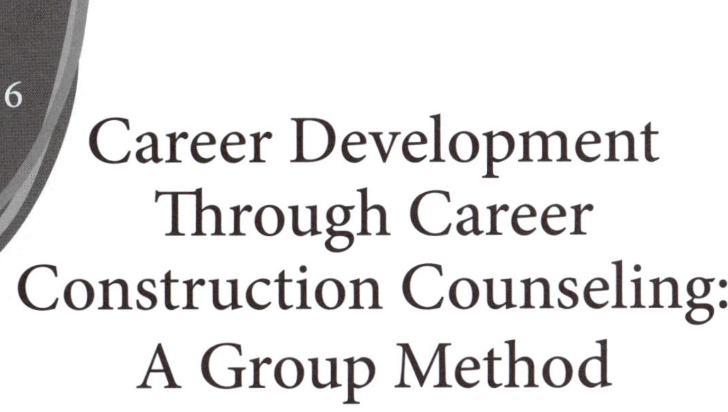

Group counseling is an approach that is applicable to career exploration and development (Anderson, 1995; Cochran, 1984; Proehl, 1995; Pyle, 2007). However, group career counseling models have not referenced recent changes in the career paradigm. Brown (1998), Ebberwein, Krieshok, Ulven, and Prosser (2004), Hall (1996), Ruffolo (1993), and Wise and Millward (2005) have all suggested that the traditional cycle of finding a single career that represents the self-concept and that lasts throughout the life span is not relevant in today's new economy. Thus, group career counseling models and approaches must reflect the changing work environment. This chapter describes an approach to group career counseling that links interventions to the new concepts of the protean career (Hall, 1996).

E5 groups (Wingett & Milliren, 2008) are counseling groups designed to provide *empowerment* to individual group members in an "atmosphere characterized by *equality*, *empathy*, *encouragement*, and *education*" (p. 494, italics added). These E elements are based on the individual psychology theory of Alfred Adler (1979) and serve as the foundation for all of the group meetings. Believing that individuals face life challenges and resolve difficulties more successfully in a group counseling setting that focuses on the personal strengths and assets of the individual group members, Wingett and Milliren developed this highly structured group to facilitate a process of self-discovery around life themes and problem solving. In addition to emphasizing the five E elements, group meetings follow "principles of respect, routine, rules, rights, and responsibilities" (Wingett & Milliren, 2006, p. 1), all established at the outset of the meetings.

Embedding the Career Style Interview Within the E5 Group Framework

The effectiveness of group counseling for career exploration and development is well documented (Anderson, 1995; Cochran, 1984; Proehl, 1995; Pyle, 2007). Although Wingett and Milliren (2008) developed the E5 group format and script as "a structured psychoeducational group experience" (p. 494) for adults and adolescents, the same format is appropriate for use in developmental career counseling with college students of all ages. Replacing the E5 script with the Career Style Interview (Savickas, 1998) within the E5 group framework (Wingett & Milliren, 2008) and extending the group session by an additional week offers an excellent opportunity to assist students in understanding and supporting the adaptable worker self. In addition, use of the E5 framework involves all group members in the process of identifying and communicating assets and strengths to fellow group members, which, according to Luft (1984), permits each member to learn about abilities, qualities, and aptitudes that were previously imperceptible to him or her. Keeping in mind that the primary intention of E5 groups is "to empower others and self" (Wingett & Milliren, 2008, p. 498), using the Career Style Interview in the E5 group setting produces an ideal space in which students can support and encourage one another as they redevelop and strengthen their career self-concepts in the adaptability paradigm. The E5 format supplies the structure and the Career Style Interview provides the exploratory guide for supporting and growing personal career adaptability (Handout 6.1). This process allows for the engagement of each member in his or her own career and life planning process.

Group Plan

Session 1: Group Introductions and Orientation
- Introduce yourself.
- Facilitate the introduction of group members (the use of an activity, perhaps a career-oriented activity, is appropriate).
- Review the consent form with group members and secure informed consent.
- Review ethical issues for the group.
- Establish group rules together.
- Ask each member to identify and briefly discuss a specific career challenge that he or she is facing.
- Just prior to ending the meeting, solicit and answer any questions or concerns group members have.

Session 2: Interview of Group Member 1

- Remind members of the previously established group rules (1–2 minutes).
- Answer any questions or concerns group members have (5 minutes).
- Ask for a volunteer to sit in a chair facing you.
- Ask the remaining group members to form a semicircle (with their chairs in a horseshoe shape) around the volunteer.
- Ask the remaining group members to listen for themes, strengths, and assets in the responses the volunteer gives to the interview prompts. Group members should remain quiet during the interview but may make notes regarding items they hear.
- Remind the group of the previously identified career challenge the volunteer is facing.
- Conduct the Career Style Interview (Handouts 6.1 and 6.2) with the volunteer. Throughout the interview, listen for themes, strengths, and assets in the responses of the volunteer.
- Upon completion of the interview, ask the volunteer for feedback as to his or her experience with the process and any themes, strengths, and assets that he or she heard or identified during the interview.
- Solicit feedback from the group members, asking them to identify the themes, strengths, and assets they heard during the interview. Allow for a lot of time in this activity because group interaction is limited during the other activities.
- Ask a member of the group other than the volunteer to write these items on the board or flip chart.
- Ask the volunteer to respond to the lists of items on the board.
- Ask the volunteer to identify 5–7 of the items that are new or a surprise to him or her.
- Ask the volunteer to explain how he or she over- or underuses some of the items.
- Finish by collaborating with the volunteer in narrating a story with a hero, challenge, and outcome and discuss how the narration relates to career adaptability for the volunteer.

Sessions 3–7: Interview of Group Members 2–6

- Sessions 3–7 are identical to Session 2 other than the fact that there is a different volunteer each week. In addition, there is no need to review the group rules after the second meeting (unless violations of the rules occur). Continue to rotate the volunteers in such a way that every group member is interviewed.
- As the group proceeds, search for common themes from different interviews and attempt to make connections.
- Although this format is highly structured, keep in mind group process observations and feedback.

Session 8: Debriefing and Closing

- Facilitate a conversation with group members regarding the total group experience.
- Ask each group member to share what was most meaningful to him or her and how that has clarified his or her career direction. Use this as a closing activity and ask whether any member has anything else he or she wants to tell the group at the end.

References

Adler, A. (1979). *Superiority and social interest.* New York, NY: Norton.

Anderson, K. J. (1995). The use of a structured career development group to increase career identity: An exploratory study. *Journal of Career Development, 21*(4), 279–291.

Brown, B. (1998). *Career mobility: A choice or necessity?* (ERIC Document Reproduction Service No. ED414436). Retrieved from http://www.eric.ed.gov/PDFS/ED414436.pdf

Cochran, D. (1984). Group approaches. In H. Burck & R. Reardon (Eds.), *Career development interventions* (pp. 124–140). Springfield, IL: Charles C Thomas.

Ebberwein, C. A., Krieshok, T. S., Ulven, J. C., & Prosser, E. C. (2004). Voices in transition: Lessons on career adaptability. *The Career Development Quarterly, 52,* 292–308.

Hall, D. T. (1996). *The career is dead—Long live the career: A relational approach to career.* San Francisco, CA: Jossey-Bass.

Luft, J. (1984). *Group process: An introduction to group dynamics.* Palo Alto, CA: National Press Books.

Proehl, R. A. (1995). Groups in career development: An added advantage. *Journal of Career Development, 21*(3), 249–261.

Pyle, K. R. (2007). *Group career counseling: Principles and practices.* Broken Arrow, OK: National Career Development Association.

Ruffolo, J. F. (1993). Voluntary midlife career change: A study of factors associated with voluntary midlife career change among professionals in urban and suburban southern California. *Dissertation Abstracts International, 54*(10), 5412B. (UMI No. 9407220)

Savickas, M. L. (1998). Career style assessment and counseling. In T. J. Sweeney (Ed.), *Adlerian counseling: A practitioner's approach* (4th ed., pp. 329–359). Philadelphia, PA: Accelerated Development.

Wingett, W., & Milliren, A. (2006). *E5 group: First session guide.* Unpublished manuscript.

Wingett, W., & Milliren, A. (2008). Psychoeducational E5 groups for use in schools. *Journal of Individual Psychology, 64,* 494–505.

Wise, A. J., & Millward, L. J. (2005). The experiences of voluntary career change in 30-somethings and implications for guidance. *Career Development International, 10,* 400–419.

Handout 6.1

Understanding the Career Style Interview

Question to Volunteer	Underlying Question	Underlying Process
Who do you admire? Who would you like to pattern your life after? If you could become anyone, who would it be? How are you like this person? How are you unlike this person?	What is your self-concept?	Exploration and attachment
What magazine, books, or television shows do you prefer? Why? What is it that attracts you to these?	What environments do you prefer?	Understanding how the world is organized
What do you like to do in your free time? What are your hobbies? What do you enjoy about these hobbies?	What are you getting ready to do?	Implementing developing aspects of the self-concept
What is your favorite saying or motto?	What steps are you taking to address your preoccupations?	Conducting autotherapy
What were your three favorite school subjects in high school? What subjects did you dislike? What subjects did you like? Why?	What talents do you like to exercise and avoid? Why?	Differentiating the aspects of the self-concept
What are your earliest recollections? What are the three earliest stories you recall about things happening to you when you were 3–6 years old?	What's eating at you? What are you trying to overcome? What matters most to you? What is your preoccupation?	Using the self-concept to resolve a core suffering or challenge

Note. Adapted from handouts provided for *Career Construction Counseling: Principles and Practice*, by P. Hartung, M. Savickas, H. Briddick, C. Briddick, S. Burns, K. Glavin, . . . B. Taber, 2008, July, presentation at the annual conference of the National Career Development Association, Washington, DC.

Handout 6.2

Career Style Interview

1. Who did you admire when you were growing up? Who would you like to pattern your life after? Name three heroes/role models:

    a. What did you admire about each of these heroes/role models?
    b. How are you like each of these persons?
    c. How are you different from each of them?

2a. What magazines do you read regularly?

    • What do you like about each of these magazines?

2b. What television shows do you really enjoy or view regularly?

    • What do you enjoy about each of these shows? Why?

2c. Tell me about your favorite movie/book.

2d. Tell me about your favorite website(s).

3. What do you like to do with your free time? What are your hobbies?

    a. What do you enjoy about these hobbies?

4. What is your favorite saying or motto? What is a saying/motto you remember hearing?

5. What were your favorite school subjects in high school? Why? Explain.

    • What subjects did you loathe or dislike strongly? Why? Explain.

6. Take a moment and tell me the three earliest incidents you can recall from your childhood.

    a. What is the "snapshot" moment in each incident?
    b. If a story is published in tomorrow's newspaper, what would the headline be for each incident?

Note. Adapted from handouts provided for *Career Construction Counseling: Principles and Practice*, by P. Hartung, M. Savickas, H. Briddick, C. Briddick, S. Burns, K. Glavin, . . . B. Taber, 2008, July, presentation at the annual conference of the National Career Development Association, Washington, DC.

Chapter 7

A Group Intervention for First-Generation College Students

Sherri L. Rings and Mara Washburn

Earning a college degree has become increasingly necessary for many careers and for upward social mobility. As college and university enrollments have increased, so has the number of first-generation college students (Engle & Tinto, 2008). Definitions of *first-generation college student* vary. Some definitions include only students from families in which neither parent pursued any education beyond high school, whereas others include students whose parents may have attended some college but did not earn a bachelor's degree. Research shows that regardless of the definition used, students from families in which neither parent earned a bachelor's degree are less likely to earn a bachelor's degree themselves. Among high school seniors who graduated in 1992 and enrolled in college between 1992 and 2000, only 24% whose parent(s) never attended college and 39% whose parent(s) attended some college earned a college degree compared to 68% whose parent(s) earned a bachelor's degree (Chen, 2005).

Many factors likely contribute to the low retention and graduation rates of first-generation college students. Demographically speaking, such students are likely to be older, to be female, and to come from minority and low-income backgrounds (Chen, 2005; Engle & Tinto, 2008). Low-income students are at particular risk for dropping out. In fact, 60% of low-income first-generation students (i.e., those with an annual family income less than $25,000) who leave postsecondary education do so within the first year, and their 6-year graduation rate is only 11% (Engle & Tinto, 2008).

Researchers have described a host of disadvantages that impede first-generation students from completing a degree (e.g., Chen, 2005; Engle & Tinto, 2008; Hsiao, 1992; Pascarella, Pierson, Wolniak, & Terenzini, 2004). For example, these students are likely to enroll in less selective institutions (e.g., community colleges), be less prepared academically when entering college, withdraw from and repeat more classes, complete fewer credits, stop out (e.g., take a semester off and then come back), and earn lower grades. They also are more likely to attend college part time, live off campus, and have work and family responsibilities that limit the amount of time they spend on campus.

For first-generation students, attending college can be a time of transition and separation from the past. They might feel like they are straddling two cultures—college versus friends and family (Cushman, 2007; Hsiao, 1992). Parents, siblings, and friends who have no college experience may not support them and may even hinder their efforts to earn a college degree (Hsiao, 1992). Furthermore, compared to their peers with college-educated parents, first-generation students are less likely to benefit from parents' social connections, knowledge of how to successfully navigate the college environment, and understanding of why a college degree is important.

A 7-session group plan for first-generation college students is outlined here, although group content may vary depending upon the needs of group participants. The overarching goal is to provide a supportive, informative environment in which first-generation students can openly share experiences, discuss stressors, and learn strategies for achieving academic and social success in college. This group is designed as a closed group—participants who start the group will be expected to attend all sessions, and no new participants will be added after the group starts. Participants in the group should be students whose parents either never attended college or attended some college but never earned a degree.

Group Plan

Session 1: Concerns of First-Generation College Students

- Have the group facilitators introduce themselves and describe their professional backgrounds, the general group format, and their role within the group.
- Discuss group ethics and expectations (e.g., members are expected to attend all groups and participate, information shared by members is confidential and is not to be shared with others outside of the group, members should be respectful of one another).
- Ask group members to introduce themselves.
- Ask members to share what brought them to the group (e.g., some of their concerns as first-generation college students) and what they are hoping to get out of it.
- To encourage discussion, have facilitators share common concerns of first-generation college students: (a) straddling two cultures—family and friends versus college; (b) staying true to their culture and who they are while adjusting to college; (c) feeling like they don't fit in; (d) having less academic preparation, money, and confidence than peers; (e) having concerns about race and class; (f) finding a sup-

port system on campus; (g) managing time and balancing multiple demands (Collier & Morgan, 2008; Cushman, 2007).
- Summarize group members' concerns and describe some of the topics planned for subsequent groups.
- Distribute Handout 7.1 (College Expectations). Ask members to complete at least Questions 1–3 for the next session. (Session 2 will likely focus on Questions 1–3, and Session 3 will focus on Questions 4–6.)

Session 2: The Transition From High School to College
- Use Handout 7.1 as a framework for exploring members' perceptions of this transition and fears/concerns about college.
- Begin with a discussion about members' perceptions of the differences between high school and college, including differences in the school environment, academic expectations, changes in schedule/routine, peer culture, and so on.
- Discuss members' reactions to these changes. Did they anticipate these differences? Which changes are/were exciting or welcome? What feels/felt overwhelming or difficult about this transition?
- Encourage each member to share one fear about college. If members have difficulty discussing fears, have each participant anonymously write his or her fears on an index card, collect the index cards, and use the cards to guide discussion.
- Ask members about changes they need(ed) to make in their schedule, behavior, attitudes, and relationships to adjust to college. Provide information about college expectations and behaviors that may not have been necessary in high school but are essential to college success.
- In preparation for the next group, ask members to think about these changes in the context of their current relationships (i.e., Questions 4–6 on Handout 7.1). How are parents and friends responding to the changes members are experiencing? Where can members find support during this transition? What additional support might they need in college?

Session 3: Building a Support System, Relationship Changes, and Parental Expectations
- Discussion will focus on building a strong support system and understanding the challenges presented by relationships with family and friends. Discussion questions can include the following:
  - Whom do members consider part of their support system? How have members' support systems, or their need for support, changed since they have started college?
  - To what extent do members feel pressure from others to succeed? How do they deal with this?
  - In what ways are parents' or others' expectations similar to or different from members' expectations? (Cultural expectations might also be important.)

- How have members coped with expectations that are different from their own? How has this affected their relationships?
- What do members wish their family or friends understood about the challenges of going to college?
- How can a friend or significant other show their support?

- As members share their experiences, facilitators and other group members can share any helpful hints for building a support system and balancing college demands and the needs of family and friends.
- Role playing also might be helpful, depending upon the situations described by members. Role plays might include talking to friends about needing to socialize less, explaining to parents why members would prefer to study a major different from what parents expect, or helping family understand why school demands might decrease family time.
- Distribute Handout 7.2. Ask members to complete it for the next group.

Session 4: Time Management

- Begin the discussion by asking members how they spent their time over the past week. It can be informative for members to calculate the actual number of hours they spent sleeping, eating, grooming/showering, commuting, attending classes, studying, working at a job, caregiving (for siblings or others), socializing (either in person or online, via text, or via telephone), spending time with family, surfing the Internet, watching television, or doing other activities.
- Discussion questions can include the following:
  - Which activities took the most time? The least?
  - Which were the biggest time-wasters?
  - How many hours did members sleep? Was this too much or too little? How does too little sleep affect time management and stress levels?
  - How many hours per week are members employed? How do they balance work and school responsibilities?
  - How much time did members spend with friends and family? Has the amount of time spent with family changed since high school? How are members managing others' expectations of their time?
  - How many hours did members spend studying?
  - What challenges did members encounter when managing time?
- Discuss the importance of studying 2–3 hours for each hour spent in class. How does this guideline compare to the number of hours members currently are studying? Which activities can they reduce to increase study time? What time of day is most effective for studying?
- Review common barriers to effective time management, including procrastination, too many commitments, perfectionism, and not being comfortable saying no to others. Explore underlying fears and anxieties that perpetuate these habits. Also explore the ways in which these habits can create stress and anxiety. How do members react emotionally and physiologically when time is mismanaged?

- Ask members for strategies they have used to get organized and successfully manage time. Emphasize the importance of prioritizing study-time tasks. Explain the difference between short-term and long-term goals and the importance of making a to-do list each week.
- Optional homework: Have members create a schedule that includes adequate study time and a to-do list for the upcoming week.

Session 5: Getting Involved and Using Available Resources

- Follow-up from time management group: Have any changes been made since the last group? How much time do members spend engaged in academic or extracurricular activities on campus?
- Ask about members' experiences, both positive and negative, with campus support services and student clubs. What are some of the barriers to using these college resources (e.g., time, negative perceptions or stereotypes about students who seek help, thinking that they don't need help, shyness or lack of confidence)?
- Share with members the research finding that involvement in these types of activities can be particularly beneficial for first-generation students.
- Review campus services available to students (e.g., wellness and counseling services, academic advising, tutoring center, career center, office of student life, disability support services, financial aid) and give them a handout containing contact information for these services.

Session 6: Self-Advocacy: Communicating Effectively With Professors and Other College Personnel

- Discuss the importance of advocating for oneself with professors and other college personnel. Provide examples of times when self-advocacy is critical (e.g., seeking help with an assignment, having concerns about financial aid, contesting a grade).
- Explore group members' experiences, both positive and negative, communicating with professors or other college personnel.
- Describe the communication styles commonly used: passive, aggressive, passive-aggressive, and assertive. Ask members for examples of these communication styles from their own lives. Explain that people often learn to use different communication styles in different circumstances. However, assertiveness is the most effective communication style for self-advocacy in the college environment. Assertiveness involves confidently expressing one's own needs while also showing respect for others.
- Have members brainstorm examples of assertive behavior that might be useful when meeting with a professor.
- If time permits, have members role play assertive communication. Ask for two volunteers: one to play the professor and one to play the student. First have the student use an ineffective communication style with the professor and have the professor react accordingly. Next have the student try communicating assertively.

- Debrief both role plays. What worked well and what didn't? Was assertiveness effective? What other strategies might have been helpful?
- Provide members with concrete tips for meetings with professors, such as the following:
  - Sign up for the professor's office hours and arrive on time for the meeting.
  - Know what you want to discuss. Write down specific questions to help you remember them in the meeting.
  - Professors generally want to help—try to relax and be yourself.

Session 7: The Importance of Choosing an Appropriate Major and Earning a College Degree

- Find out how many members have declared their major or have some idea what they want to major in. Ask members to describe the process they have gone through to choose a major. What challenges have they faced? If any members have changed their major, why have they done so? What are members' career goals?
- If members have not yet declared majors, discuss the college's policy about when a major must be declared and any consequences of not doing so (e.g., in terms of financial aid, academic progress). Describe the resources available for undecided students.
- What are members' reasons for earning a college degree? How do these reasons affect their choice of major?
- Ask how members believe their lives will change when they earn a college degree. What do they predict will happen if they don't reach their academic goals?
- Share statistics regarding earnings and unemployment by education level. The Bureau of Labor Statistics and U.S. Census Bureau websites provide helpful information. For example:
  - 2008 unemployment by education level: http://www.bls.gov/emp/ep_chart_001.htm
  - 2007 educational attainment in the United States: http://www.census.gov/prod/2009pubs/p20-560.pdf
- Ask how this information affects members' motivation to earn a college degree.
- Ask members to summarize what they have learned from the group and how they plan to use this information.

References

Bureau of Labor Statistics (2009). *Graph of unemployment rates and median weekly earnings in 2008 by degree type.* Retrieved from http://www.bls.gov/emp/ep_chart_001.htm

Chen, X. (2005). *First-generation students in postsecondary education: A look at their college transcripts* (National Center for Education Statistics Publication No. 2005–171). Washington, DC: U.S. Government Printing Office.

Collier, P., & Morgan, D. (2008). "Is that paper really due today?" Differences in first-generation and traditional college students' understandings of faculty expectations. *Higher Education, 55,* 425–446.

Crissey, S. R. (2009). *Educational attainment in the United States: 2007.* U.S. Department of Commerce, U.S. Census Bureau. Washington, DC: U.S. Government Printing Office. Retrieved from http://www.census.gov/prod/2009pubs/p20-560.pdf

Cushman, K. (2007). Facing the culture shock of college. *Educational Leadership, 64*(7), 44–47.

Engle, J., & Tinto, V. (2008). *Moving beyond access: College success for low-income, first-generation students.* Washington, DC: Pell Institute for the Study of Opportunity in Higher Education.

Hsiao, K. P. (1992). *First-generation college students* (ERIC Digest Report No. EDOJC-00-04). Los Angeles, CA: ERIC Clearinghouse for Junior Colleges. (ERIC Document Reproduction Service No. ED351079)

Pascarella, E., Pierson, C., Wolniak, G., & Terenzini, P. (2004). First-generation college students: Additional evidence on college experiences and outcomes. *Journal of Higher Education, 75*(3), 249–284.

Handout 7.1

College Expectations

1. Describe some of the differences you've noticed between high school and college.

    ____

    ____

2. Describe the changes you personally will have to make (in your schedule, behavior, relationships, thinking, etc.) or have made to adjust to these differences.

    ____

    ____

3. What are some of the fears you have/had about coming to college?

    ____

    ____

4. What expectations does your family have for you now that you are in college?

    ____

    ____

5. In what ways do your family's expectations for you differ from your own expectations?

    ____

    ____

6. Who can you go to for support as you are adjusting to college? (Include any family members, friends, mentors, role models, or other resources you could turn to for help or support.)

    ____

    ____

Handout 7.2

How Do You Spend Your Time?

Directions: For each hour of the next week, record ALL your activities. (Include sleeping, eating, studying, text messaging, e-mailing, watching TV, showering, etc.)

Time	Monday	Tuesday	Wednesday	Thursday	Friday	Saturday	Sunday
6 a.m.							
7							
8							
9							
10							
11							
12 p.m.							
1							
2							
3							
4							
5							
6							
7							
8							
9							
10							
11							
12 a.m.							
1							
2							
3							
4							
5							

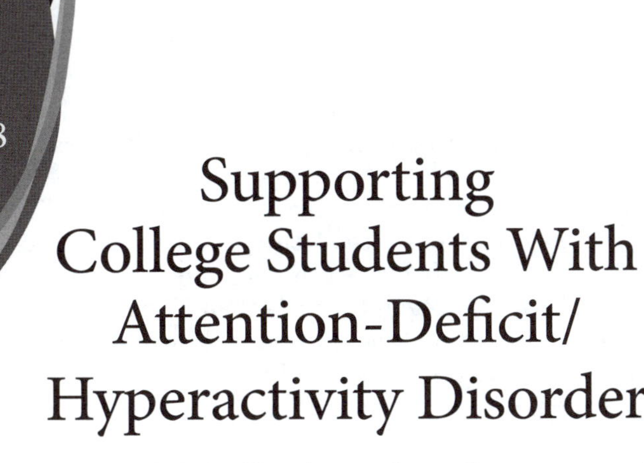

Supporting College Students With Attention-Deficit/ Hyperactivity Disorder

Miranda Hellenbrand and Kari Much

Attention-deficit/hyperactivity disorder (ADHD) is a neurobiologically based disorder described by the *Diagnostic and Statistical Manual of Mental Disorders, Fourth Edition, Text Revision* (*DSM–IV–TR*; American Psychiatric Association, 2000) as a persistent pattern of inattention and/ or hyperactivity-impulsivity that is more frequent and severe than is typically observed in individuals at a comparable level of development. Symptoms of note include inattention to detail, lack of follow-through, disorganization, easy distractibility, and frequent forgetfulness. In addition, individuals may also struggle with sustained sitting, running or climbing (in children), restlessness (in adolescents), difficulty playing or engaging in leisure activities quietly, excessive talking, often being on the go or acting as if driven by a motor, difficulty waiting turns, and interrupting and/or intruding on others. Although this developmental syndrome may persist into adulthood, symptoms must have been present before age 7 and must occur in two or more settings, and clear evidence of clinically significant impairment must be found.

ADHD symptoms often manifest themselves very differently across individuals. Whereas some individuals may exhibit more prominent symptoms of inattention, others may struggle more with hyperactivity or a combination of both. In addition, symptoms can vary depending on a person's age and developmental stage, making ADHD somewhat difficult to diagnose and treat.

Research suggests that 30% to 50% of children continue to meet *DSM–IV–TR* criteria for ADHD as adults (Filipe, 2009; Jackson & Farrugia, 1997; Ramsay & Rostain, 2006; Reilley, 2005). Additional research has found that 2% to 11% of college students exhibit symptoms of ADHD (Ramsay & Rostain, 2006; Reilley, 2005). College students may have unique challenges as a result of their ADHD symptoms, including academic difficulties, relationship difficulties, and job performance issues. Time management difficulties may not be as evident in a controlled high school environment, but many college students may find this a significant struggle when they attend college. Poor time management creates academic struggles and may contribute to occupational difficulties as well. Procrastination, disorganization, and distractibility can also cause similar problems. Limited communication skills, such as talking excessively, interrupting, and intruding on others, may significantly impair an individual's capacity to form relationships with peers as well as professors. In addition, individuals with ADHD often feel ineffective, incompetent, and different from friends and coworkers, which may negatively affect their self-esteem.

The purpose of this psychoeducational support group is to provide students with strategies to better their skills for improving academics and relationships. In addition, the group ideally provides a source of recognition for challenging tasks, may be intrinsically motivating, and may increase the self-esteem of group members.

Group Plan

Session 1: Introduction and Review of ADHD

- Introduction to group rules, confidentiality, and informed consent should be reviewed. Group members should be given an opportunity to introduce themselves, stating their year in school and what they are hoping to obtain from the group.
- Psychoeducation about the ADHD diagnosis should be provided, as should a forum for members to discuss any reservations about the group.
- Members are encouraged to share how symptoms of ADHD have affected them throughout their lives. In addition, a pretest can be given with the intention of administering a posttest at the conclusion of the group (a sample ADHD screening quiz is available at http://counsellingresource.com/quizzes/adhd/index.html). A baseline assessment can be a valuable tool for enabling group members to recognize their individual strengths and areas of growth and for providing a comparative analysis at termination.
- A short debriefing of the pretest can act as a segue into a discussion of how symptoms of ADHD have affected each member academically, socially, and occupationally. Many students list distractibility and maintaining attention as their primary difficulty; it is suggested to begin with this topic and interweave related discussions throughout the remaining sessions. Including both visual and verbal formats is useful in addressing distractibility and providing members with concrete techniques to maintain their attention.

Session 2: Procrastination and Time Management

- The definition of procrastination is reviewed, and functional reasons why procrastination persists are given. Group members take a short quiz to determine their procrastination style, and strategies for dealing with each style are presented.

- The homework assignment is to write a brief reflection on how each member's style of procrastination has hindered him or her. In addition, members are encouraged during the group to select a tip or strategy for combating procrastination to try for the next week. The group session is also devoted to identifying time management styles, and group members are encouraged to discover their individual time management tendencies.
- Members are then asked to identify their biggest time-wasters, and skills to enhance each individual's time management are processed. Homework includes prioritizing members' current responsibilities and creating a planner or electronic organizer in a fashion that reflects those priorities.

Session 3: Organization and Goal Setting

- Members are provided a forum to discuss the role that organization (or a lack thereof) plays in their lives.
- Members are reminded that following a routine will likely be a challenge but can be very helpful in eliminating some of the negative consequences of being disorganized.
- Group members are encouraged to think about and discuss a slightly altered Chinese proverb that states, "If you don't know where you are going, how will you know when you get there?"
- This provides the introduction to the importance of goal setting, and the concept of SMART goals (Specific, Measurable, Attainable, Realistic, Timely) is provided.
- Group discussion pertaining to the SMART theory is encouraged. The homework assignment for the week is to form a goal using the SMART theory, addressing who, what, how, and when.

Session 4: Relationship Skills and Enhancing Communication

- The session begins by having group members process how symptoms of ADHD affect their interpersonal relationships and discussing strategies group members have used to overcome these issues.
- A discussion follows regarding characteristics that either enhance or interfere with social relationships (e.g., having poor follow-through, having difficulty listening, being distracted, being late, making unrealistic time commitments, having trouble setting limits, being creative, knowing how to have fun, bringing excitement and energy to life, having a sense of humor, seeing new perspectives, and possessing varied interests).
- Group members then write down ways in which they would like to see their communication skills improve, and a list of techniques for improving their skills (e.g., being mindful, pacing the conversation, avoiding promises, observing how others interact, showing one's strengths) is reviewed.
- All facets of communication are discussed, including body language and other social cues that individuals with ADHD may frequently misinterpret or miss altogether.

- Strategies for how to be a good listener (giving 100% of your attention, responding in a verbal or nonverbal manner, rephrasing what has been stated, etc.) are reviewed, and members are encouraged to practice these skills during the group.
- Homework includes thinking about one or more conversations that went badly and imagining how the conversation could have gone better with more responsive listening. Members are encouraged to write down an alternative version of the conversation.

Session 5: Self-Acceptance

- Review myths and facts about the diagnosis of ADHD and process these within the group; individuals are encouraged to share what negative messages they have heard about themselves or their abilities as a result of their symptoms.
- Individuals are asked to identify who in their lives relayed these messages to them, how the messages made them feel, and whether the messages contribute to how they feel about themselves or conclusions they have made about their abilities.
- Group members are encouraged to think about the detrimental effects such comments have had on their self-esteem. Following this discussion, group members are asked to identify positive traits they possess and strategies they can use to strengthen their self-esteem.

Session 6: Conclusion

- This final session is focused on terminating the group. Group members are administered the posttest and are debriefed, and members further analyze their progress.
- Individuals are asked to identify specific techniques, strategies, and/or goals they have learned that they plan to use in the future.
- Members are also asked to provide a written evaluation of the group, the group leader, and their overall experience of the group.

References

American Psychiatric Association. (2000). *Diagnostic and statistical manual of mental disorders* (4th ed., text rev.). Washington, DC: Author.

Filipe, C. N. (2009). Adult ADHD: An under-diagnosed condition. *European Psychiatry, 24,* S13.

Jackson, B., & Farrugia, D. (1997). Diagnosis and treatment of adults with attention deficit hyperactivity disorder. *Journal of Counseling & Development, 75,* 312–319.

Ramsay, J. R., & Rostain, A. L. (2006). Cognitive behavior therapy for college students with attention deficit/hyperactivity disorder. *Journal of College Student Psychotherapy, 21*(1), 3–20.

Reilley, S. P. (2005). Empirically informed attention-deficit/hyperactivity disorder evaluation with college students. *Journal of College Counseling, 8,* 153–164.

Chapter 9

Psychodrama and Family Relationships

Trey Fitch and Stephen Giunta

Blatner (2000) stated, "Psychodrama is a method of exploring psychological and social problems by having participants enact the relevant events in their lives instead of simply talking about them" (p. 1). The techniques used in psychodrama help participants develop self-awareness and give them the opportunity to hone new skills. Group participants engage in warm-up activities prior to the enactment and a sharing component following the enactment. Moreno (1972), a pioneer in psychodrama, used terms associated with drama to outline the different roles played during enactments. These enactments are dramatic expressions of events that are important to the *protagonist*, or the person who is the focus of the enactment. The *director* role is assumed mainly by the group leader, and this person guides the group through the enactment and the warming and sharing phases. *Auxiliary protagonists* interact as people in the scene or as inner elements of the self, such as the *double*, or someone who expresses inner feelings and hidden thoughts. The *audience* not only witnesses the scene but also interacts in the sharing phase. Using these various components provides an endless number of possibilities that help all members gain insight and new skills.

Following the enactment, the audience and others are asked to provide personally relevant feedback on the enactment and the protagonist's issue (Blatner, 2000). The comments should reflect personal experience and commonality, and they are guided away from objective analysis. The director will steer the feedback away from comments in which an audience member attempts to explain the problems and the perceived solution. Instead, he or she will ask for similar experiences, thoughts, and feelings that are relevant to the situation. As a result, audience members directly

69

benefit from the process and are not just witnesses. The sharing provides for self-reflection and insight building as well. Psychodrama is corrective in nature, and the sharing phase is a crucial element to finding meaning and commonality in the enactment.

Psychodrama is particularly well matched to helping students cope better with family conflict. The techniques help students to explore relationships, practice new behaviors, and gain insight and support from others. Typical family issues are pressure to perform well academically, conflict about finances and college, over-engagement or under-engagement between parents and students, and sibling conflicts and rivalries. These conflicts and stressors are reenacted in a safe milieu in an effort to gain new skills and enhanced self-awareness.

Group Plan

Session 1: Group Introduction and Warm-Up

- Introduce yourself and describe your professional background.
- Review ethical issues for the group, focusing on privacy and respect.
- Get introductions from group members, including their names and their goals for the experience.
- Establish group rules together.
- Explain that psychodrama involves group members acting out the significant events and situations in their lives. Each person in the group has to participate at some level for the group to be successful. Sometimes a certain member will be the focus, and sometimes he or she will be helping to support others. One person will describe a troubling scenario or situation, and the group will act out that event to gain awareness and practice new reactions. After each enactment the group members will discuss reactions and similar experiences. They will not be allowed to analyze or advise; they can only observe and report similar situations and how they reacted.
- Initiate a warm-up activity from those listed on Handout 9.1.
- After the warm-up activity, set up the following scenario:

The protagonist is a 21-year-old man living on campus who is having frequent arguments with his mother. His mother is very strict and is very opposed to his partying and lifestyle. However, she wants to stay close to him and wants to know what is going on in his life. Every time he talks about his weekend or activities, it leads to an argument. The student wants to be able to talk to his mother without it turning into a conflict.

Describe this scenario to the group and ask for someone to play the role of the student and someone else to act as the mother. He has called her on the phone Sunday night and they are talking about their week. Ask other group members to serve as auxiliary members who state what the person is thinking but not saying. Have one for the mother and one for the son. After the role play, ask the nonparticipating group members to report their observations and similar experiences and reactions.

- After the group has enacted and discussed this role play, explain to the group that they are going to "sculpt" their families to show alliances and positions in the family. Ask a volunteer to use group members to represent members of his or her family. Describe the family members and then place them in a position that represents their place in the family. For example, an authoritarian father might be placed standing on a chair looking down on the family, whereas a disengaged brother is facing away in the corner. The volunteer will place each family member, and afterward the group will provide reactions and discuss similar situations and how they have coped.
- Repeat the sculpting activity for at least half of the group members, and plan on the other half completing the activity in Session 2.
- At the end of the group, summarize the group experience and ask group members about their reactions to the session.

Session 2: Family Sculpting

- Initiate a warm-up activity from those listed on Handout 9.1.
- After the warm-up activity, ask each group member to engage in a role reversal. The members are to assume the role of someone in their family and describe themselves from that family member's perspective. For example: "My big brother is off to college now and I am happy to get his room. We used to be close, but now he's too caught up with his college buddies to worry about me. I don't think he really cares about the family or me much anymore." Rotate around the group, giving each member a chance to participate. Afterward, ask members to share their reactions to what they heard and how they have coped with similar experiences.
- Complete the family sculpting activity from Session 1 until all members have participated. At the end of each sculpting, ask for sharing from the other group members.
- Based on the sculpting activity, identify a concern that one member would like to enact and share. That person will serve as the protagonist, and the group members will assume the roles of the family. Make sure the protagonist provides enough description for the group members to assume the roles well. Enact the event and then ask group members to share similar experiences and their reactions, reminding them not to offer analysis or advice.
- Repeat with another group member as time permits.
- Summarize the events of the group and ask for reactions from the group members.

Session 3: Enactments and Role Reversals

- To help identify positive aspects of family relationships, as a warm-up activity have each group member assume the role of a family member and complete the following sentence: "What I like most about my brother/sister/son/daughter is ______________."
- Expand the use of enactments in this session. Ask for volunteers to identify a stressful family event or situation and describe it to the group. Get volunteers to assume the roles of family members and reenact the event or situation. Previously, the focus had been on awareness and insight. Starting with this session, the group will also start looking for new reactions and skills. Add additional enactments to demonstrate a resolution or a more desired outcome. Allow other group members to assume the role of the protagonist so that he or she can observe alternative reactions. The original protagonist will assume the role of other family members.
- Complete each enactment with a sharing session. Ask members to share similar experiences and reactions. As members become comfortable they might be more inclined to analyze and advise; make sure this is redirected to supporting and sharing.
- End by summarizing the session and asking for reactions from the group members.

Session 4: New Voices

- Initiate a warm-up activity from those listed on Handout 9.1.
- After the warm-up activity, introduce new voices to the enactments by asking each member to verbalize a debate between different parts of the self for a current conflict. For example, a student may be in conflict between going home on weekends to visit family or staying to be with friends on campus. Have these competing entities debate each other. Remember to engage in sharing afterward to get reactions and support.
- Add new components to enactments. Ask auxiliary members to verbalize the thoughts of people in the enactments. Or use group members to represent competing parts of an inner conflict relating to a family issue. For example, have one member verbalize the moral and parental self while another represents the more impulsive and childlike self. Another component is to add a coping voice to the scenario, asking a member to recite helpful thoughts to the protagonist during the enactment.
- At the end of this group meeting, ask members to restate their goals and what progress has been made. Ask about their likes and dislikes about the group and what they have learned. Ask whether anything can be changed to help them better meet their goals.

Sessions 5–7: Working Stage

- All of the components to be used in this group have now been introduced with the exception of the empty chair technique, which is addressed in this group. Sessions 5–7 are a continuation of these approaches using different protagonists and mixing approaches as appropriate.

- As groups develop, members often gain more comfort and confidence. The methods of warm-up, enactment, and sharing while using protagonists and auxiliary members continue in Sessions 5–7, but the content and comfort level are expected to change. Remain flexible in directing group members using a variety of techniques. Although early sessions often focus on insight, the later group sessions can be especially helpful for facilitating catharsis and practicing new behaviors and skills.
- Guide the activities based on the needs of the group members. For example, does the main goal appear to be gaining insight, achieving emotional release, or learning new behaviors?
- Enactments are very helpful for gaining insight and practicing skills, and they can also provide emotional release. Some methods, such as the empty chair, can provide a more intense experience and greater catharsis. For this technique, place an empty chair in front of a member and have him or her pretend a family member who is a focus of the conflict is sitting there. Ask the member to use language that is directed to the person, such as "you" or their name. Have the group member communicate thoughts and feelings that he or she would normally repress in an effort to release blocked affect. Note that group leaders should have training and practice in these approaches so that they are aware of the risks and benefits involved. Novice counselors might not be capable of addressing the intense emotions or may not know how to monitor and react to them.
- Complete the session with a summary and ask for reactions. Be sure to monitor both the group process and individual reactions. Ask yourself whether the sharing is equitable and supportive. Are any group members being exploited or avoided? Do any members appear to need individual sessions?

Session 8: It's a Wrap

- Ask someone to take the protagonist role and to complete two enactments, the first one representing their old way of reacting to a situation and the second showing their new manner of reacting internally or externally.
- Repeat this with other group members with a sharing session after each enactment to highlight progress and similar experiences in growth.
- Conclude by asking each member what he or she would most like to take away from this experience.

References

Blatner, A. (2000). *Foundations of psychodrama: History, theory, and practice.* New York, NY: Springer.

Moreno, J. L. (1972). *Psychodrama* (4th ed.). Beacon, NY: Beacon House.

Handout 9.1

Warm-Up Activities

The success of any warm-up activity is often contingent upon the moments that immediately precede the activity. When working with a group of individuals who are unfamiliar to you and/or to one another, positive first impressions can go a long way and negative first impressions can be difficult to overcome. The more effective group facilitator will take the time to make the physical environment friendly to the participants and will present himself or herself as open and engaging. Remember, often something as simple as a smile and a comment about the weather can help lay the groundwork for successful warm-up exercises and subsequently successful psychodrama activities.

Activity 1: Introductions as a Member of a Family

The purpose of this exercise is to have the group members consider their familial role and any concerns that they bring to the group that are based on familial contexts.

1. Explain that in lieu of any formal introductions, groups members will first define their individual role within their family unit and then state their name.
2. Use yourself as an example (e.g., "Hello. I am Margaret's husband, Henry's grandfather, and the father of three sons: Joey, Stevie, and Mac. Oh yeah, and I'm Rachael's father-in-law. My name is Steve").

   A number of variations can be used to further flesh out the group members' familial context. For example, members could further define themselves by their cultural or ancestral background (e.g., "I'm half Italian and half Irish") or their perceived responsibilities within the family (e.g., "I'm the breadwinner" or "I'm the scapegoat"), or they could complete an assigned sentence (e.g., "I'm the most ______________ person in my family").

Activity 2: The Group Handshake

The purpose of this well-known exercise, when used within the context of psychodrama, is to break down the physical barriers between individual group members. This is a particularly valuable warm-up exercise if sculpting activities are planned for the group.

1. Formally introduce yourself to the group, keeping in mind that you will be asking participants to disclose the same information (possibly in lesser detail) when they are introduced.
2. Explain to the group members that they will be providing a formal introduction of another member of the group to the whole group and that the introduction will take place as they shake hands with the person they are introducing.

3. Determine whether you have an odd or an even number of partici-pants. If there is an odd number of group members, demonstrate the process by taking the hand of one group member, asking his or her name, and, while still holding hands, broadcasting that information to the group. For example, if working with a group of individuals going through a divorce, you might ask their first name; the age and gender of their children; and whether they are just beginning the divorce process, are in the middle of the process, or are reaching the end of the process. After you have demonstrated this process, have the group members take one another's hands and make introductions. If there is an even number of group members, supervise the activity as it takes place between the first two group members.

Activity 3: The Family Collage

The group members create a collage using pictures that symbolize or represent members of their family. The purpose of this activity is to allow group members to consider their family structures, both their roles and the roles of other family members.

1. Before the group session, collect various images from magazines, organize them by category (people, food, animals, nature, etc.), and place them in large (8.5″ × 12″) envelopes or manila folders. Ensure that a large selection of images is available, giving the group mem-bers many options to choose from within each individual category. At your discretion, participants may receive only one category of images to choose from or may have access to all of the categories. Together with the collection of images, provide each group member with construction paper, glue, and markers.
2. After the materials are distributed, advise the group members that they have 10 minutes to select one image that reminds them in some sense of each family member, including themselves, to glue the images to the construction paper, and then to label each family member on the paper.
3. Have group members use the collages to introduce themselves and their family members.

Chapter 10

Creative Counseling to Raise Self-Awareness in College Students

Allison Smith

The concept of creativity in counseling is not a novel one (Carson & Becker, 2004). As a process, counseling is creative; for example, being able to think on one's feet, be in the moment, or deal with resistance involves creativity on the part of the counselor. *Creative* can also describe the type of approach used by the counselor. Creative approaches in counseling can include the use of music, dance and movement, imagery, visual arts, drama, and play and humor (Gladding, 2011).

Creative approaches in counseling allow a client the opportunity to experience. The advantages of experiencing in counseling have been noted (see Carpenter, 2002) and include the notion that experiencing is a powerful teacher and that learning is increased through this mechanism. People access emotions more quickly and in a more authentic way when experiencing. In addition, typical defenses that normally serve as protective features are not as readily available when one is experiencing. Experiential approaches often feel playful to clients; this way of working is unexpected and unfamiliar to clients, so perhaps they are more open (Carson & Becker, 2004). Other benefits of using creative approaches have been noted (Gladding, 2011) and include offering a new energy to clients that in turn might increase their sensitivity to themselves. Creative counseling also helps clients become more invested in the counseling process. In addition, presenting concerns can become more concrete when creativity is used. Something tangible assists the client in remembering, visualizing, and actively working on a specific struggle. Creative counseling is multicultural in nature because creative approaches such as music or visual art can reach many different types of people from various backgrounds (Gladding, 2011).

Creativity can be used in various counseling settings (Carson & Becker, 2004). Authors (e.g., Bowman & Boone, 1998) have discussed the benefits of using creativity in a group setting, in particular to raise self-awareness and develop a sense of community. In fact, compared to more linear approaches to counseling, creative counseling provides clients with different opportunities for bringing thoughts and feelings into awareness. It allows clients to express themselves in multiple ways, which can lead to increased awareness of self and others (Gladding, 2011).

The following 8-week group program encourages self-awareness in college students through the use of creative approaches. The group program is structured around a different art area each week so that in addition to increasing their self-awareness, group members have the opportunity to develop a level of comfort with each creative art. Art areas included in the group are imagery/visual art, music, literature, photography, movement, and drama. The first activity is an adaptation of *My Metaphor* (Smith & Hall, 2011a). Sessions 6 and 7 encourage deeper sharing, as students are encouraged to discuss their "shadows" together during a dramatic activity (Smith & Hall, 2011b).

Group Plan

Session 1: Imagery/Visual Art

The following creative activity is designed to allow group members to build cohesion. The activity could take place over the course of one or two sessions, depending on the number of group members.

As group leader, you should first introduce the idea of metaphor and give an example, if needed (e.g., "I feel as if the weight of the world is on my shoulders"). Next encourage group members to explore the idea of metaphor as it relates to a presenting concern or a way to describe each group member. The majority of the time should be used to create the metaphor using art materials. The final portion of the group should be used for group members to take turns sharing their metaphor with the group.

Materials

Paper; drawing materials such as pastels, colored pencils, and crayons; clay or play dough; collage materials, such as magazines, scissors, and glue; and any other art materials that you and the members deem necessary to create the metaphor.

Instructions

1. Encourage each group member to use a metaphor to describe the presenting concern that motivated him or her to come into group counseling. If a member does not have a specific presenting concern, he or she can create a metaphor that describes his or her personality in some way. You can give an example of a metaphor, if needed. For example, if the college student wants to get more serious about academics, a metaphor to describe this might be "I'm shifting gears."

2. Have group members create the metaphor using art materials. For example, the student might use magazine pictures to create a collage depicting a car shifting gears.
3. Once group members have created the metaphors, begin a group sharing of each metaphor. Allow each group member to describe his or her metaphor and state why it is a representation of himself or herself or a presenting concern. Use the following process questions or others to promote discussion.

Process Questions
- What does your metaphor represent?
- How do you hope to use this metaphor in this group?
- Is there something you want to change (i.e., how might your metaphor be different at the end of the group)?

4. Use the metaphor throughout group sessions so that group members will remember the reason that brought them to the group. For example, you might keep the collage of the shifting gears on the wall of the group room throughout the group meetings and reference it when appropriate. Group members can reference the metaphors of other members when appropriate.
5. Assign homework for the next week (Handout 10.1). Explain the following: "Next week in group, we're going to continue to raise awareness using music. Please take some time before the next group meeting and think of a song that describes either you or a specific situation that you are in. For example, if you are feeling 'stuck' for some reason, you might use the song *Stuck in the Middle With You*. Please bring the song or written lyrics to the group next week and be prepared to play or read the song to the group. Also bring the worksheet to the group."

Session 2: Music

This activity is designed to continue to build group cohesion among members. It also encourages creative self-expression and awareness through music.

Materials
The group can decide what is most convenient to use for playing the songs—either an iPod docking station so that members plug in iPods, a laptop computer with speakers so that members bring CDs, or a CD player or something else so that everyone can play each song to the group. Bring one or more of these to play the songs.

Instructions
1. Each group member takes a turn sharing his or her song with the rest of the group. Songs should be no longer than 4 minutes for the sake of time. If a particular portion of the song captures the essence of what the group member wants to portray, then the group member can share only this portion of the song.

2. After each group member shares a song, he or she uses the worksheet to discuss how the song captures himself or herself.
3. After each group member has had the chance to share a song, have group members get into dyads or triads (depending on the size of the group) and ask them process questions. Have the dyads and triads discuss them.
4. After discussing the questions as a dyad or triad, each small group reports to the large group what the members discussed.

Process Questions
- What did you notice about your group after hearing the songs?
- Are there similarities among group members? Differences?
- How would we summarize what is needed from the group? How can we accomplish this together?
- Is there anyone in particular who might need some time today to discuss his or her song or situation in more detail?
- How can we use the information that we learned today in future group meetings?

Session 3: Literature

Group members are encouraged to use the first 30 minutes of the group to journal about the music and songs from last week. After group members finish journaling, each person reads the journal entry to himself or herself to see what themes or patterns are present in the writing.

Materials
Paper, pens, and markers.

Instructions
1. Have the students write a title or headline that captures something important that came out of their song and journal entry. This headline should read in a similar way to a newspaper headline. For example, if *Stuck in the Middle With You* was the song that described how a student felt, she might journal about this, notice themes of feeling stuck, and create a headline that reads "Woman So Stuck! Will She Ever Find Her Way?" to capture her situation.
2. After each member creates his or her headline, have group members take turns sharing with the large group. Facilitate discussion about these and other topics that come up based on the sharing for the remainder of group time.
3. Assign homework for next week: "Bring in photographs or copies of photographs of your family members or other people in your life whom you rely on for support. We will make collages with these, so make sure that the pictures are duplicates or ones that you don't mind using for an art project."

Session 4: Photography

In this group activity, students use the medium of photography to explore the notion of a support system. The majority of the session includes each group member making a collage of his or her individual support system. The final portion of the session should be reserved for group members to take turns sharing their support systems with the group.

Materials
Photographs that each group member brings in; paper; drawing materials, such as pastels, colored pencils, and crayons; collage materials, such as magazines, scissors, and glue; and any other art materials that you and the members deem necessary to create the support system.

Instructions
1. Encourage group members to create their support system using the photographs they brought to the meeting. Have the students use materials to create a collage that depicts their support system.
2. Once group members have created their support systems, begin a group sharing of each support system. Allow each group member to describe his or her support system and state why each person in that system is important to him or her. Use the following process questions or others to promote discussion.

Process Questions
- How do you ask for support?
- Have you asked for support recently?
- Are there people in your support system who also ask you for support when they need it? How do you offer support?
- What type(s) of support will you need in the next few months?

Session 5: Movement
This group focuses on movement and the body as a vehicle for self-awareness and expression. It introduces the topic of emotions and how group members express their emotions.

Instructions
1. Facilitate a discussion about emotions and how each member expresses emotions. The focus should stay on how group members hold and show emotion in their bodies. A prompt might be "How do you know when you're angry? Where do you feel it in your body?"
2. After a discussion about the body and emotions, introduce the concept of an emotions sculpture—a frozen image that the group will create with their bodies that depicts a specific emotion.
3. Next ask the group members to think of one emotion that they can create a sculpture to represent. If needed, the group can use Handout 10.2 to decide which emotion they would like to create. For example, a group member might decide to create an emotions sculpture that depicts the emotion shock.
4. In an open space, perhaps the middle of a circle or the front of the room, one group member assumes a body posture or position that shows shock, for example covering his or her face with the hands.

Next another group member adds to the sculpture. This could be done by standing across from the first person, as if he or she were telling the other some shocking news. One at a time other group members add to the shock sculpture by assuming positions that convey shock until it feels complete. There should be no talking during the process.

5. The process can continue with other emotions, so that other emotions sculptures are created for the remainder of the group. The last 20 minutes of the group should include a discussion led by you using the following process questions or others.

Process Questions
- How do you express negative emotions? Positive emotions?
- Are there people to whom you cannot show these emotions?
- In your family, how are emotions expressed?
- Are you satisfied with your emotional expression? How might you practice expressing emotions more openly?

Students can use the emotions worksheet (Handout 10.2) to expand their emotions vocabulary.

A variation of the emotions sculpture activity can include group members creating a sculpture that depicts a specific challenging or difficult event or moment that a group member wants to share with the group. For example, if a group member confronted his or her roommate about using illegal drugs in the dorm room, then that person might choose a group member to assume the role of the roommate and another group member to assume to role of himself or herself. Then that person could create a sculpture that depicts this moment and the emotions involved in the event.

Sessions 6 and 7: Drama

In this two-session activity, group members are encouraged to increase their self-awareness related to judgments of others. During a "shadow party," students increase self-awareness as they embody what they reject in others and have the opportunity to shift away from stereotyped patterns of responding. Session 6 is used to introduce the concepts, encourage reflection and discussion, and allow group members to consider how they want to embody their shadows. Group 7 is the actual shadow party, which takes between 45 and 90 minutes to facilitate, depending on the size of the group. In Session 7, 10–15 minutes should be allowed for an initial phase of unstructured interactions, followed by 15–30 minutes of more formal introductions and 15–20 minutes of debriefing.

Materials
Each student is responsible for creating his or her own costume. This may be regular dress with an accessory or something more elaborate, depending on the person's preference and the role that is being assumed (e.g., a person coming as an extremely depressed person might come in her pajamas and robe with a box of tissues; a scrutinizer may bring a magnifying glass).

Instructions: Session 6

1. Group members are asked to consider the following questions:
   - What behaviors or traits in others do you find the most irritating?
   - What would be the worst insult someone could say about you?
   - What are some of the adjectives that you would use to describe your least favorite person?
2. The concept of the shadow is then introduced. The shadow is described as representing parts of ourselves that are present but that we try to hide or disown, parts that may be evident in what we find disdainful in others. The shadow sometimes emerges when an early reaction to another occurs and results in a disowning of all associated elements. For example, when witnessing a verbally aggressive adult, a child may subconsciously reject that way of being and disown not just the aggression but also potentially useful but associated elements such as power, strength, and assertiveness. Consequently, the person may be withdrawn and passive and may harshly judge others who are assertive as "demanding."
3. Group members are invited to reflect on the questions asked to assist them in identifying one of their shadow parts. Group members are asked to keep their shadow identity secret from other group members.

Instructions: Session 7

1. Group members dress up to embody their shadows and arrive at the beginning of the group acting as their shadow (it helps to meet in a new location or somehow set up the group space as a party).
2. For 10–15 minutes, group members embody their shadows and interact with other members of the group as their shadow would.
3. Members are invited to sit in a half circle (still in their roles; e.g., a depressed person might curl up and cry, a scrutinizer might be overly critical of others). Invite each member individually to introduce himself or herself and ask a few questions of the shadow:

   a. Do you have a name?
   b. Is there anything you would like us to know about you?
   c. What do you think of this party?
   d. Are there people here you like or dislike?
4. Group members are then invited to guess what shadow the person is embodying and to get affirmation or clarification from the actor. This continues until all group members have been introduced.
5. Members are invited to shake off their shadow role in whatever way seems appropriate and to come together to debrief the experience.

   a. What was your experience being in this role?
   b. What feelings, thoughts, or ways of acting emerged?
   c. How was it to interact with others from this role?
   d. Did you see parts of yourself in others' shadows?
   e. What are the positive aspects of this shadow? The negative aspects of the shadow?

f. Are there elements of the shadow that could be drawn on or adapted to serve you?

Session 8: Imagery/Visual Art

Closing session: Repeat the metaphor activity from Session 1.

Instructions
See Session 1.

Process Questions
- How are you similar to/different from the metaphor that you created during Week 1?
- How would you like to see yourself continue to grow after the group is finished?
- How did this group assist you in raising your self-awareness?

References

Bowman, V. E., & Boone, R. K. (1998). Enhancing the experience of community: Creativity in group work. *Journal for Specialists in Group Work, 23,* 388–410.

Carpenter, J. (2002). *Effective clinical strategies for improving relationships.* Eau Claire, WI: PESI HealthCare.

Carson, D. K., & Becker, K. W. (2004). When lightning strikes: Reexamining creativity in psychotherapy. *Journal of Counseling & Development, 82,* 111–115.

Gladding, S. (2011). *The creative arts in counseling* (4th ed.). Alexandria, VA: American Counseling Association.

Smith, A. L., & Hall, H. K. (2011a). My metaphor. In S. Degges-White & N. Davis (Eds.), *Bringing the arts to the science of counseling: Expressive arts interventions across theoretical constructs* (pp. 191–192). Lanham, MD: Jason Aronson.

Smith, A. L., & Hall, H. K. (2011b). Shadow party. In S. Degges-White & N. Davis (Eds.), *Bringing the arts to the science of counseling: Expressive arts interventions across theoretical constructs* (pp. 144–146). Lanham, MD: Jason Aronson.

Handout 10.1

Song Activity

What is the name of the song that describes you/your presenting concern?

____

____

Do other songs also describe this? If yes, list below:

____

____

How would you describe you/your presenting concern in a few sentences?

____

____

What was it about the song that made you pick it?

____

____

What is a particular lyric/verse of the song that really describes you/your concern?

____

____

What do you want the group to know about this?

____

____

How would you like things to be different?

____

____

Handout 10.2

Emotions

Fear
- anxiety
- apprehension
- distress
- dread
- tenseness
- uneasiness
- worry
- alarm
- fear
- fright
- horror
- hysteria
- mortification
- panic
- shock
- terror

Joy
- amusement
- ecstasy
- gaiety
- euphoria
- bliss
- elation
- delight
- happiness
- jubilation

Love
- fondness
- attraction
- adoration
- sentimentality
- caring
- desire
- passion
- infatuation
- obsession

Sadness
- depression
- unhappiness
- misery
- melancholy
- gloom
- dispair
- insecurity
- alienation
- homesickness
- embarrassment
- humiliation

Anger
- fury
- wrath
- bitterness
- loathing
- resentment
- hate
- agitation
- aggravation
- grouchiness
- revulsion
- contempt

Surprise
- astonishment
- amazement

Interpersonal Process Groups in College and University Settings

Mary Kate Reese

Despite the potential obstacles, there is definitely support for the relevance of group work with students in college and university settings. Kincade and Kalodner (2004) posited that college students are at a unique developmental stage that includes addressing issues related to forming an individual identity, separating from parents, and establishing new relationships. According to these authors, college and university counseling centers have used group interventions with students for personal growth since the 1960s; these groups have been an efficient use of diminishing staff resources as well as a developmentally appropriate intervention for students. Group therapy is described as being "superior to individual therapy in the provision of social learning, developing social support, and improving social networks" (Yalom & Leszcz, 2005, p. 232). M. S. Corey, Corey, and Corey (2010) noted that by participating in groups students can focus on personal development (versus academics, which is the predominant focus of the college setting) and explore areas that may be causing difficulties in their interpersonal relating.

Many groups offered in college and university counseling centers are psychoeducational in nature, but there is obviously an important niche for groups that focus on relationships and interpersonal processes. In a survey of college and university counseling centers, Golden, Corazzini, and Grady (1993) found that 59% of the centers offered process-oriented psychotherapy groups. Hogg and Deffenbacher (1988) found that interpersonal process group therapy was just as successful as cognitive group therapy in reducing depressed thinking and increasing self-esteem in college students. These authors defined interpersonal process groups as those that "examine the interpersonal communications and emotional transactions among group members and focus on here-and-now group dynamics to help clients express their feelings more directly, act more independently, and feel more connected to others" (p. 304).

Johnson (2009) described a model for facilitating interpersonal process therapy groups for university students that is short term, developmental, and designed to increase cohesiveness and commitment to the group, thus decreasing early terminations. This chapter briefly outlines the basic components of interpersonal process groups in college and university settings and provides a variety of resources for conducting the group.

Group Plan

Sessions 1–2: Introduction and Self-Reflection

- In the first session, the group leader should orient group members by explaining group processes, the roles and skills needed for effective group participation, and the overall goals and objectives of the group. This orientation can have a positive impact on group cohesiveness, as the group members come to understand what they can expect and what is expected of them.
- Specific attention should be paid to ways in which each group member's individual goals or concerns might be manifested and worked on in future group sessions, as an early understanding of the group as a sort of "laboratory" in which to identify patterns and practice different behaviors can be helpful.
- According to Johnson (2009), the first group sessions should consist of some fairly structured activities that are focused on getting students oriented to the group, illuminating group process, and getting students accustomed to sharing here-and-now reactions with the group.
- G. Corey, Corey, Callanan, and Russell (2010) described some excellent structured exercises that enhance self-reflection and that structure group members to begin to share their reactions and to interact with one another.
- See Handout 11.1 for some examples of group exercises and activities that may be useful in this phase of the group.

Sessions 3–6: Transition to the Working Stage

- During the transition and working stages of a group, some typical characteristics are seen (Tuckman, 1965).
- Defensiveness, resistance, and conflict are very common during the transition stage, and it is often the successful resolution of these (or at least the recognition of them) that propels the group forward into an even more meaningful experience.
- In the working phase, there is often a greater sense of willingness to initiate topics for exploration and a greater focus on the here and now of the group experience, as well as how this relates directly to members' patterns and experiences outside of the group.

- Group norms—such as speaking for oneself; honestly expressing thoughts, feelings, and reactions to occurrences in the group; and being willing to experiment with new behaviors and take risks—often become a part of the underlying framework of the group, and members hold themselves and their peers accountable for the maintenance of these.
- See Handout 11.1 for some examples of group exercises and activities that may be useful in this phase of the group.

Sessions 7–10: Working Stage and Conclusion

- Group leaders who regularly acknowledge the time-limited nature of a group and who remind members of this reality over the entire course of the group are more likely to facilitate the transfer of learning to the outside lives of the group members.
- Awareness of the finite nature of the group in every session can prevent a feeling of abruptness when the end occurs.
- During the final stage of the group, learning is consolidated and action plans are created by each member to continue forward with identified goals after the group ends (Tuckman, 1965).
- See Handout 11.1 for some examples of group exercises and activities that may be useful in this phase of the group.

References

Corey, G., Corey, M., Callanan, P., & Russell, J. M. (2010). *Group techniques* (4th ed.). Pacific Grove, CA: Brooks/Cole.

Corey, M. S., Corey, G., & Corey, C. (2010). *Groups: Process and practice* (8th ed.). Pacific Grove, CA: Cengage.

Golden, B. R., Corazzini, J. G., & Grady, P. (1993). Current practice of group therapy at university counseling centers: A national study. *Professional Psychology: Research & Practice, 24,* 228–230.

Hogg, J. A., & Deffenbacher, J. L. (1988). A comparison of cognitive and interpersonal-process group therapies in the treatment of depression among college students. *Journal of Counseling Psychology, 35,* 304–310.

Johnson, C. V. (2009). A process-oriented group model for university students: A semi-structured approach. *International Journal of Group Psychotherapy, 59,* 511–528.

Kincade, E. A., & Kalodner, C. R. (2004). The use of groups in college and university counseling centers. In J. L. DeLucia-Waack, D. A. Gerrity, C. R. Kalodner, & M. T. Riva (Eds.), *Handbook of group counseling and psychotherapy* (pp. 366–377). Thousand Oaks, CA: Sage.

Tuckman, B. W. (1965). Developmental sequence in small groups. *Psychological Bulletin, 63,* 384–399.

Yalom, I., & Leszcz, M. (2005). *The theory and practice of group psychotherapy* (5th ed.). New York, NY: HarperCollins.

Handout 11.1

Sample Group Activities for an Interpersonal Process Group in a College Setting (10 Sessions)

- *Icebreaker:* Start the group with some sort of icebreaker activity that allows members to share something personal yet safe with the group. For example, ask members to select one item from their pocket or purse that they think represents something important about them and have them share one at a time about the item and what it represents.
  - Discuss the group contract, confidentiality, and individual goals for each member.
- *Two Truths and a Lie:* Ask participants to make three statements about themselves, two that are true and one that is false. The rest of the group then votes to identify which statement is false ("Two Truths and a Lie," n.d.).
  - Be sure to allow time at the end of the first group session for reflection. Say, "I would like to ask each of you to share your thoughts about the group and about your comfort level."
- *Dyad Activity:* At the beginning of the group, ask participants to pair up with someone they do not know and to spend 5 minutes talking to each other about their thoughts and feelings prior to coming to the group meeting that day. When the group reconvenes, ask members to share something that they told their partner and to note any similarities in their experiences.
- *Fear in a Hat:* Distribute note cards and pencils to group members and ask members to write down a fear or something that they worry about; encourage them to be as specific as possible without giving away their identity. Take up all of the papers in a hat or a basket and then pass the hat around. Ask each person to draw one card from the hat, read it out loud, and then elaborate on what the person who wrote this may have meant. Tell group members that if they draw their own card, they do not have to tell the group, as no one will know if they don't acknowledge it. Ask the group to discuss what some of the common fears were ("Fear in a Hat," n.d.).
- *Chronological Lineup:* Put masking tape on the floor in a straight line long enough for everyone in the group to stand side by side on the tape. Tell members that you are going to give them a group task and that their goal is to complete this task. There are only two rules to keep in mind: (a) They must keep one foot on the line at all times, and (b) there is absolutely *no* talking during the activity. Watch the process and do not answer any more questions after the exercise starts. Have the group process the activity afterward: What did they notice/learn about themselves during this exercise? What did they notice/learn about this group overall during this exercise? What feelings/

reactions did they experience during the task? Did their feelings/reactions/behaviors during this exercise in any way reflect how they typically interact in the outside world?

- *Crocodile River/Magic Shoes:* Put some sort of tape or line on the floor to designate a 6- to 8-foot span of floor that will be the "river" in this exercise. There should be enough space on either side of the line for people to stand. Everyone in the group starts on one side of the river. Their task is to cross this river, which is full of crocodiles. There are hungry, person-eating pygmies coming from behind them in the forest, so time is of the essence. The only tool they have to get across the river are these (pretend to pull something from out of your pocket) invisible magic shoes. Wearing these shoes, each person can cross the river a maximum of two times (one way each time). The shoes must be handed from person to person (i.e., they cannot be thrown across the river to another group member). They have to get *all* members across safely, and if anyone's foot touches the water, he or she forfeits and must start over again.

  Various strategies may be developed by the group; several different ones can work. Have the group members process the activity afterward: What did they notice/learn about themselves during this exercise? What did they notice/learn about this group overall during this exercise? What feelings/reactions did they experience during the task? Did their feelings/reactions/behaviors during this exercise in any way reflect how they typically interact in the outside world?

- *Termination Activity:* Distribute note cards to group members (enough so that each member has a note card for every other member). Using a guided imagery or description of a magical shop, explain to the group members that they are going to go shopping for a gift for each of their group members. The magical store contains all sorts of attributes, characteristics, or items that represent something that they can give the group member to take away from the group with him or her. There are no boundaries to the creativity that can be used with this exercise, but you may wish to give a few examples to get members started. For example, "You might want to give someone in the group a mirror that has the magical powers to tell her, when she looks into it, how beautiful she is on the inside and the outside, whenever she forgets this fact" or "You may give someone a shield that has the ability to filter out any verbal attacks and deflect him from the person holding it, sort of like a boundary that prevents him from being hurt by the words of others." Of course, group members may choose to write a simple word or phrase on each card (e.g., "hope and courage"). Each gift should be written, drawn, or depicted in some way on the note card so that each group member makes a card for every other member of the group. Once all have finished, ask for a volunteer to go first to receive gifts, and have the group members explain their gifts and give the cards to the group member to take home.

- For additional ideas on group exercises, games, and activities that you may wish to use, see Corey, Corey, Callanan, and Russell (2010), Belmont (2006), DeLucia-Waack, Bridbord, Kleiner, and Nitza (2006), and various websites on group games and activities (e.g., www. wilderdom.com, www.icebreakers.ws).

References

Belmont, J. (2006). *The therapeutic toolbox: 103 group activities and tips.* Eau Claire, WI: PESI HealthCare.

Corey, G., Corey, M., Callanan, P., & Russell, J. M. (2010). *Group techniques* (4th ed.). Pacific Grove, CA: Brooks/Cole.

DeLucia-Waack, J., Bridbord, K. H., Kleiner, J. S., & Nitza, A. (2006). *Group work experts share their favorite activities* (Rev. ed.). Alexandria, VA: Association for Specialists in Group Work.

Fear in a hat. (n.d.). Retrieved from http://www.icebreakers.ws/team-building/fear-in-a-hat.html

Two truths and a lie. (n.d.) Retrieved from http://www.icebreakers.ws/small-group/two-truths-and-a-lie.html

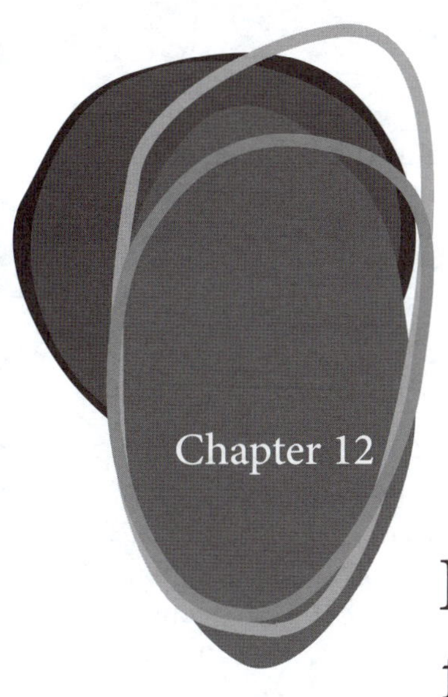

A Spiritual Development Group for College Students

Gayle L. Reed

Spiritual wellness, which is located at the center of the wellness model (Myers, Sweeney, & Witmer, 2000), is considered to be the core of overall wellness. The components of spiritual wellness involve formal and informal practices that are key elements of identity development and values clarification. According to Chickering and Reisser (1993), the clarification of beliefs and values is a developmental concern of college students. About 25% of college students report that they become more spiritual during college, whereas only 7% report becoming less spiritual (Harvard University Institute of Political Affairs, 2006)

Reed (2009) developed a model for exploring spiritual development using interventions that apply well to a group format and that do not promote any particular religious viewpoint. They highlight personal values and awareness and are designed for use in nonchurch settings.

Three key elements in the model present the foundations for spirit, ethics, and culture as defined by the awareness of or relationship between self and the larger world. The three elements are explained and established in the course of spiritual direction and can offer a student heightened clarity of self, beliefs, and values that can assist in promoting overall health and well-being, many times in cooperation with a professional counselor. Religious context is incorporated into the elements of this model as identified by the student (Reed, 2009).

The first element in the process is the identification and establishment of a personal mission statement. The personal mission is not related to physical objects or hopes for other people (e.g., a new car or the happiness of children). The individual cannot control these activities. Working from a personal mission should induce a sense of calm and warmth as a visceral experience. The student should choose words for his or her personal mission that identify behaviors he or she is able to control (e.g., *friendly*, *happy*, and *kind*). The second element in the process is the integration of words and actions within the context of the mission statement. If a student says, "I want to be a friendly person," but he or she continually walks into class without talking to other students, then the interpretation of the word *friendly* may need some discussion, as matching words and actions in life activities can be diluted by misinterpretation or opposing interpretations of words between the student and other individuals (Reed, 2009).

The third foundational element of the model is beliefs and reality. This element emerges from the psychological premise that suggests a relationship between distress and perceptions. The level of distress increases as beliefs/perceptions and reality/descriptive events move further apart. If what a student believes is not integrated with events that have occurred, a sense of frustration, anger, sadness, or irritation increases. Personal energy is focused on trying to justify the discrepancy (Reed, 2009).

If an individual places his or her energy into living out this personal mission statement in thoughts, words, and actions, then little energy and time can be spent on life away from this central focal point. According to this perspective, spirit also supports the religious context of the individual as he or she gains clarity with regard to his or her interconnectedness with others and the world. The goal of the spiritual process is to ask the questions that will help the individual find the answers that are buried deep within at this core point of human potential.

Group Plan

Session 1: Things You Appreciate

- Introduce yourself and offer some background information about who you are and what you do.
- Review ethical issues for the group.
- Ask for introductions from all group members and also request a brief synopsis of each person's personal background only if he or she is comfortable sharing.
- Establish group rules.
- Explain that the purpose of these activities is to help members become more intentional about the decisions they make and how those decisions can impact them and the people around them. The goals are to teach them a way of seeing the world so that they can be more at peace with themselves and their decisions.
- Start with a minute of quiet time. Encourage the group to sit quietly and listen to the sounds around them. Challenge them to see how many different sounds they can hear as they sit without speaking. Tell them to try not to think about other things; just focus on the sounds they hear.

- After 1 minute ask the members to open their eyes. Say, "There are things going on all around you. If you are so busy thinking about those things, you forget to listen to the other things that are happening around you. You can even forget to listen to the parts of life that are important to you."
- Discuss which activities they love the most, things they take for granted, and things they appreciate:
    1. Encourage each person in the group to make sure they "feel" a lightness or excitement when writing about the things they love. What activities do they do that make time disappear?
    2. Encourage each person to list all the things they take for granted (e.g., moving arms and legs, breathing, reading). You can give examples of how many people have challenges moving their arms and legs, challenges breathing without help, intellectual challenges, and so on.
    3. Encourage each person to list all the things they appreciate. These can be people, things, activities, or behaviors.
- Have members share this information with others in the group if they would like to do so. If they do not want to share, invite them to sit quietly and reflect on how the words of the other people might impact their way of thinking.
- Challenge for the week: Offer each person in the group the challenge of making a list (mental or written) of what things they appreciate (behaviors of self or others, activities like reading or walking) and what things they take for granted (walking, writing, seeing).
- As you end the meeting time, offer the people in the group the opportunity to sit in the room silently and think about the discussion if they would like.

Session 2: Scarcity and Abundance

- Welcome the members and remind them of the group rules.
- Reinforce the purpose of these activities: to help members become more intentional about the decisions they make and how those decisions can impact them and the people around them. They are working on the goal of finding new ways to see the world so that they can be more at peace with themselves and their decisions.
- Start with a minute of quiet time. Encourage the group to sit quietly with eyes closed and listen to the sounds around them. Challenge them to see how many different sounds they can hear as they sit without speaking. Tell them to try not to think about other things; just focus on the sounds they hear. If they were to think of anything it would be okay for them to think of the list they have made of what they appreciate in life, no matter how small the items on the list.
- After 1 minute ask the members to open their eyes. Say, "Remember the last meeting. Activity is going on all around you. If you are so

busy thinking about things, you might miss something that is there in the background."

- Encourage the people in the group to share at least one thing they found that week that they appreciated. Next have them discuss things they took for granted. You may share your own experiences or list simple examples (e.g., trees, books, a smile from a stranger) to promote discussion.
- Refer to Handout 12.1, Meeting 2. Follow the guide here to work through Handout 12.1, Meeting 2, with the group.
  1. Read "For your consideration . . ."
  2. Ask the members to give examples of where the scarcity model was used. Then have them give examples of how the abundance model was used. If they do not want to talk, then encourage them to write their thoughts on the handout.
- Have members share this information with others in the group if they would like to share, or they may sit and reflect on how the discussion applies to their life.
- Challenge for the week: Offer each person in the group the challenge of thinking about how he or she looks at situations. Encourage them to look at each situation using both the scarcity model and the abundance model. Which model do they tend to use more for each situation?
- As you end the meeting time, offer the people in the group the opportunity to sit in the room silently and think about the discussion if they would like.

Session 3: The Role of Fear

- Welcome the members and remind them of the group rules.
- Reinforce the purpose of these activities: to help members become more intentional about the decisions they make and how those decisions can impact them and the people around them. They are working on the goal of finding new ways to see the world so that they can be more at peace with themselves and their decisions.
- Start with a minute of quiet time. Encourage the group to sit quietly with eyes closed and listen to the sounds around them. Challenge them to see how many different sounds they can hear as they sit without speaking. Tell them to try not to think about other things; just focus on the sounds they hear. If they were to think of anything, it would be okay for them to think about how the abundance model and the scarcity model impacted the way they looked at situations this past week.
- After 1 minute ask the members to open their eyes. Say, "Last time we met we talked about the scarcity and abundance models. Let's spend some time hearing your stories about this past week."
- Encourage the people in the group to share at least one event that they looked at using the scarcity model and one that they looked at

using the abundance model. You may share your own experiences or other stories you have heard. If a person does not wish to share, then encourage him or her to reflect on how the other stories may impact his or her way of thinking.

- Refer to Handout 12.1, Meeting 3. Follow the guide here to work through Handout 12.1, Meeting 3, with the group.

  1. Read "For your consideration . . ."
  2. Encourage each person to answer the following question on the handout: "I am afraid of __________."
  3. Have members sit quietly for a minute looking at their list and adding to it if anything else comes to mind. Encourage them to listen to the sounds around them as they are contemplating their list. Encourage them to write down any new thoughts that come to mind. Ask them to focus not on the list but on the sounds around them.
  4. Encourage the people in the group to share their lists with the others.
  5. Ask the second question on the handout: "What would I do if I were not afraid . . .?" Have members write a list and sit quietly looking at the list. Once again encourage them to listen to the sounds around them as they consider the answer to this question. If they are religious, they can use this time to pray silently.

- Challenge for the week: Offer each person in the group the challenge of finding a situation this week and naming a fear or responding without fear. Then ask them to find one thing that they would love to do but have not done, and participate in the activity. Encourage them to take it slowly. Encourage them to sit quietly and listen to all the activity going on around them when they feel afraid. See what sounds they can hear around them when they are not worrying about what they fear.

Note: The goal of this meeting is to have each person reset his or her expectations. It is another step in the process of taking a little deeper look at life. You may let people sit in silent reflection if they are not willing to speak.

Session 4: Expectations and Reality

- Welcome the members and remind them of the group rules.
- Reinforce the purpose of these activities: to help members become more intentional about the decisions they make and how those decisions can impact them and the people around them. They are working on the goal of finding new ways to see the world so that they can be more at peace with themselves and their decisions.
- Start with a minute of quiet time. Encourage the group to sit quietly and listen to the sounds around them. Challenge them to see how

many different sounds they can hear as they sit without speaking. Tell them to try not to think about other things; just focus on the sounds they hear. If they were to think of anything, it would be okay for them to think about how fear played a role in their week.

- After 1 minute ask the members to open their eyes. Say, "Last time we met we talked about fear. Let's spend some time hearing your stories about this past week."

- Encourage the people in the group to share at least one event they feared and what they could do when fear was not motivating them. You may share your own experiences or other stories you have heard. If people do not wish to share, they may sit and reflect on how the discussion applies in their life.

- Refer to Handout 12.1, Meeting 4. Follow the guide here to work through the activity on Handout 12.1, Meeting 4, with the group.

  1. Read "For your consideration . . ."
  2. Talk about situations in which perception could have clouded what was happening. Have someone tell a story that made him or her mad. As the person tells the story, ask the group to help put parts of the story into the perceptions/expectations side of the list and other parts of the story into the reality/observations side of the list.
  3. After you have completed the story or stories, have the group members sit quietly for a minute looking at the list and adding to it if anything else comes to mind. Encourage them to listen to the sounds around them as they are contemplating their lists. It is important that they try not to make judgments about the list. They should just sit and listen to the sounds around them so they can focus on the inside.
  4. After the minute of contemplation, encourage the people in the group to share their examples with the others. If someone has a difficult time separating expectations and reality, continue to give examples and ask the people in the group to identify whether the statement is an expectation or a reality (see the list of examples on Handout 12.1).

- Challenge for the week: Offer each person in the group the challenge of finding a situation this week and listing out its expectations and realities. Encourage them to take time to see how looking at situations in this way changes how they respond.

Session 5: Matching Words and Actions

- Welcome the members and remind them of the group rules.
- Reinforce the purpose of these activities: to help members become more intentional about the decisions they make and how those decisions can impact them and the people around them. They are working on the goal of finding new ways to see the world so that they can be more at peace with themselves and their decisions.

- Start with a minute of quiet time. Encourage the group to sit quietly and listen to the sounds around them. Challenge them to see how many different sounds they can hear as they sit without speaking. Tell them to try not to think about other things; just focus on the sounds they hear. If they were to think of anything, it would be okay for them to think about their expectations of situations.
- After 1 minute ask the members to open their eyes. Say, "Last time we met we talked about expectations and reality. Let's spend some time hearing your stories about this past week."
- Encourage the people in the group to share at least one event for which they divided out expectations and reality. If someone had difficulty seeing the differences, you can walk through the story with them and the group and model what is an expectation and what are reality/observations. You may share your own experiences or other stories you have heard. Encourage members to first look at the situation without emotion. Identify observations about what was occurring without judgment. If members become emotional, ask them to put the emotion away for now and try to find the observation (describe what actually happened).
- Refer to Handout 12.1, Meeting 5. Follow the guide here to work through the activity on Handout 12.1, Meeting 5, with the group.

  1. Read "For your consideration . . ."
  2. Encourage the group to talk about what matching words and actions can mean in their lives. Discuss how matching words and actions can build trust with others and also help people stay true to themselves.
  3. Have members sit quietly for a minute thinking about their words and actions. Encourage them to listen to the sounds around them as they are contemplating their list. They can write on the handout any thoughts about matching words and actions that come to mind during this time.
  4. After the minute of contemplation, encourage the people in the group to share their thoughts about matching words and actions with the others. Remind them that if words and actions don't match, actions are the true representation of who they are as a person. This can be true for them and for others.

Note: If there is a discussion about feelings toward other people when words and actions don't match, you can encourage them to remember Session 4 ("Expectations and Reality").

- Challenge for the week: Because this is the last meeting, encourage the group members to take all the information they have learned in the meeting and look at ways to incorporate it into their lives. If they would like to continue looking deeper, they can work with a counselor or a spiritual director (see Spiritual Directors International, www.sdiworld.org) or both if warranted.

- When the meeting is over, you may let people sit in silent reflection if they would like to spend some time thinking about what was discussed this week and listing the expectations and realities. Encourage them to take time to see how looking at situations in this way changes how they respond.

References

Chickering, A. W., & Reisser, L. (1993). *Education and identity* (2nd ed.). San Francisco, CA: Jossey-Bass.

Harvard University Institute of Political Affairs. (2006). *Spring 2006 youth survey.* Boston, MA: Author.

Myers, J. E., Sweeney, T. J., & Witmer, J. M. (2000). The Wheel of Wellness counseling for wellness: A holistic model for treatment planning. *Journal of Counseling & Development, 78*(3), 251–266.

Reed, G. L. (2009). *Fixing the problem: Making changes in how you deal with challenges.* Bloomington, IN: iUniverse.

Handout 12.1

Abundance, Fear, Expectations, and Matching

Meeting 2

For your consideration . . .

There are two models that look at the way people think about the same situation. One model is called the *scarcity model*. The other model is called the *abundance model*. According to the scarcity model, people become fearful and hold on to things (behaviors, items, beliefs) because they are afraid that without these things they will never have "enough" in their life. According to the abundance model, sharing things and being open with oneself can bring abundance and peace because it is a good feeling to share regardless of the outcome. These two models were observed in situations as significant as the concentration camps during the Holocaust, as discussed by Viktor Frankl.

Look at the Same Situation From Each Way of Thinking

Scarcity Abundance

Meeting 3

For your consideration . . .

Fear is a major motivator. Sometimes you don't even know you are afraid of something. Sometimes it is easier to pretend it doesn't exist. Fear can stand in the way of you finding peace within yourself.

I am afraid of ____

What would I do if I were not afraid? _____________________________

Meeting 4

For your consideration . . .

Sometimes your beliefs, expectations, and perceptions can cloud your ability to be at peace with yourself and with others. If you get mad at people, then you are not at peace. To be able to find a place where peace can reside it is helpful to be able to separate a situation into beliefs/expectations/perceptions versus reality/observations.

Expectations/Beliefs/Perceptions Reality/Observations

Examples

Joe is frowning 

 Because Joe is frowning
he is mad.

Meeting 5

For your consideration . . .

As you look at who you wish to become, it is important that your words and actions match. Matching words and actions can help you build trust with others and stay true to yourself. If your words and actions don't match, then your actions become the true representation of who you are as a person. This can be true for yourself and for others. Think about the confusion that can be created by a person saying one thing and doing something different.

Words	Actions

Do they match?

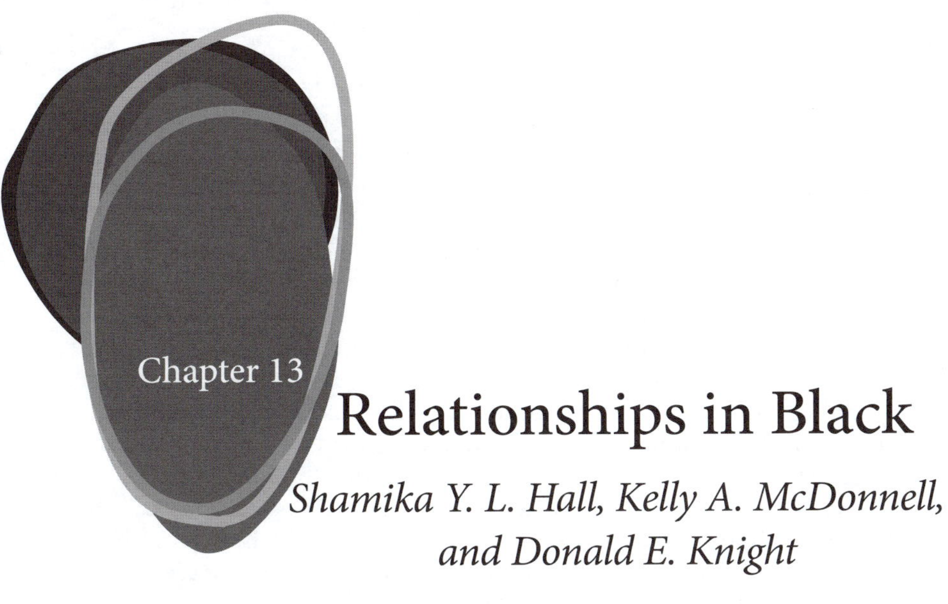

Chapter 13

Relationships in Black

*Shamika Y. L. Hall, Kelly A. McDonnell,
and Donald E. Knight*

Minority students have more difficulty adjusting to college than White students (Bonner, 1997; Taylor, 1986). In addition, Taylor reported that African American students may be beginning to develop their identity when they enter college. Although enrollment for African American students has increased throughout the years, historically this population has not sought out psychological services. These services are thus often underutilized by African American students on campuses (Bonner, 1997; Duncan, 2003; Rollock, Westman, & Johnson, 1992). Moreover, minority students may not seek out services until they are under immense psychological distress (Duncan, 2003; Rollock et al., 1992). There are many perceived barriers to seeking services, including the perception that there are no African American counselors or therapists in college counseling centers who would understand their problems (Bonner, 1997; Duncan, 2003). Furthermore, Bonner reported that there may also be some mistrust among African Americans that prevents them from seeking services at predominantly White institutions. This could result in students suffering from a mental disorder and yet going undiagnosed and untreated.

College counseling centers may need to become more proactive in their outreach efforts to this population. They could begin by developing culturally sensitive programs and support groups specifically for minority students (Bonner, 1997; Roach, 1999). The effective use of the group modality for therapy with African American clients has been supported in the literature for decades (Davis, 1984; Elligan & Utsey, 1999; Franklin & Pack-Brown, 2001; Lee, 1987; Muller, 2002; Rollock et al., 1992; Shipp, 1983; Wright & McCreary, 1997). This modality allows for the validation of shared experiences (Ford, 1997), stresses the collective over the individual expression of identity (Bailey & Bradbury-Bailey, 2007; Sue & Sue, 2003), and supports the notion of having "safety in numbers" (Merta, 1995), which may be important given the mistrust Blacks often have toward the helping professions (Terrell & Terrell, 1984). It is important for group facilitators to plan for and modify the group type in congruence with the population being served, especially when they are working with racial and ethnic minorities (Helms & Cook, 1999).

When preparing to facilitate a group with Black students, coleaders must take into account a host of considerations. First and foremost, they may need to use nontraditional approaches to gain access to this population, such as developing relationships with campus departments in which minority students feel most comfortable, like multicultural or diversity centers. Group leaders may want to arrange to serve as guest lecturers for an Africana/Black Studies course, volunteer time with a Black/minority student organization, and/or become involved in orientation activities in which they can engage with Black students new to the campus. They could also cultivate authentic relationships with student leaders, staff, and faculty throughout campus, as these individuals can serve as points of contact for potential group members. Group leaders should also assess where they are in relation to their own racial identity development and what knowledge they have about the Black experience (Helms & Cook, 1999; Shipp, 1983). Otherwise, leaders could run the risk of missing nuances in cultural communication (both verbal and nonverbal) and/or impeding the development of the group and its individual members (Bailey & Bradbury-Bailey, 2007; Muller, 2002). Possessing knowledge of one's racial self is significant for not only non-Black facilitators but Black facilitators as well, because Black racial identity attitudes vary within the Black community. Coleaders should discuss these issues as well as their group facilitation styles and how they will work together.

Group Plan

Session 1: Overview of the Group, Including Introductions and Informed Consent

- Provide each member with an individual copy of the group informed consent document, discuss and address any concerns or questions, and have group members sign their copies. This document should include such aspects as the importance of confidentiality and its limitations; expectations for attendance and member participation; and information about the leaders, as applicable (e.g., credentials, training, experience; and in the case of leader trainees, information about being supervised). Provide group members with a copy of the informed consent document to keep.
- Discuss group rules such as punctuality and attendance (e.g., calling if not able to attend) and respect for others. When discussing confidentiality, address what it means to group members and the implications of breaking confidentiality (i.e., that doing so impacts trust in the group). This is important in this type of group because of the increased

potential for members of the African American community to see one another on campus outside the context of the group.

- Have group members introduce themselves (stating their name, academic major, motivation for joining the group, and what they want to get out of the group experience). Then introduce yourself and reiterate information that was shared in the prescreening of members. This initial self-disclosure begins the process of sharing, establishing relationships, and building trust and cohesion.
- Discuss goals by having the members talk about their individual goals and their goals for the group as a whole. Also talk about some of your goals for the group.
- In preparing for the group, it would be helpful to develop a list of potential weekly discussion topics that might be of interest to the members. Rather than sharing those at the outset, you might first want to give the group members an opportunity to generate topics of interest to them. This will empower the members and help them establish some ownership of the group. If the members initially have difficulty generating topics, you could offer some suggestions from your list in order to get the discussion started.
- Some examples of interesting topics to discuss:
  - Black Love
  - Interpersonal communication
  - Infidelity
  - Interracial relationships/dating
  - Male/female ratio imbalance
- Talk about the format of the group.
  - It is designed to be a process-oriented counseling-type group wherein the responsibility for the group is shared among the members and the leaders.
  - Consider how to begin the discussions. Will any readings related to the weekly topics be used to encourage discussions?
- Get started.
  - Use an icebreaker to facilitate discussion and interaction in the initial session.
  - Talk about the group members' experiences in intimate relationships.
  - Encourage members to share their current relationship status and how they feel about that.
  - How have the members' views of relationships been shaped thus far?
  - What do they hope to learn about intimate relationships?
- At the end of the first session, and for each subsequent session, group members should decide the topic for discussion during the next group meeting.

Session 2: Black Love (Loving Oneself, Self-Acceptance)
- Address any unfinished business from the previous meeting.
- Questions/subtopics for discussion:

- What does Black Love mean to the group members?
- How have they experienced Black Love? What models have they had? What have they observed in others (e.g., family of origin, pop culture)?
- How does one achieve it? What challenges do members face on campus and/or in society in their journey?
- How is Black Love perceived in society today?
- Discussion points may include intimate relationships in general, how they have developed and evolved for the members over time, and how they are maintained.
- Wrap up the meeting by asking if anyone has anything they need to say before the group ends for the week. It is recommended that you initiate this about 15 minutes before the end of the group session.

Session 3: Interpersonal Communication

- Address any unfinished business from the previous meeting.
- Questions/subtopics for discussion:
  - How (process) are men and women in our community communicating with one another?
  - What (content) are we talking to one another about with regard to intimate relationships?
  - What impact has society or the media had on Black relationships?
  - What constitutes healthy and unhealthy interpersonal communication?
  - How do the group members feel about their communication with their significant others and previous or current relationship partners?
- Include a focus on the here-and-now process in the group, and explore the group members' interpersonal communication.
- Wrap up the meeting by asking if anyone has anything they need to say before the group ends for the week. It is recommended that you initiate this about 15 minutes before the end of the group session.

Session 4: Infidelity

- Address any unfinished business from the previous meeting.
- Questions/subtopics for discussion:
  - Encourage members to discuss whether they believe individuals in relationships can be faithful to each other.
  - What is considered cheating? Physical or emotional cheating or both (e.g., spending extended time with someone, holding hands, kissing, e-mailing or using the Internet)?
  - Is cheating okay? Why or under what circumstances, or why not?
  - What role does society or the media play in infidelity?
- Explore the different values and perspectives held by group members and how they are similar and/or different; consider the impact one's perspective and experiences have on his or her relationships (e.g., why one person would choose to stay in a relationship whereas another member would end the relationship); what does that say about the person, that relationship?

- Wrap up the meeting by asking if anyone has anything they need to say before the group ends for the week. It is recommended that you initiate this about 15 minutes before the end of the group session.

Session 5: Interracial Relationships/Dating

- Address any unfinished business from the previous meeting.
- Questions/subtopics for discussion:
  - How do the group members feel about interracial relationships?
  - What are some of the challenges of interracial relationships or interracial dating?
  - How do group members feel interracial dating is perceived by the larger society?
  - What experiences, if any, have the group members personally had with interracial relationships?
- Wrap up the meeting by asking if anyone has anything they need to say before the group ends for the week. It is recommended that you initiate this about 15 minutes before the end of the group session.

Session 6: Male/Female Ratio Imbalance

- Address any unfinished business from the previous meeting.
- Questions/subtopics for discussion:
  - Explore with group members the relative imbalance of men to women available for forming intimate relationships. This could include a discussion of the higher ratio of available women to available men and the higher concentration of women to men on college campuses.
  - How do group members feel about the gender imbalance?
  - Do group members feel there are enough single/eligible/suitable mates with whom to partner? Why or why not?
  - What impact does the male/female ratio imbalance have on relationships (e.g., intimate relationships, friendships)?
- Wrap up the meeting by asking if anyone has anything they need to say before the group ends for the week. It is recommended that you initiate this about 15 minutes before the end of the group session.

Session 7: Review and Continuation

- Address any unfinished business from the previous meeting.
- Questions/subtopics for discussion:
  - Open the session to questions members have for one another to gain a better understanding of intimate relationships.
  - Members could continue to discuss topics that have been addressed thus far or introduce other topics of interest to them.
- If your group has more than eight sessions, you can continue to discuss topics already broached or generate additional topics with group members.

- Wrap up the meeting by asking if anyone has anything they need to say before the group ends for the week. It is recommended that you initiate this about 15 minutes before the end of the group session.

Session 8: Termination

- Encourage group members to talk about their experience in the group and what they feel they have gained from the discussions about intimate relationships.
- Help members articulate what they have learned about themselves with regard to forming and sustaining intimate relationships.
- Explore where members will go from here (after the group), how they will continue the work they have started, what their future goals are, and how they will apply the learning to their life beyond the group and continue to grow.
- Help group members process how they feel about the final group meeting and the end of the group.
- Elicit group members' feedback about the group, including whether they would consider being a member again and/or whether they feel this group would be beneficial to others.
- The entire last session (or the last two sessions, if the group has been meeting longer) includes a wrap-up of unfinished business. Leave sufficient time to help members make sense of the group experience and what they have learned and to process the ending of the group. Do not encourage group members to bring up new topics for which there would be insufficient time for exploration and processing.

References

Bailey, D. F., & Bradbury-Bailey, M. E. (2007). Promoting achievement for African American males through group work. *Journal for Specialists in Group Work, 32*(1), 83–96.

Bonner, W. W. (1997). Black male perspectives of counseling on a predominantly White university campus. *Journal of Black Studies, 27,* 395–408.

Davis, L. E. (1984). Essential components of group work with Black Americans. *Social Work With Groups, 7*(3), 97–109.

Duncan, L. E. (2003). Black male college students' attitudes toward seeking psychological help. *Journal of Black Psychology, 29,* 68–86.

Elligan, D., & Utsey, S. (1999). Utility of an African-centered support group for African American men confronting societal racism and oppression. *Cultural Diversity and Ethnic Minority Psychology, 5*(2), 156–165.

Ford, D. Y. (1997). Counseling middle-class African Americans. In C. C. Lee (Ed.), *Multicultural issues in counseling: New approaches to diversity* (2nd ed., pp. 81–107). Alexandria, VA: American Counseling Association.

Franklin, R. B., & Pack-Brown, S. (2001). Team brothers: An Africentric approach to group work with African American male adolescents. *Journal for Specialists in Group Work, 26*(3), 237–245.

Helms, J. E., & Cook, D. A. (1999). Racial and cultural dynamics of group interventions. In J. E. Helms & D. A. Cook (Eds.), *Using race and culture in counseling and psychotherapy* (pp. 226–253). Needham Heights, MA: Allyn & Bacon.

Lee, C. C. (1987). Black manhood training: Group counseling for male Blacks in Grades 7-12. *Journal for Specialists in Group Work, 12*(1), 18–25.

Merta, R. J. (1995). Group work: Multicultural perspectives. In J. G. Ponterotto, J. M. Casas, L. A. Suzuki, & C. M. Alexander (Eds.), *Handbook of multicultural counseling* (pp. 567–585). Thousand Oaks, CA: Sage.

Muller, L. E. (2002). Group counseling for African American males: When all you have are European American counselors. *Journal for Specialists in Group Work, 27*(3), 299–313.

Roach, R. (1999). Succeeding on White campuses: Elite institutions explain why initiatives that support Black student success are essential to achieving the goal of diversity. *Black Issues in Higher Education, 15*(26), 42–43.

Rollock, D. A., Westman, J. S., & Johnson, C. (1992). A Black student support group on a predominantly White university campus: Issues for counselors and therapists. *Journal of College Student Personnel, 17,* 243–252.

Shipp, P. L. (1983). Counseling Blacks: A group approach. *Personnel and Guidance Journal, 62,* 108–111.

Sue, D. W., & Sue, D. (2003). *Counseling the culturally different: Theory and practice* (4th ed.). New York, NY: Wiley.

Taylor, C. A. (1986). Black students on predominantly White college campuses in the 1980s. *Journal of College Student Personnel, 27,* 196–202.

Terrell, F., & Terrell, S. (1984). Race of counselor, client sex, cultural mistrust level, and premature termination from counseling among Black clients. *Journal of Counseling Psychology, 31,* 371–375.

Wright, R. C., & McCreary, M. L. (1997). The talented ten: Supporting African American male college students. *Journal of African American Men, 3*(1), 45–68.

Supporting Students of Color on Campus

Sam Steen, Dana Griffin, and Qi Shi

More than 4.5 million students of color from low-income backgrounds are currently attending U.S. colleges and universities as first-generation students (Pell Institute for the Study of Opportunity in Higher Education, 2007). Often, students—particularly first-generation students, students of color, and students from low-income backgrounds—do not make it successfully through the first year of college because of limited academic support (Cole, 2009). For instance, compared with 93% of high school graduates from higher income families, only 69% of students from low-income families graduate from high school (Mortenson, 2007). Of these 69%, only 12% have attained a college degree by age 24. In contrast, the graduation rate for their higher income peers was 73% (Mortenson, 2007).

Time and again many students—regardless of their cultural and/or socioeconomic background—are not prepared for college from the very beginning of this transition (Hicks & Heastie, 2008). Even though many students take more and more challenging courses during high school, a number are entering postsecondary education unprepared. In other words, public schools are struggling to provide explicit and consistent evidence of what it takes to be ready for college beyond simply obtaining a high school diploma. This is particularly problematic for students of color, first-generation college students, and students from impoverished backgrounds.

We propose that a group counseling program for students of color, first-generation college students, and students from impoverished backgrounds can provide academic and personal-social support as well as strategies and insights from others facing some of the very same issues. Here we offer some suggestions for a group format that includes sample activities, processing questions, and teaching strategies that can be used with such students.

Group Plan

Session 1: Introductions, Ground Rules, and Administration of the Preassessment

Objectives

To introduce one another, generate a list of ground rules, administer the preassessment, and discuss the number of group sessions.

Materials Needed

Whiteboard, markers, Blackboard (or other electronic platform), preassessment (e.g., Multigroup Ethnic Identity Measure [MEIM]; Phinney, 1992), and a poem (e.g., "Diversity Is a Good Thing" by Deidre Blair). (Please see http://www.poemhunter.com/ for all poems referenced in this group plan.)

Opening/Introduction

- Ask students to discuss (a) reasons they thought they were attending the group; (b) whether they would be interested in exploring ways to be successful as they transition to college; (c) whether they would be interested in learning strategies for dealing with different issues students encounter in postsecondary school; and (d) whether they would commit to using an electronic medium (e.g., Blackboard) to post questions, resources they come across, and blogs of their struggles and successes in their studies.

Activities

1. Have everyone introduce themselves by sharing their names and where they are from.
2. Generate ground rules
   - Brainstorm with students the ground rules that all members would be willing to follow.
   - Consider posting the ground rules to the Blackboard site, if appropriate, and obtain agreement from each member to uphold the ground rules.
   - Be sure to stress and explore the issue of confidentiality. Encourage the students to feel free to discuss their experiences with other members from the group outside the group. However, stress that in order to ensure that information remains in confidence, they should not share with others who are not participating in the group. Other examples of ground rules include listening with respect, taking turns talking, being open minded, providing support and encouragement, and being honest with one another.
3. Administer the preassessment (e.g., the MEIM can be accessed using a Google search)
   - The preassessment is used to determine a baseline for the students regarding the perceptions of themselves in relation to their cultural backgrounds.

- Administer the preassessment in the ways that would best match the group situation (e.g., individually, in paper-and-pencil format, or electronically via a survey website such as Survey Monkey).
- The analysis of the results can be shared with the group in the following session by guiding the students to calculate the average score of their preassessment (e.g., the MEIM) and providing further explanations on how to interpret the scores. This measurement can serve as a fundamental starting point for students in this group that may relate to other areas for improvement and change in future sessions.

Closing

- Have a volunteer read aloud a selected poem (e.g., "Diversity Is a Good Thing" by Deidre Blair).
- Briefly explore reactions to the poem and interpretations of the poem.
- Inform the students of the total number of group sessions.
- Have the students share one new insight that they had in the group today.
- Encourage students to think about one individual goal they would like to establish for this academic semester.

Session 2: Brief Review, Acquaintance, and Individual Goals

Objectives

To review previous session, to get to know one another in an unconventional manner, and to explore individual goals.

Materials Needed

Whiteboard, markers, Blackboard (or other electronic platform), and a poem (e.g., "The Diversity of People" by Jessica Gouldreault).

Opening/Brief Review

- Ask students to discuss (a) one thing they remember from the last session, (b) whether they would be interested in getting to know one another more deeply, and (c) one individual goal that they would like to accomplish this academic semester.

Activity

Nontraditional introductions

- Explain to the students that this exercise is an opportunity to meet the other members of the group and to begin building group cohesion.
- Ask the students to think about what someone usually asks another person when meeting for the first time.
- Generate a list of these questions on the whiteboard (e.g., Where are you from? How old are you? Do you have any siblings? What's your major? What do you want to do when you graduate?).
- After soliciting these questions, tell each person to pair up with someone in the group with whom they are least familiar. Tell the students that they are to get to know each other without using any of the questions mentioned previously.

- Provide students about 5–7 minutes to talk with their partners.
- After time is up, bring the students back together and discuss what they learned about each other by having them share with the rest of the group some aspects about their partner.
- Some follow-up questions that can be posed include the following: What was that activity like for you? How did you feel initially? Did your feelings change as you continued? Did you take any risks? How well did you get to know your partner? What did you get out of this activity?

Goals
- Teach students the definition of goals and goal orientations (e.g., performance goals vs. mastery goals). For instance, mastery-oriented students strive to gain understanding of a concept, whereas performance-oriented students aim to outperform their peers and display their competence. A mastery goal orientation has been linked to higher achievement than a performance goal orientation.
- Discuss the idea that the strategies one uses to accomplish one's goal are just as important as the goal itself.
- Have students generate one individual short-term goal they would like to accomplish during this semester and 3–4 specific strategies or steps that they would need to take in order to accomplish this goal.
- Use the Blackboard site to post the goals that the students come up with. Encourage the students to blog their successes and challenges when striving to achieve their goals.

Closing
- Have a volunteer read aloud a selected poem (e.g., "The Diversity of People" by Jessica Gouldreault).
- Briefly explore reactions to the poem and interpretations of the poem.
- Inform the students of the number of sessions the group has left.
- Have the students share one new insight that they had in the group today.
- Encourage students to look up the definition of *self-advocacy*, which will be discussed during the next session.

Session 3: Brief Review and Self-Advocacy

Objectives
To review the previous session, to generate a definition of *self-advocacy*, and to explore strategies to advocate for oneself.

Materials Needed
Whiteboard, markers, Blackboard (or other electronic platform), and a poem (e.g., "For Unity in Diversity" by Florence Wiener).

Opening/Brief Review
- Ask students to discuss (a) how well they are doing in accomplishing their individual goals, (b) whether they would be interested in sharing any definitions of *self-advocacy* that they gathered since the

last session, and (c) whether they would be interested in learning strategies to advocate for themselves.

Activities
1. Define *self-advocacy*
   - Ask students to share their definitions of *self-advocacy*. One definition is the ability to seek, evaluate, and use information for one's own benefit. Write the examples on the whiteboard.
   - Collectively decide on a working definition of *self-advocacy* relevant to the members' experiences at the university based on the examples generated by the group.
2. Self-advocacy strategies
   - Show a video clip that shows a character advocating for himself or herself (e.g., in the movie *Hitch*, the character Albert Brenneman seeks assistance from Dr. Hitch).
   - Discuss strategies the character takes in order to achieve the desired outcomes or to overcome certain challenges or barriers.
   - Talk about some difficulties or barriers that the students may have had in their lives, what they did to overcome those difficulties, and how they felt after overcoming those hardships.
   - Incorporate into the discussion the relationship between self-advocacy and success in college (e.g., seeking help from a professor, establishing a support network of friends and study partners, balancing school and social life). Self-advocacy strategies can also be used to seek out leadership roles within the university or to address needs in the local community.
   - Use the Blackboard site to post the definitions and strategies generated during the session. Encourage the students to blog their successes and challenges when advocating for themselves throughout the semester.

Closing
- Have a volunteer read aloud a selected poem (e.g., "For Unity in Diversity" by Florence Wiener).
- Briefly explore reactions to the poem and interpretations of the poem.
- Inform the students of the number of sessions the group has left.
- Have the students share one new insight that they had in the group today.
- Encourage students to look up the definition of *self-concept*, which will be discussed during the next session.

Session 4: Brief Review and Self-Concept

Objectives
To review the previous session, to generate a definition of *self-concept*, and to explore academic and personal self-concept.

Materials Needed
Blank 8" × 11" sheets of paper, whiteboard, markers, Blackboard (or other electronic platform), and a poem (e.g., "Unity in Diversity" by Rajaram Ramachandran).

Opening/Brief Review
- Ask students to discuss (a) how well they are doing in accomplishing their individual goals, (b) whether they would be interested in sharing any definitions of *self-concept* that they gathered since the last session, and (c) whether they would be interested in exploring the academic and personal perceptions of themselves.

Activities
1. Define *self-concept*
   - Ask students to share their definitions of *self-concept*. One definition is the composite of ideas, feelings, and attitudes that a person has about his or her own identity, worth, capabilities, and limitations. Write the examples on the whiteboard.
   - Collectively decide on a working definition of *self-concept* relevant to the members' experiences at the university based on the examples generated by the group.
   - Differentiate between academic self-concept and personal self-concept.
   - Use the Blackboard site to post a definition of *self-concept* that includes both personal and academic self-concept.
2. What do you think about me?
   - The purpose of this activity is to compare what one thinks in relation to how others may perceive them. First have students individually write down a list of things that they feel about themselves (both positive and negative) on one 8″ × 11″ sheet of paper. Be sure that the students' names are on the papers.
   - Collect the sheets and then pass out another set of blank 8″ × 11″ sheets of paper, each with a group member's name, to someone other than that member.
   - Have students compose both positive comments and areas for improvement about the individual's personal attributes and their academic characteristics on the paper they received.
   - Collect these sheets and then pass them to someone else for that person to offer his or her perceptions of the student. Repeat this process two to three times, and then pass all of the sheets to the people they belong to, including the sheet that they first completed about themselves. Allow the students a few minutes to read the other students' responses and compare them to what they initially wrote about themselves.
   - Explore with the students what it is like to read these comments confirming or discrediting their personal perceptions. Some processing questions include the following: What did you learn from others? Was it difficult being honest when writing on others' sheets? How can we balance what we feel about ourselves in comparison to how others perceive us? How does this relate to our academic self-concept?

Closing
- Have a volunteer read aloud a selected poem (e.g., "Unity in Diversity" by Rajaram Ramachandran).
- Briefly explore reactions to the poem and interpretations of the poem.
- Inform the students of the number of sessions the group has left.
- Have the students share one new insight that they had in the group today.
- Encourage students to look up the definition of *empowerment*, which will be discussed during the next session.

Session 5: Brief Review, Empowerment, and Self-Regulation

Objectives
To review the previous session, to generate a definition of *empowerment*, and to discuss self-regulatory strategies.

Materials Needed
Whiteboard, markers, Blackboard (or other electronic platform), and a poem (e.g., "Cultural Diversity" by Gregory Pickett).

Opening/Brief Review
- Ask students to discuss (a) how well they are doing in accomplishing their individual goals, (b) whether they would be interested in sharing any definitions of *empowerment* that they gathered since the last session, and (c) whether they would be interested in exploring self-regulatory strategies that they can use to be successful in college.

Activities
1. Define *empowerment*
   - Ask students to share their definitions of *empowerment*. One common definition is to increase personal, interpersonal, or political power so that individuals and/or communities can do something to improve their current situations (Gutierrez, 1990). Write their examples on the whiteboard.
   - Collectively decide on a working definition of *empowerment* relevant to members' experiences at the university based on the examples generated by the group.
2. Self-regulation strategies
   - Explore with the students the concept of self-regulation, which refers to the degree to which students are metacognitively, motivationally, and behaviorally active participants in their own learning process. In other words, students who are self-regulated learners use and differentiate effective versus ineffective learning strategies to accomplish their goals in school.
   - Generate strategies to ensure academic success. Include tips and strategies for writing, test taking, and studying large amounts of information.

- Invite a guest speaker to lead a discussion on how to write college-level essays, take exams, or study large amounts of information. A field trip to the reference section of the university library or the office through which one can receive academic assistance might be useful.
- Use the Blackboard site to post the definitions and strategies generated during the session. Encourage the students to blog their successes and challenges when using self-regulatory strategies throughout the semester.

Closing
- Have a volunteer read aloud a selected poem (e.g., "Cultural Diversity" by Gregory Pickett).
- Briefly explore reactions to the poem and interpretations of the poem.
- Inform the students of the number of sessions the group has left.
- Have the students share one new insight that they had in the group today.

Session 6: Brief Review and Internal and External Assets

Objectives
To review previous session, to acknowledge personal strengths, and to discover support networks within and outside of the university community.

Materials Needed
Whiteboard, markers, Blackboard (or other electronic platform), and a poem (e.g., "As I Grew Older" by Langston Hughes).

Opening/Brief Review
- Ask students to discuss (a) how well they are doing in accomplishing their individual goals, (b) whether they would be interested in learning the definitions of *internal* and *external assets*, and (c) whether they would be interested in brainstorming about support networks within and outside of the university community.

Activity
Define *internal* and *external assets*
- Generate one definition of *internal* and *external assets*. The Search Institute (2010) is useful in accomplishing this. One common definition for *internal assets* is aspects within the self that are strengths (e.g., sense of purpose, personal power); *external assets* are aspects outside of the self that are provided by the family, school, and/or community and that enable a person to be successful (e.g., a caring university climate, positive adult role models). Write the examples on the whiteboard.
- Discuss and brainstorm a list of individuals or organizations who could serve as support networks inside the school and within the surrounding community.
- Help students identify barriers that might deter them from connecting with individuals within and outside of the university.

- Acknowledge the role of environmental factors and systemic oppression in students' difficulties. Teach students strategies for overcoming these barriers.
- Explore with the students the importance of learning about support networks and how these relate to success in college.
- Use the Blackboard site to post the definitions and strategies generated during the session. Encourage the students to blog their successes and challenges when using, identifying, and connecting with external assets.

Closing
- Have a volunteer read aloud a selected poem (e.g., "As I Grew Older" by Langston Hughes).
- Briefly explore reactions to the poem and interpretations of the poem.
- Inform the students that the next session is the final session.
- Have the students share one new insight that they had in the group today.
- Encourage students between now and the next session to identify and connect with one person in the school via e-mail or in person and be prepared to share their interactions at the next session.

Session 7: Brief Review of the Entire Group, Identification of Support Networks, and Closure

Objectives
To briefly review individual goals, to identify support networks within and outside of the university community, to complete postassessments, and to negotiate a follow-up meeting.

Materials Needed
Whiteboard, markers, Blackboard (or other electronic platform), and a poem (e.g., "Tomorrow's a Brand New Day" by Resty Rivera).

Opening/Brief Review
- Ask students to share where they currently stand regarding accomplishing the goals they established at the beginning of the group. Allow students who volunteer to share (a) what goal(s) they have accomplished and (b) what steps they took to do so.
- Encourage students who do not believe they were successful to share where they currently stand.

Activities
1. Support networks
   - Generate a list of individuals on the whiteboard whom the students contacted to be a part of their support network within or outside of the university community. Feel free to list additional individuals whom the students can seek out for support in the future (e.g., a student affairs contact, a sports coach, or an alumnus still living in the community).

- Encourage students to discuss their interactions with the person they contacted in between the group sessions and what it was like to begin establishing a relationship with someone who may be called upon in the future.
- Use the Blackboard site to post the list of individuals and their contact information generated from the discussions for the students' future reference.

2. Group summary
- Allow students to review any previous discussions involving goals, academic self-concept, self-advocacy, empowerment, self-regulation, and finding support networks within and outside of the university community.

3. Postassessment(s) (e.g., the MEIM, the Critical Incidents Questionnaire [Kivlighan & Goldfine, 1991]).
- The MEIM can be used as the postassessment to compare the students' perceptions of themselves in relation to their cultural backgrounds.
- The Critical Incidents Questionnaire asks students to share their reactions to the following prompt: "Of all the events that occurred in the group, which one do you feel was most important to you. Describe the event, what took place, who were the students involved with, and what were their reactions. Why was this important to you? What did you learn?" (Kivlighan & Goldfine, 1991, p. 152).
- In order to gather additional information that could be useful for improving future groups, you can include other open-ended questions at the end of this questionnaire. Sample questions include the following: What did you learn during these group sessions? Did the group help you improve your grades? What are your recommendations to make the group better?

Closing and Follow-Up
- Students should be encouraged to keep in contact with the individuals they identified as resources within and outside of the university community. You can also negotiate when the group could have a follow-up meeting in the future (e.g., at the end of the semester, at the beginning of the semester, before exams). During the follow-up meeting the students can meet together to check in, to encourage one another to continue using their internal and external assets, and to complete the surveys again to see if any of the learning that took place was retained.
- Have a volunteer read aloud a selected poem (e.g., "Tomorrow Is a New Day" by Susan Polis Schutz).
- Briefly explore reactions to the poem and interpretations of the poem.
- Have the students share one new insight that they had in the group today.

- If applicable, encourage students between now and the follow-up meeting to seek out help and to support one another if or when the need arises.

References

Cole, D. L. (2009). Staying within the margins: The educational stories of first-generation, low-income college students. *Dissertation Abstracts International: Section A. Humanities and Social Sciences, 70*(2A), 689.

Gutierrez, L. M. (1990). Working with women of color: An empowerment perspective. *Social Work, 3,* 150–153.

Hicks, T., & Heastie, S. (2008). High school to college transition: A profile of the stressors, physical and psychological health issues that affect the first-year on-campus college student. *Journal of Cultural Diversity, 15*(3), 143–147.

Kivlighan, D. M., Jr., & Goldfine, D. C. (1991). Endorsement of therapeutic factors as a function of stage of group development and participant interpersonal attitudes. *Journal of Counseling Psychology, 28,* 150–158.

Mortenson, T. (2007). *Bachelor's degree attainment by age 24 by family income quartiles, 1970 to 2005.* Oskaloosa, IA: Postsecondary Education Opportunity.

Pell Institute for the Study of Opportunity in Higher Education. (2007). *Demography is not destiny: Increasing the graduation rates of low-income college students at large public universities.* Washington, DC: Author.

Phinney, J. (1992). The Multigroup Ethnic Identity Measure: A new scale for use with adolescents and young adults from diverse groups. *Journal of Adolescent Research, 7,* 156–176.

Search Institute. (2010). *Developmental assets tools.* Retrieved from http://www.search-institute.org/assets/

Support Group for Gay and Lesbian Students

M. Carolyn Thomas and Paul F. Hard

Few publications are available describing homogeneous groups for gay, lesbian, bisexual, transgender, or questioning (GLBTQ) youth (Christner, Stewart, & Freeman, 2007). Brabender, Fallon, and Smolar (2004) described how prior to the gay rights movement of the 1970s groups for these populations were often reparative or conversion attempts to change what was believed to be a psychopathology. Puglia and Hall (2010) described several theme-specific groups for sexual minorities with specialized concerns, such as coming out, living with HIV/AIDS, drug and alcohol addictions, suicide, parenting, and aging. Of only three articles in the *Journal for Specialists in Group Work* about groups for sexual minorities, two described groups for men living with HIV/AIDS (Norsworthy & Horne, 1994; Smiley, 2004) and one described groups for women (Firestein, 1999). Even the Puglia and Hall chapter about group work with gay, lesbian, and bisexual clients in the Capuzzi, Gross, and Stauffer (2010) text described a group exclusively for men diagnosed with HIV. Muller and Hartman (1998) outlined a group for sexual minority youth that included both boys and girls, but similar articles about developmental homogeneous groups that are not designed for specific populations within the sexual minority community have rarely been described in the literature.

Despite the paucity of articles describing groups for sexual minorities, the beneficial effects of group work are often described. Christner et al. (2007) mentioned that cognitive behavioral group therapy was especially appropriate for use with GLBTQ youth because groups were particularly helpful in restructuring distorted and negative beliefs associated with being other than heterosexual. Getting rid of the distortions relieves depression, anger, shame, guilt, and confusion and also increases communication skills, assertiveness, and emotional coping skills. Bringaze and White (2001) studied the effects of sexual minorities having access to healthy resources, a gay community, and counseling. They found that these factors definitely contributed to positive identity development and reduced alienation. Because of their findings, they strongly urged counselors to identify gay and lesbian community centers, campus organizations, and support groups. Puglia and Hall (2010) asserted that gays, lesbians, and bisexuals share their own situations and feelings with others who have similar problems and learn new ways of coping with discrimination. The affirmation in groups helps counteract the family, community, and spiritual difficulties experienced outside the group. The group inclusion also helps overcome alienation and hopelessness.

Description of a Group for Gay and Lesbian College Students

The group for gay and lesbian college students described here is a general support/counseling group that is planned for 13 weeks of a 15-week semester. Although the group includes psychoeducation, it is primarily designed as a developmental, personal growth counseling experience. The objectives are the result of findings from a previous group offered in the Auburn Montgomery Counseling Center (Montgomery, Alabama) and the expressed needs of student members of a recently formed GLBTQ student social organization.

Group Objectives

The objectives of the group are as follows:

1. Relieve isolation by providing a supportive environment.
2. Dispel myths about homosexuality.
3. Reduce negative self-labeling and challenge internalized homoprejudice.
4. Provide positive strategies for coming out.
5. Facilitate growth through the stages of positive identity development.
6. Identify healthy resources.
7. Explore positive sexual minority portrayals and images in the arts, music, and literature.
8. Learn how to build a supportive community and family of choice.
9. Improve family-of-origin, peer, and professional relationships.
10. Explore sources of healthy spirituality.

Group Plan

Session 1: Orientation and Gay/Lesbian Stories
- Review group goals, group rules, rights, and responsibilities.
- Sign confidentiality agreement and informed consent.

- Ask members to spend about 10 minutes sharing their gay/lesbian stories, including how they came to realize their orientation, the extent to which they are out, and an example of a positive and negative experience with the straight world.
- Invite the members to identify and directly address others with whom they identify, sharing the similarity of their short life stories.
- Ask the members what they learned about themselves from listening to others' stories.
- Summarize themes that arose from the stories, and list the important issues for subsequent group sessions.

Session 2: Cleaning House: Getting Rid of Myths and Negative Self-Labels

- Ask members to write down all of the negative labels they have heard used about gays and lesbians and consolidate the lists on a chalkboard or flip chart.
- Invite members to share situations when some of those labels have been used about them and how they felt. Make certain that members identify the feeling and the depth of the feeling.
- Have each member scratch out a negative label someone personally used with them and write beside it a positive true characteristic. When a member has difficulty replacing the insult with a positive characteristic, you or other members can help find a positive replacement.
- Ask members to share myths they have heard expressed about gays and lesbians, and the effects of hearing people believe falsehoods about them. You and the other members can dispel the myths and replace the falsehoods with truths.
- Make a short presentation on internalized homophobia and how negative labels and myths can damage feelings about the self, even when the person knows the labels and myths are false.
- Seek closure by asking members to share what they have learned about themselves and to finish the statement "I am ..." with a positive affirmation. You may also ask members to give one or two other members affirmations by telling them "I see you as ..."

Session 3: Images in the Arts, Music, and Literature

- Select a variety of vignettes of movies or plays, songs, poems, books, paintings, or short stories that include both negative and positive images or portrayals of gays and lesbians. The selections should be carefully chosen so that the formats appeal to participants who may be culturally diverse.
- Show, play, or distribute for reading the examples of negative portrayals of gays and lesbians, and ask the members to identify why each example is negative. Also ask them how the portrayal can damage opinions about gays and lesbians and how it can perpetuate negative self-labeling.

- Avoid an extensive philosophical discussion by getting members to share their own personal reactions to the negative portrayals.
- Show, play, or distribute for reading the examples of positive and truer portrayals of gays and lesbians, and ask members to compare their feelings engendered by the negative and positive portrayals.
- Assignment: Invite members to bring to the next session a movie, song, or piece of literature they would like to share with a family member or friend to help that family member or friend better understand how the group member feels and develop a truer and more positive understanding of the group member.

Session 4: This Is Who I Am

- Invite each member to share the movie, song, or literature he or she has chosen to possibly share with a close person to help the family member or friend better understand the group member. Movies or novels too lengthy to include can be summarized by identifying the important points. Encourage members to explore examples with honest, genuine, affirming, and uplifting portrayals of sexual minorities rather than choosing examples with only entertainment value.
- After all examples have been shared, ask the participants to identify how other members' contributions have influenced their own feelings and self-image.
- Summarize emerging themes in the examples and member responses.
- Ongoing assignment: Start a resource list of positive gay and lesbian images in the arts, media, and literature. (Members can continue to read and search for examples and compile a comprehensive resource list by the end of the semester.)

Session 5: Where Am I in My Identity Development?

- Provide an outline and chart of Cass's (1979) stages of gay and lesbian identity development, and explain the developmental nature of the process and the characteristics of each stage. Perhaps choose characters in the media or literature the members previously brought to the group to explain the stages.
- Ask members to identify the stage through which they are currently progressing and provide reasons for their belief. Invite other members to provide feedback to each participant that might verify or gently challenge the chosen stage.
- Invite members to share their behaviors, feelings, and relationships in previous stages and how they progressed through each of the previous stages.
- Seek closure by inviting members to tell others how their own progression has been similar.
- Summarize the session by identifying common themes in members' identity development.

Session 6: Where Am I Going and How Will I Get There?

- Given the identification in the previous session of each member's current stage of identity development, ask each member to envision his or her next stage and describe how life will be in the next stage.
- Get the members to close their eyes and conduct a Future Day Fantasy Exercise (see Handout 15.1).
- Ask the members to share their future day, describing how it will be representative of the next stage of identity development.
- Invite other members to give each member feedback to verify or gently challenge whether the future day really is representative of the next stage.
- Ask members to share commonalities they share with other members in their journey through a healthy identity development.
- Assignment: Invite the members to devise a plan for specific changes in their lives so that they can progress to the next stage of identity development. The plan should include what, when, and how they can make changes. Resources needed to facilitate the changes can also be identified.

Session 7: The Coming Out Process: A Personal Choice

- Distribute the Coming Out Process and Assessment (Handout 15.2) for members to complete and ask them to share their results with other members. Emphasize that whether they come out to themselves only, significant others, or most people is strictly a personal choice. It also can be a lifelong process.
- Invite the members who came out to significant others in nonaffirming ways to share how they might change how they revealed their orientation and how the results may have been different.
- Ask members who experienced acceptance to describe why their experiences were more affirming.
- Assignment: Ask members to choose a person with whom they might someday want to share their orientation and visualize how they might come out to that person using helpful strategies taken from the Coming Out Process and Assessment (Handout 15.2). They will be asked to role play coming out to that person in the next group session. Assure them that this exercise is in no way a pressure to come out to anyone. Rather, the intention is to develop an affirming personal style should they ever choose to come out more than they currently have.

Session 8: Coming Out: Role Play "What If I Do"

- Have each member share the person to whom they may potentially come out and role play with another member or other members how they will share their orientation. Use dyad role plays in larger groups.

- Ask other members to give feedback about how the coming out style would make them potentially more or less accepting if they were the person to whom the member was coming out.
- Seek closure by asking each member whether the helpful strategies and role play made him or her less afraid of disclosure. Reinforce that coming out is a personal choice and a lifelong process.

Session 9: Building a Supportive Community

- Distribute the Community Support Worksheet (Handout 15.3) and have members write in their known *current* and *available* healthy supports and resources. The categories include (a) social support, (b) cultural identity, (c) intellectual growth, (d) spiritual support, (e) political and legal protection, (f) career and professional growth, and (g) health resources.
- After members share their resources, they may be able to add previously unknown resources they discover from other members' worksheets. You may also provide lists of available healthy resources unknown to members.
- Ask members to identify gaps in their support.
- Assignment: Invite members to try and locate healthy resources to fill in gaps. If needed resources are not available, ask members to devise a plan to create resources when feasible. Provide a sampling of Internet resources members may find helpful (see Handout 15.4, Internet Resources).

Session 10: My New Community

- Have members share the new resources they discovered and add these resources to their worksheets. Where needed resources do not exist, members may commit to creating the resources in their community or finding alternative methods for completing their community.
- Seek closure by asking members to tell other members what they have learned from them and share how increased knowledge and awareness of healthy resources and support has affected their feelings of isolation.

Session 11: Creating a Family of Choice

- Differentiate between family of origin and family of choice, and ask members to describe how they fit in their family of origin. Ask them how their sexual minority status is treated and what unmet needs they may have.
- Ask the members to define what *family* means to them and to describe a potential family of choice in which they would be respected, loved, and positively affirmed members. These families of choice may include members of the students' families of origin.
- Ask members what they can do to improve their acceptance in their family of origin and how they can build a new family to compensate for unmet needs in their family of origin.

- Seek closure by identifying common themes in family values. Also invite each member to identify strengths and characteristics in other members that would make them valuable to their own family of choice.

Session 12: The Path to Finding a Spiritual Self

- Provide a definition of *spirituality*, such as "the capacity and tendency in all human beings to find and construct meaning about life and existence and to move toward personal growth, responsibility, and relationship with others" (Myers & Williard, 2003, p. 149). Ask the group to define what spirituality personally means to them, being careful to distinguish it from religion.
- Identify and explore themes of spirituality within group responses such as wholeness, wellness, meaning, centeredness, balance, harmony, values, compassion, celebration of life, and connectedness.
- Ask which paths members have taken to find meaning and purpose and how they have made progress toward finding their own personal spirituality. Ask in which area(s) of spirituality they have strengths and in which areas they would like to grow.
- Invite members to share where they see, or have seen, spiritual strengths in other members.
- Seek closure by asking members to tell how their spiritual journeys have been similar.

Session 13: A Parting Gift

- Ask each member to share how the group may have created changes in his or her internalized homoprejudice, acceptance of self, stage of identity development, fear of being more open, and worldview.
- Invite members to thank another member or other members for specific gifts of affirmation they might have received or something they learned from the member(s) that made a significant difference in their lives.
- Finally, ask each member to write down a symbolic gift for each of the other members and give the written gift to each member to keep with him or her so that the benefits of the group can continue to grow.

References

Brabender, V., Fallon, A., & Smolar, A. (2004). *The essentials of group therapy.* Hoboken, NJ: Wiley.

Bringaze, T. B., & White, L. J. (2001). Living out proud: Factors contributing to healthy identity development in lesbian leaders. *Journal of Mental Health Counseling, 23,* 162–173.

Capuzzi, D., Gross, D. R., & Stauffer, M. D. (Eds.). (2010). *Introduction to group work* (5th ed.). Denver, CO: Love.

Cass, V. C. (1979). Homosexual identity formation: A theoretical model. *Journal of Homosexuality, 9,* 219–235.

Christner, R. W., Stewart, J. L., & Freeman, A. (2007). *Handbook of cognitive-behavior group therapy with children and adolescents: Specific settings and presenting problems.* New York, NY: Taylor & Francis Routledge.

Firestein, B. A. (1999). New perspectives on group treatment with women of diverse sexual identities. *Journal for Specialists in Group Work, 23,* 306–315.

Muller, L. E., & Hartman, J. (1998). Group counseling for sexual minority youth. *Professional School Counseling, 1,* 38–41.

Myers, S. E., & Williard, K. (2003). Integrating spirituality into counselor preparation: A developmental, wellness approach. *Counseling and Values, 47,* 142–155.

Norsworthy, K. L., & Horne, A. M. (1994). Issues in group work with HIV-infected gay and bisexual men. *Journal for Specialists in Group Work, 19,* 112–119.

Puglia, B., & Hall, S. F. (2010). Group work: Gay, lesbian, and bisexual clients. In D. Capuzzi, D. R. Gross, & M. D. Stauffer (Eds.), *Introduction to group work* (5th ed., pp. 537–566). Denver, CO: Love.

Smiley, K. A. (2004). A structured group for gay men newly diagnosed with HIV/AIDS. *Journal for Specialists in Group Work, 29,* 207–224.

Handout 15.1

Future Day Fantasy Exercise

Instructions: Close your eyes and spend a few minutes envisioning an ordinary and pleasant day in the future 5 years from now. This future day should be representative of a day if you are in your next stage of identity development.

Think about your answers to the following questions:

Where are you living?

What kind of environment?

What kind of neighborhood and community?

What kind of house?

What time do you awaken?

Do you awaken alone or with someone?

Is he or she a life partner? If so, describe the person with whom you live.

Who else is in your house?

What is the family atmosphere?

What do you do when you first get up?

What do you do after you dress?

Go to school? If so, what are you studying?

Go to work? If so, what kind of job do you have? What kind of work atmosphere is present? How gay friendly is your workplace? Do your coworkers/supervisors know your sexual orientation? If not, what do you do to hide your orientation? If they know your orientation, how do they treat you? What do you do for lunch? If you go out with coworkers, what do you talk about?

What do you do after work/school?

What kind of recreation do you have?

Who are your friends? Are they mostly gay/lesbian? Mostly straight? Equally gay/lesbian and heterosexual?

When do you go back home? Who is there? Are you alone? Children? Life partner?

What do you do for dinner? Who cooks? What do you eat?

While you are going to sleep and think about the good things in your day, what are the good things?

If you think of things about your day you would like to change, what are those things?

Final instructions: Decide whether a future day in the next stage of identity development is more desirable than an ordinary day in your current stage. Assume you want to continue in your development and progress to the next stage.

Handout 15.2

Coming Out Process and Assessment

Coming out or choosing a degree of openness about your sexual orientation is an ongoing, lifelong process that can occur at three levels. The level of openness a sexual minority member chooses is a personal choice and should be made only by the person coming out. The first level is when a person accepts his or her homosexuality and incorporates that self-knowledge into a healthy self-concept. Perhaps it is healthy for every sexual minority member to come out at this first level, regardless of subsequent choices. The second level is when a person shares his or her orientation with a close person or a few significant friends or family members. The third level of coming out is a public phase in which a sexual minority member is generally open.

At which level of coming out are you?

    a ______ Level 1
    b. ______ Level 2
        To whom have you come out?________________________________
    c. ______ Level 3

If you are at Level 2, how did you share your orientation?

a. Did you wait until you felt good about yourself?
b. What did you want and expect to happen?
c. Did you first choose a person who was most likely to react in an affirmative manner to you?
d. Did you choose affirming words to describe yourself and orientation? Use "I" statements? Share your feelings? Avoid defensive or accusing language? Make the disclosure a close and sharing occasion?
e. Did you select an appropriate time and place? Did you avoid a time of crisis when other issues were more important? Did you choose a private place conducive to the honest expression of feelings?
f. Did you allow time for the other person to adjust and accept the new information? Did you remember that it may have taken you years to come out, so it may take your close person some time to learn and accept the new information?
g. Did you make healthy learning and support resources available to your close person that might help them adjust (e.g., resources from the Parents, Families and Friends of Lesbians and Gays [PFLAG])?

Note. Handout compiled by M. Carolyn Thomas using information from *Men's Bodies, Men's Selves* by S. Julty, 1979, New York, NY: Dell.

Handout 15.3

Community Support Worksheet

Instructions: Part 1. Write in known current and available healthy resources and support systems for sexual minorities under the appropriate categories. Part 2. Search your community to find existing but previously unknown healthy resources and support systems. Part 3. Identify gaps in needed resources and support systems that would complete a healthy community for sexual minorities.

A. Social Support: Family, friends, or organizations
   1. Known and currently available resources
   2. Discovered and available resources
   3. Needed resources not available
B. Cultural Identity: Literature, music, art, theater
   1. Known and currently available resources
   2. Discovered and available resources
   3. Needed resources not available
C. Intellectual Growth: Educational opportunities
   1. Known and currently available resources
   2. Discovered and available resources
   3. Needed resources not available
D. Spiritual Support
   1. Known and currently available resources
   2. Discovered and available resources
   3. Needed resources not available
E. Career and Professional Growth
   1. Known and currently available resources
   2. Discovered and available resources
   3. Needed resources not available
F. Political and Legal Protection
   1. Known and currently available resources
   2. Discovered and available resources
   3. Needed resources not available
G. Health Resources: Physical, mental, emotional
   1. Known and currently available resources
   2. Discovered and available resources
   3. Needed resources not available

Final Instructions: It may be feasible to acquire or organize some of the needed but unavailable resources and support systems. Make a plan for how you might feasibly obtain or build the needed resource or support system.

1. What steps need to be taken to make the resource or support system available?

2. Who might be involved in making the resource or support system available?
3. What is the timeline for acquiring or building the resource or support system?
4. What is the cost, and how will the funds be provided?

Note. Handout compiled by M. Carolyn Thomas from numerous counseling organization presentations and class units on counseling gay and lesbian students.

Handout 15.4

Internet Resources

General Resources

Human Rights Campaign
http://www.hrc.org/

Gay & Lesbian Alliance Against Defamation (GLAAD)
http://www.glaad.org/Page.aspx?pid=183

Gay, Lesbian, and Straight Education Network (GLSEN)
http://www.glsen.org/cgi-bin/iowa/all/home/index.html

Parents, Families and Friends of Lesbians and Gays (PFLAG)
http://community.pflag.org/Page.aspx?pid=194&srcid=-2

National Gay and Lesbian Task Force (NGLTF)
http://www.thetaskforce.org/

Religious or Spiritual Resources

Soulforce
http://www.soulforce.org/

Soulforce seeks freedom from religious and political oppression for lesbian, gay, bisexual, transgender, queer, and questioning people.

Integrity
http://www.integrityusa.org/

Since 1974, Integrity has been a faithful witness of God's inclusive love to the Episcopal Church and the lesbian, gay, bisexual, and transgender community. It is working for the full inclusion of all of the baptized in all of the sacraments.

DignityUSA
http://www.dignityusa.org/

DignityUSA works for respect and justice for all gay, lesbian, bisexual, and transgender persons in the Catholic Church and the world through education, advocacy, and support.

Association of Welcoming and Affirming Baptists (AWAB)
http://rainbowbaptists.org/

AWAB seeks to encourage church leadership to welcome and affirm lesbian, gay, bisexual, and transgender people into full participation in the faith community.

World Congress of Gay, Lesbian, Bisexual, and Transgender Jews:
Keshet Ga'avah
http://gaylife.about.com/gi/dynamic/offsite.htm?zi=1/
XJ&sdn=gaylife&zu=http://www.glbtjews.org/

The World Congress holds conferences and workshops representing the interests of lesbian, gay, bisexual, and transgender Jews around the world. The focus of these sessions varies from regional to national, continental, and global.

Chapter 16

Group Work for College Students With Eating Issues

*Amanda M. Thomas-Evans, John L. Klem,
Jamie S. Carney, and Mary A. Belknap*

Reports suggest that an estimated 8 million Americans have an eating disorder, with 1 million of those (10%–15% of the total population of diagnosed individuals) identified as male (Carlat & Camargo, 1997; South Carolina Department of Mental Health, 2009). Clients diagnosed with an eating disorder are at the highest risk for mortality within the spectrum of mental illness, and studies indicate that 80% of females diagnosed have not received the recommended level of treatment because of health care constraints and the expense of the treatment (South Carolina Department of Mental Health, 2009). Women are overly identified within the eating disorder literature, and statistics show that 90% of females identified as having an eating disorder are between the ages of 12 and 25 (Alliance for Eating Disorders Awareness, 2009). With these statistics in mind, it is recommended that college counseling centers offer affordable, available, and reliable therapeutic support to college-age students who are experiencing eating issues.

The therapeutic intervention described here is a 6-week structured counseling group prepared for college-age students who have been identified as experiencing eating issues within the academic environment. A counseling format was selected for this group to provide members with the opportunity to garner interpersonal support as well as engage in problem solving (Capuzzi, Gross, & Stauffer, 2010). The model recommended here can be facilitated by one or two counselors based on agency practices or funding. Furthermore, facilitators may want to consider offering homogeneous composition group opportunities in a closed format, if possible, as supported by the literature (Wanlass, Moreno, & Thomson, 2005).

A feminist group counseling format with cognitive behavioral interventions has been selected to provide group members with multiple-method benefits (Vitousek, Watson, & Wilson, 1998). This approach provides both structured and empowering opportunities for group members to experience within the confines of group treatment. The overall goals for this group include (a) providing participants with a community of peers to assist in the normalization of experiences, (b) educating and assisting members in identifying and refuting negative thought processes associated with eating issues, (c) discussing society's influence on personal eating or body image perceptions, and (d) identifying more appropriate and personalized eating behaviors.

Group Plan

Session 1: Initial Stage

- As this is the introduction to the group process, members are encouraged to participate in the development of group norms to be upheld throughout the group experience. This activity can promote early empowerment for the group by allowing members to determine personal and peer expectations. These norms may include attendance policies, requesting time to discuss members' own needs, or related topics.
- Once group norms have been identified, members should be educated on the group process with an additional consideration for specific approaches to be used. In this case, members will be introduced to both feminist and cognitive behavioral group approaches.
- Ultimately for this session, the facilitator works toward providing an environment for group building with a focus on (a) forming interpersonal relationships and (b) instilling hope in the group counseling process (Black, 2003). These goals can be attended to through various initiatives, including identifying group norms, committing to the group process, focusing on the here and now, and encouraging the use of "I" statements. In addition, as identified in cognitive behavior therapy, members should be encouraged to learn and participate in a mood-check activity whereby they begin to acknowledge their own feelings in the here and now.
- Once the Session 1 agenda has been completed and members acknowledge a working comprehension of the group process (including contact information if a crisis occurs, confidentiality practices, risks to participants, and group expectations), members are encouraged to complete a mood-check homework assignment in which they record their mood associated with various activities several times a day throughout the week to develop a baseline.

Sessions 2 and 3: Transitioning

- As the transitioning stage is most commonly associated with group member anxiety and fear of exposure within the group (Corey, Corey, & Corey, 2010), Session 2 requires the facilitator to model appropriate transitioning behaviors. After standard greetings, members should be encouraged to review their completed mood-check homework and provide any personal insights into their findings (i.e., What has occurred both positively and negatively for you since the last time the group met?).

- This review can be followed by a discussion of societal influences on perceptions of the self (Black, 2003). Topics may include society's view of individuals who are obese, an assessment of one's relationship to the individual self and worldview, and cognitions associated with one's culture (Handout 16.1). In addition, members may be reminded that society's expectations for them as college-age individuals may be unique as they are striving toward acceptance within the realm of higher education. These peer-to-peer dialogues can promote interpersonal relationship development and reduce anxiety associated with self-disclosure.
- As previously acknowledged, facilitator demonstration of appropriate transitioning behaviors, including conflict resolution, is advised. Homework for the transitioning stage should include exploring one's relationship with current perceptions and one's relationship to society through narrative activities (journaling, therapeutic letter writing) and cognitive interventions (assessment of core beliefs, identification of rules associated with eating, and acknowledgment of schemata).

Sessions 4 and 5: Working

- These sessions should begin with a mood check and discussion of positive and negative experiences that are important to share with the group. Although some groups may never reach the working stage because of limiting factors, the activities suggested here may still be implemented to encourage growth.
- After members discuss relevant experiences since their last meeting, the facilitator can continue to work from a narrative and cognitive technique approach by encouraging continued discussion of subjective/individualized experiences related to eating issues.
- These repeated structured opportunities to share and discuss can promote self-growth and challenging behaviors. Throughout this process, members should continue member-specific homework assignments to promote additional self-reflection. In addition, termination preparations should begin by way of group discussion and reminders.

Session 6: Termination

- As this is the final session, members are encouraged to discuss their personal relationship to the group, identify sources of growth, and prepare a continued plan for success.
- A continued plan for success may include a review or identification of personal triggers and a proposal for how to decrease the power or triggers, recognize dysfunctional thought patterns, and make a continued commitment to the self.
- Referral resources may be provided.

References

Alliance for Eating Disorders Awareness. (2009). *Eating disorder statistics.* Retrieved from http://www.eatingdisorderinfo.org/Resources/Eating-DisordersStatistics/tabid/964/Default.aspx

Black, C. (2003). Creating curative communities: Feminist group work with women with eating disorders. *Australian Social Work, 56*(2), 127–139.

Capuzzi, D., Gross, D. R., & Stauffer, M. D. (2010). *Introduction to group work* (5th ed.). Denver, CO: Love.

Carlat, D. J., & Camargo, J. (1997). Review of bulimia in males. *American Journal of Psychiatry, 154,* 1127–1132.

Corey, M. S., Corey, G., & Corey, C. (2010). *Groups: Process and practice.* Belmont, CA: Brooks/Cole.

South Carolina Department of Mental Health. (2009). *Eating disorder statistics.* Retrieved from http://www.state.sc.us/dmh/anorexia/statistics.htm

Vitousek, K. B., Watson, S., & Wilson, G. T. (1998). Enhancing motivation for change in treatment-resistant eating disorders. *Clinical Psychology Review, 18,* 391–420.

Wanlass, J., Moreno, J. K., & Thomson, M. T. (2005). Group therapy for eating disorders: A retrospective case study. *Journal for Specialists in Group Work, 30,* 47–66.

Handout 16.1

Society's View of the Self

According to my perception, society views individuals who are overweight as

____

____

Society is very important to me because

____

____

I can remember a time when I was not interested in society at large, and it felt like

____

____

In my society, I have learned that eating is

____

____

To me, society includes these people

____

____

If I continue to abide by society's rules, one day I will

____

____

Views within society are fluid. I can remember a time in society when it was not acceptable to

____

____

I cope with changes in society by

____

____

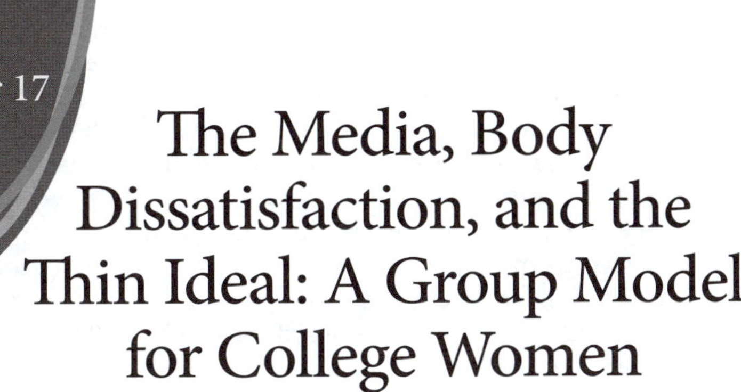

Chapter 17

The Media, Body Dissatisfaction, and the Thin Ideal: A Group Model for College Women

Juleen K. Buser

Body dissatisfaction is considered to be quite common among women in Western societies (Striegel-Moore, Silberstein, & Rodin, 1986) and has been associated with the development of eating disorders (Stice & Shaw, 2002). Media images that promote a thin body ideal have been linked to the development of body dissatisfaction in college-age women (Groez, Levine, & Murnen, 2002). Researchers have documented that group models that focus on and deconstruct these media messages can reduce levels of body dissatisfaction among group participants (e.g., Stice, Chase, Stormer, & Appel, 2001). This chapter presents a 4-week group model for college women that emphasizes the media's role in the genesis of body dissatisfaction.

In setting up group membership, it is imperative to screen for diagnosable eating disorders; individuals struggling with such disorders are not appropriate for this group. Counselors can use clinical interviews in order to assess for eating disorder symptoms. The Eating Disorder Diagnostic Scale (Stice, Telch & Rizvi, 2000) is a validated instrument that can be used to diagnose clinical levels of anorexia nervosa, bulimia nervosa, and binge-eating disorder. Students who are assessed as having serious eating disorder symptoms can then be referred for counseling and medical attention (American Psychiatric Association, 2006).

Research has revealed that high percentages of college women report problematic eating behaviors, such as the use of diet pills, binge eating, and chronic dieting (Celio et al., 2006; Mintz & Betz, 1988; Tylka & Subich, 2002). These women do not meet clinical levels for a diagnosis of an eating disorder as determined by the *Diagnostic and Statistical Manual of Mental*

Disorders, Fourth Edition, Text Revision (American Psychiatric Association, 2000); nonetheless, these behaviors are troubling. Participants who report subclinical symptoms are likely acceptable candidates for this group, but their disordered eating practices should not be ignored. Studies have shown that, for some women, subclinical levels of an eating disorder progress to clinical diagnoses (Shisslak, Crago, & Estes, 1995). Referral for counseling that addresses these symptoms is vital.

In addition, it is important to screen for other related and comorbid disorders among potential group participants. Specifically, individuals with obsessive-compulsive disorder and body dysmorphic disorder (BDD) would likely benefit more from individual counseling than from participation in the current group. Obsessive-compulsive disorder is correlated with eating disorder symptoms (Swinbourne & Touyz, 2007) and therefore should be screened in a clinical interview or with the use of instruments such as the Obsessive-Compulsive Inventory (Foa, Kozak, Salkovskis, Coles, & Amir, 1998). BDD is a concern with one's physical appearance that is distinct from body dissatisfaction. In this disorder (which is often comorbid with eating disorders), individuals are fixated on what they see as flaws in their appearance (American Psychiatric Association, 2000; Ruffolo, Phillips, Menard, Fay, & Weisburg, 2006). Individuals with BDD may be obsessed with very minor physical imperfections or may imagine that physical flaws exist (Allen & Hollander, 2004). A clinical interview and/or the Body Dysmorphic Disorder Examination (Rosen & Reiter, 2006) can be used to assess for BDD.

The group presented here aims to reduce the detrimental influence of media images and messages through educational presentations, experiential activities, group sharing, and personal application. This group model uses methods that actively involve the members, as researchers have found that interactive elements are effective components of eating disorder prevention programs (Stice & Shaw, 2004).

Group Plan

Session 1: Media and Body Image

- The first group begins with member introductions, the establishment of group rules, a discussion of confidentiality, and a summary of group goals and structure.
- Participants are provided with information about the media portrayal of a thin body ideal; the group leader(s) can outline the following points as examples of media messages:
  - Barbie represents an impossible body shape, in that her back would not be stable enough to support her weight and her waist would be too thin and constricted to have enough room for a liver (Media Awareness Network, 2008).
  - Eating disorders are often glorified in the media. Popular magazines tend to focus more on reporting the techniques individuals with

eating disorders use to lose weight than the physical impact of
the disorders (Inch & Merali, 2006).
- Watch the Dove© (2009) *Evolution* video (1 minute, 14 seconds)
  - http://www.dove.us/#/features/videos/default.aspx[cp-
    documentid=7049579]/
  - This video shows the alterations that are part of media images.
- The group leader(s) then facilitate a group discussion using the fol-
  lowing prompts:
  - What reactions do you have to the Dove© video?
  - What reactions do you have to the statistics on media images?
  - What role does the Dove© video play in counteracting other media
    images?

Session 2: Critical Consumption

- Watch the 34-minute video *Killing Us Softly 3: Advertising's Image of
  Women* (created by Jean Kilbourne; produced, directed, and edited
  by Sut Jhally). This video is available from the Media Education
  Foundation: http://www.mediaed.org
- The group leader(s) facilitate a group discussion about the video.
- Critical consumption of media messages
  - The National Eating Disorders Association (NEDA) has a useful
    handout on its website (www.nationaleatingdisorders.org) titled
    Tips for Becoming a Critical Viewer of the Media (NEDA, 2005).
  - The group leaders(s) facilitate a discussion about how to be critical
    consumers of media.
  - In what ways do the videos we watched in this group help you
    view media images differently?
  - What will help you view media images through a more critical lens?
  - Suggestions: reminding oneself about the falsity of many media
    images (e.g., airbrushing); reminding oneself of the consumer-
    driven motives of the media (NEDA, 2005).
- Participants are reminded that in the next two sessions they will be
  prompted to share more intimately about the influences media mes-
  sages have on them personally.
- *Homework for next week:* Participants are asked to bring in a media mes-
  sage or image that promotes the thin ideal (complete Handout 17.1).

Session 3: Personal Mantras

- Sharing of media messages/images
  - Group members share their media images and their answers to
    Handout 17.1.
  - The group discusses ways in which these negative images can be
    combated personally (e.g., through self-talk, by not buying
    certain magazines) and on a wider scope (e.g., by writing letters
    to advertisers who promote the thin ideal; NEDA, 2005).

- Group activity
  - Group members work on creating a personal mantra to counteract the negative messages of the media (Handout 17.2).
- *Homework for next week:* Group members prepare (on note cards) a *positive* element they learned/appreciated from the group in general and each group member specifically. They will share this with the group in the next session and give each member her note card.

Session 4: Mantra Sharing and Termination

- Opening discussion about the helpfulness of the mantra created last week.
- Note card sharing and exchange activity.
- The group leader(s) facilitate a closing discussion about how the participants will apply the group material and group experience to their daily lives.

References

Allen, A., & Hollander, E. (2004). Similarities and differences between body dysmorphic disorder and other disorders. *Psychiatric Annals, 34,* 927–933.

American Psychiatric Association. (2000). *Diagnostic and statistical manual of mental disorders* (4th ed., text rev.). Washington, DC: Author.

American Psychiatric Association. (2006). *Practice guideline for the treatment of patients with eating disorders* (3rd ed.). Retrieved from http://www.psychiatryonline.com/pracGuide/loadGuidelinePdf.aspx?file=Ea tingDisorders3ePG_04-28-06

Celio, C. I., Luce, K. H., Bryson, S. W., Winzelberg, A. J., Cunning, D., Rockwell, R., . . . Taylor, C. B. (2006). Use of diet pills and other dieting aids in a college populations with high weight and shape concerns. *International Journal of Eating Disorders, 39,* 492–497.

Dove©. (2009). *Evolution.* Available from http://www.dove.us/#/features/videos/default.aspx[cp-documentid=7049579]/

Foa, E. B., Kozak, M. J., Salkovskis, P. M., Coles, M. E., & Amir, N. (1998). The validation of a new obsessive-compulsive disorder scale: The Obsessive-Compulsive Inventory. *Psychological Assessment, 10*(3), 206–214.

Groez, L. M., Levine, M. P., & Murnen, S. K. (2002). The effects of experimental presentation of thin media images on body satisfaction: A meta-analytic review. *International Journal of Eating Disorders, 31,* 1–16.

Inch, R., & Merali, N. (2006). A content analysis of popular magazine articles on eating disorders. *Eating Disorders, 14,* 109–120.

Kilbourne, J. (Creator), & Jhally, S. (Producer, Director, Editor). *Killing us softly 3: Advertising's image of women.* Available from http://www.mediaed.org

Media Awareness Network. (2008). *Beauty and body image in the media.* Retrieved from http://www.media-awareness.ca/english/index.cfm

Mintz, L. B., & Betz, N. E. (1988). Prevalence and correlates of eating disordered behaviors among undergraduate women. *Journal of Counseling Psychology, 35,* 463–471.

National Eating Disorders Association. (2005). *Tips for becoming a critical viewer of the media.* Retrieved from http://www.nationaleatingdisorders. org/nedaDir/files/documents/handouts/MediaTip.pdf

Rosen, J. C., & Reiter, J. (2006). Development of the Body Dysmorphic Disorder Examination. *Behavior Research and Therapy, 34,* 755–766.

Ruffolo, J. S., Phillips, K. A., Menard, W., Fay, C., & Weisburg, R. B. (2006). Comorbidity of body dysmorphic disorder and eating disorders: Severity of psychopathology and body image disturbance. *International Journal of Eating Disorders, 39,* 11–19.

Shisslak, C. M., Crago, M., & Estes, L. S. (1995). The spectrum of eating disturbances. *International Journal of Eating Disorders, 19*(3), 209–219.

Stice, E., Chase, A., Stormer, S., & Appel, A. (2001). A randomized trial of a dissonance-based eating disorder prevention program. *International Journal of Eating Disorders, 29,* 247–262.

Stice, E., & Shaw, H. E. (2002). Role of body dissatisfaction in the onset and maintenance of eating pathology: A synthesis of research findings. *Journal of Psychosomatic Research, 53,* 985–993.

Stice, E., & Shaw, H. E. (2004). Eating disorder prevention programs: A meta-analytic review. *Psychological Bulletin, 130,* 206–227.

Stice, E., Telch, C. F., & Rizvi, S. L. (2000). Development and validation of the Eating Disorder Diagnostic Scale: A brief self-report measure of anorexia, bulimia, and binge eating disorder. *Psychological Assessment, 12*(2), 123–131.

Striegel-Moore, R. H., Silberstein, L. R., & Rodin, J. (1986). Toward an understanding of risk factors for bulimia. *American Psychologist, 41*(3), 246–263.

Swinbourne, J. M., & Touyz, S. W. (2007). The co-morbidity of eating disorders and anxiety disorders: A review. *European Eating Disorders Review, 15,* 253–274.

Tylka, T. L., & Subich, L. M. (2002). Exploring young women's perceptions of the effectiveness and safety of maladaptive weight control techniques. *Journal of Counseling & Development, 80,* 101–110.

Handout 17.1

Critical Consumption of a Media Message/Image

Describe the media image/message you chose that promotes a thin body ideal (if you chose a picture from a magazine, bring the image with you, if possible):

____

____

____

____

How does this image promote/glorify a thin body?

____

____

____

____

What are the negative influences this image could have on females?

____

____

____

____

Given the previous two groups on how to critically consume media messages/images, discuss how you can view this media through a more critical lens

____

____

____

____

Handout 17.2

Creation of Personal Mantra

This mantra can be a phrase/sentence, such as

- "Media images are fake" or
- "I can see through the images the media throws at me" or
- "I am confident in my personal beauty"

Choose an individual mantra that affirms your self-worth apart from appearance and counteracts the media messages promoting thinness.

My Mantra

____

____

____

____

Now create an artistic representation of this phrase/sentence (use paper, markers, and other art supplies to create your mantra).

Then put this mantra in a place that will be most helpful (e.g., in your room, in your car).

Where do you think you will put your mantra?

____

____

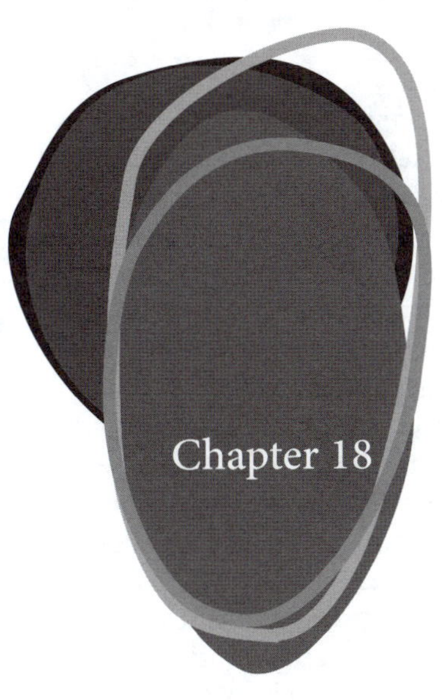

Self-Care and Eating Issues

Catherine Cook-Cottone

Effective intervention programs are critical for the reduction of eating disorders (Cook-Cottone, 2009). Once established, eating disordered behaviors can become chronic and resistant to treatment (e.g., Van Hoeken, Seidell, & Hoek, 2003). The average prevalence rates for bulimia nervosa are 1% in females and 0.1% in males, and overall incidence rates are estimated at 12 per 100,000 per year (Rastam, Gillberg, van Hoeken, & Hoek, 2004). An average prevalence rate of 0.3% in females was found for anorexia nervosa, with overall incidence rates at 8 per 100,000 population per year (Rastam et al., 2004). Research indicates that the long-term outcomes of eating disorders are serious. Specifically, Keel and Herzog (2004) reported that anorexia nervosa is associated with one of the highest risks for premature death among all psychiatric disorders, with an estimated crude mortality rate of 5%–5.9% of those diagnosed. A crude mortality rate of 0.3% has been estimated for bulimia nervosa, although this value may be an underestimate given the short duration of the currently available follow-up studies.

The self-care and eating issues group described here is based on the attunement model of self, which provides an understanding of eating disorders (Cook-Cottone, 2006). In addition, the group format integrates techniques that have been shown to be effective at preventing and treating eating disordered behavior (Cook-Cottone, 2006; Reindl, 2001; Stice, Shaw, & Marti, 2007; Striegel-Moore & Bulik, 2007). For a self-care approach to be effective at correcting eating issues, it must be undertaken within the context of an individual's relationships (Cook-Cottone, 2009; Cook-Cottone, Beck, & Kane, 2008). The goal is to build *attunement* among internal experiences (i.e., thought, feelings, and physiological processes) and external experiences (e.g., family, community and cultural experiences; Cook-Cottone, 2006). Specifically, *attunement* is defined as a reciprocal process of mutual influence and coregulation (Siegel, 2010). The *Mindful Self* (see Figure 18.1) represents the self that works to regulate internal experiences and to interact with others within external systems such as family, community, and culture (Cook-Cottone, 2006).

The attunement model of self can help explain the onset of eating disordered behavior. According to this model, over time internal processes or pressures (i.e., cognitive, emotional, and physiological processes) and external relationships or pressures (i.e., family, community, and culture), or even the interface of these processes and pressures, are experienced as too complicated, conflicted, and/or overwhelming (Cook-Cottone, 2006; Reindl, 2001; Siegel, 2010). For those at risk, engaging in eating disordered thoughts and behaviors becomes a way to manage complicated and overwhelming feelings and experiences.

Effective interventions provide a tangible (or experiential) bridge for negotiating overwhelming life experiences so that the eating disorder is no longer needed in order to cope. A group format allows for growth of the Mindful Self to occur within the context of an interpersonal and social setting (Yalom & Leszcz, 2005). Group sessions focus on building an understanding of the Mindful Self, relationships, attunement, and the practice of self-care. Sessions integrate techniques grounded in cognitive and dialectic behavior therapy (Linehan, 1993), emotional regulation techniques (Macklem, 2008; Siegel, 2010), positive psychology (Cook-Cottone et al., 2008; Siegel, 2010), and mindful and intuitive eating (Albers, 2003; Tribole & Resch, 2003). Emphasis is placed on active discussion of concepts, home practice, and construction of healthy self-care behaviors that replace the eating disordered conceptualizations and behaviors.

Group Plan

Session 1: Group Introduction: The Self-Care and Attunement Model

- Introduction to the group
  - Explain to the members that the meaning and benefit of the group is created, or coconstructed, by the group in its entirety (members

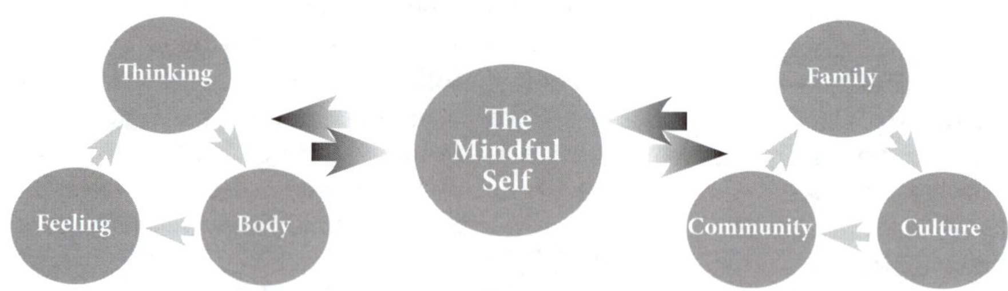

Figure 18.1
The Mindful Self

Note. Arrows represent attunement. Adapted from "The Attuned Representation Model for the Primary Prevention of Eating Disorders: An Overview for School Psychologists," by C. Cook-Cottone, 2006, *Psychology in the Schools, 43*, pp. 1–8. Copyright 2006 by John Wiley and Sons. Reprinted with permission.

and leaders) and that confidentiality and privacy create an atmosphere of comfort and safety.

- Encourage members to process questions related to connectedness; interpersonal relatedness; and the universality of emotional, cognitive, and physical experiences.
- Instruct members on the positive psychology orientation of the group and encourage them to share coping successes.
- Discourage members from sharing diagnoses or specific symptoms with the group.
- Administer a mindfulness assessment survey by asking group members to rate their stress levels and how difficult it was to take care of themselves this week (Cook-Cottone et al., 2008).
- Ask group members to rate their use of wellness practices, including yoga, meditation, pleasant activities, journaling, nutrition, setting boundaries with others, and expressing themselves appropriately (Cook-Cottone et al., 2008).
- Have group members discuss their responses.
- Encourage members to share their thoughts and reflections on the model and how attunement and pressures play a role in their struggles or challenges.
- Introduce the concepts of wellness and self-care. Using Handout 18.1, review each of the domains of the model within the context of eating disordered symptoms and wellness and self-care. Introduce the attunement model of self by reviewing the integration of thoughts, feelings, and physiological self.
- Practice a relaxation session (see Davis, Eshelman, & McKay, 2000).
- *Homework.* Encourage members to practice a relaxation technique at home and to think about the Mindfulness Worksheet as they make choices during the week.

Session 2: Thinking, Feeling, and Choice

- Readminister a mindfulness assessment survey by asking group members to rate their stress levels and how difficult it was to take care of themselves this week (Cook-Cottone et al., 2008).
- Ask group members to rate their use of wellness practices, including yoga, meditation, pleasant activities, journaling, nutrition, setting boundaries with others, and expressing themselves appropriately (Cook-Cottone et al., 2008).
- Refer to Handout 18.1, Figure 18.2, and the internal systems, with a particular focus on thoughts and feelings. Explain that true wisdom is the attuned balance between thoughts and feelings and that both are needed to make good choices.
- Introduce basic brain anatomy and describe the thinking brain (the frontal cortex) and the feeling brain (the limbic system) as working together to allow for integrated and mature responses to life's challenges (see Siegel, 2010).

- Have members visualize a feeling response in the center of the brain and a thinking response in the frontal regions near their forehead and eyes. Explain that when we are reacting emotionally, the frontal region is not active and vice versa. Explain that healthy brain functioning involves activation in both areas and an integration of both thinking and feeling information.
- Have group members give examples of times when either their emotional self or their thinking self predominated. Facilitate by explaining how it is so easy to say things we regret when we are angry or how a failure to consider emotions can also make for poor decisions.
- Explain that deep breathing and relaxation can help the thinking and the feeling parts of the brain work together, calming emotional responses and activating cognitive input.
- *Homework.* Encourage members to work on breathing and using both thoughts and feelings when approaching an emotional situation.

Session 3: Care of the Body: Nutrition, Hydration, Rest, and Exercise

- Readminister a mindfulness assessment survey by asking group members to rate their stress levels and how difficult it was to take care of themselves this week (Cook-Cottone et al., 2008).
- Ask group members to rate their use of wellness practices, including yoga, meditation, pleasant activities, journaling, nutrition, setting boundaries with others, and expressing themselves appropriately (Cook-Cottone et al., 2008).
- Describe to the members the importance of the body in supporting the thinking and feeling parts of ourselves.
  - Emphasize that caring for the body allows the body to be steady and regulated. A steady and regulated body supports regulated emotions. An unregulated body can trigger emotional dysregulation.
  - Provide an example of when lack of physical regulation can affect emotions. A good example is skipping a meal, which allows sugar levels to drop. Often this creates irritability and low frustration tolerance. Ask members to share these types of experiences
- Describe physical care of the body as including nutrition, hydration, rest, and exercise.
  - Ask group members to think of the day in 3-hour cycles (6 a.m.–9 a.m., 9 a.m.–12 p.m., 12 p.m.–3 p.m., 3 p.m.–6 p.m., 6 p.m.–9 p.m., etc.). Explain that the body works in 45- and 90-minute cycles within each 3-hour cycle. Ask them to think about how our routines, meals, classes, and work (even TV shows) are often scheduled to work around these temporal cycles.
  - Remind them that in each 180 minutes (or 3-hour cycle), an individual should eat, hydrate, and rest and that within each day there should be a period of 30 to 60 minutes of exercise.
  - Have members sketch out how the current day has progressed and assess how they did in each 3-hour cycle.

- Have members discuss particular 3-hour cycles that are a challenge and brainstorm ways that they can work toward consistent care of the body through nutrition, hydration, rest, and exercise.
- *Homework.* Encourage members to track their days using 3-hour cycles to explore challenging times and corrective self-care practices.

Session 4: Working for Good Days and Self-Reflection

- Readminister a mindfulness assessment survey by asking group members to rate their stress levels and how difficult it was to take care of themselves this week (Cook-Cottone et al., 2008).
- Ask group members to rate their use of wellness practices, including yoga, meditation, pleasant activities, journaling, nutrition, setting boundaries with others, and expressing themselves appropriately (Cook-Cottone et al., 2008).
- Discuss triggers and hungers (see Tribole & Resch, 2003).
  - Internal: *body needs like heat, hunger, relaxation*
  - Emotional: *hungry to avoid fear or hungry to escape*
  - External: *hungry to feel in control of life, social hunger*
- Ask group members to review the last time they experienced these symptoms and felt as if their response to something was unregulated.
- For each instance, ask members to rate the feeling on a scale of 1 to 10, identify what they were thinking at the time, and identify any triggers that related to the feelings and thoughts.
- Ask members to share their triggers and possible misinterpretations.
- Ask group members to review the last time they felt challenged or felt triggers yet still made a healthy choice.
- Ask members to share what made them most proud about their good day and one tip that helped them be successful.

Session 5: Self-Care and Attunement With Others

- Readminister a mindfulness assessment survey by asking group members to rate their stress levels and how difficult it was to take care of themselves this week (Cook-Cottone et al., 2008).
- Ask group members to rate their use of wellness practices, including yoga, meditation, pleasant activities, journaling, nutrition, setting boundaries with others, and expressing themselves appropriately (Cook-Cottone et al., 2008).
- Describe how relationships in our lives (with family members and friends in the community) can play a role in how we care for ourselves: Provide an example of a time when an interaction or set of interactions resulted in your not taking adequate care of yourself.
  - Ask members to share similar challenges.
  - In a discussion format, share ideas as to how to be assertive in the service of self-care.
  - Ask whether relationships present a particular challenge for any of the group members.

- Ask the group to problem-solve solutions to particular struggles presented.
- Role play some solutions to assertiveness and self-care challenges and ways to say "No."
- *Homework*
  - Ask members to continue to monitor their behaviors and record slips by tracking and journaling "I was feeling . . .," "I was thinking . . .," "The triggers were . . .," and "I could have done ____ differently."
  - Ask group members to bring in (a) a recipe for a favorite healthy food and (b) an unusual fruit or vegetable.

Session 6: *Mindful Eating and Sharing Food Passions*

- Readminister a mindfulness assessment survey by asking group members to rate their stress levels and how difficult it was to take care of themselves this week (Cook-Cottone et al., 2008).
- Ask group members to rate their use of wellness practices, including yoga, meditation, pleasant activities, journaling, nutrition, setting boundaries with others, and expressing themselves appropriately (Cook-Cottone et al., 2008).
- Describe the qualities of mindful eating (see Albers, 2003):
  - Awareness of the hunger and desire you feel associate with the food you are about to eat
  - Awareness of the sensory experience of the food you are eating (e.g., texture, weight, density, visual appearance, smell, and presentation on the dish)
  - Awareness of the process of eating the food (e.g., the feel on your lips, the taste and texture in your mouth, the aroma while you eat, the feeling of chewing, and the feeling of swallowing)
  - Awareness of the pace of your eating and the sensation of becoming satisfied
  - Prepare and serve the unusual fruits and vegetables brought in by group members.
  - Practice the qualities of mindful eating.
  - Ask group members to share their experiences as they eat.
  - Ask group members to share their recipes and to explain, using a mindful eating perspective, why the recipe is their favorite.
- *Homework*
  - Ask members to continue to monitor their behaviors and record slips by tracking and journaling "I was feeling . . .," "I was thinking . . .," "The triggers were . . .," and "I could have done ____ differently."
  - Encourage group members to practice mindful eating at home.
  - Have group members bring in media images (print ads from magazines) that they feel affect eating and body acceptance.

Session 7: Self-Care and Attunement With Our Culture

- Readminister a mindfulness assessment survey by asking group members to rate their stress levels and how difficult it was to take care of themselves this week (Cook-Cottone et al., 2008).
- Ask group members to rate their use of wellness practices, including yoga, meditation, pleasant activities, journaling, nutrition, setting boundaries with others, and expressing themselves appropriately (Cook-Cottone et al., 2008).
- Describe cultural influences on eating and body acceptance.
  - Have group members share their perspectives on cultural influences on eating and body acceptance.
  - Ask members to critically explore print ads in popular magazines.
  - Ask members to rate ads as healthy or unhealthy.
  - Ask members to share with the group why they made these particular choices and how an ad may influence eating and body acceptance.
  - Ask members to share their feelings about media pressures and to consider media images as potential triggers for unhealthy eating behaviors.
- *Homework*
  - Ask members to continue to monitor their behaviors and record slips by tracking and journaling "I was feeling . . .," "I was thinking . . .," "The triggers were . . .," and "I could have done ____ differently."

Session 8: Working for Good Days and Self-Reflection

- Readminister a mindfulness assessment survey by asking group members to rate their stress levels and how difficult it was to take care of themselves this week (Cook-Cottone et al., 2008)
- Ask group members to rate their use of wellness practices, including yoga, meditation, pleasant activities, journaling, nutrition, setting boundaries with others, and expressing themselves appropriately (Cook-Cottone et al., 2008)
- Ask members to list the most challenging triggers.
  - For each trigger, review all of the possible methods of addressing the trigger in a healthy manner.
  - Ask members to share (a) their evaluation of their individual progress and (b) share one proud moment of their work toward wellness self-care and healthy eating.
- For closure, have each member share an intention for her continued progress toward consistent self-care.

References

Albers, S. (2003). *Eating mindfully: How to end mindless eating and enjoy a balanced relationship with food.* Oakland, CA: New Harbinger.

Cook-Cottone, C. (2006). The attuned representation model for the primary prevention of eating disorders: An overview for school psychologists. *Psychology in the Schools, 43,* 1–8.

Cook-Cottone, C. P. (2009). *Success at any cost? School-based prevention of high risk, body-change strategies: Eating disorders, steroid abuse, and excessive exercise.* Buffalo, NY: GSE.

Cook-Cottone, C. P., Beck, M., & Kane, L. (2008). Manualized-group treatment of eating disorders: Attunement in mind, body, and relationship (AMBR). *Journal for Specialists in Group Work, 33,* 61–83.

Davis, M., Eshelman, E. R., & McKay, M. (2000). *The relaxation and stress reduction workbook.* Oakland, CA: New Harbinger.

Keel, P. K., & Herzog, D. B. (2004). Long-term outcome, course of illness and mortality in anorexia nervosa, bulimia nervosa, and binge eating disorder. In T. D. Brewerton (Ed.), *Clinical handbook of eating disorders: An integrated approach* (pp. 97–116). New York, NY: Marcel Dekker.

Linehan, M. (1993). *Cognitive behavioral treatment of borderline personality disorder.* New York, NY: Guilford Press.

Macklem, G. L. (2008). *Practitioner's guide to emotional regulation in school-aged children.* New York, NY: Springer.

Rastam, M., Gillberg., C., van Hoeken, D., & Hoek, H. W. (2004). Epidemiology of eating disorders: A developmental overview. In T. D. Brewerton (Ed.), *Clinical handbook of eating disorders: An integrated approach* (pp. 71–96). New York, NY: Marcel Dekker.

Reindl, S. M. (2001). *Sensing the self: Women's recovery from bulimia.* Cambridge, MA: Harvard University Press.

Siegel, D. J. (2010). *Mindsight: The new science of transformation.* New York, NY: Random House.

Stice, E., Shaw, S., & Marti, C. N. (2007). A meta-analytic review of eating disorder prevention programs: Encouraging findings. *Annual Review of Clinical Psychology, 3,* 233–257.

Striegel-Moore, R., & Bulik, C. M. (2007). Risk factors for eating disorders. *American Psychologist, 62,* 181–198.

Tribole, E., & Resch, E. (2003). *Intuitive eating: A revolutionary program that works.* New York, NY: St. Martin's Griffin.

Van Hoeken, D., Seidell, J., & Hoek, H. W. (2003). Epidemiology. In J. Treasure, U. Schmidt, & E. van Furth (Eds.), *Handbook of eating disorders* (2nd ed., pp. 11–34). West Sussex, England: Wiley.

Yalom, I. D., & Leszcz, M. (2005). *The theory and practice of group psychotherapy* (5th ed.). New York, NY: Basic Books.

Handout 18.1

Understanding the Attunement Model of Self and the Mindful Self

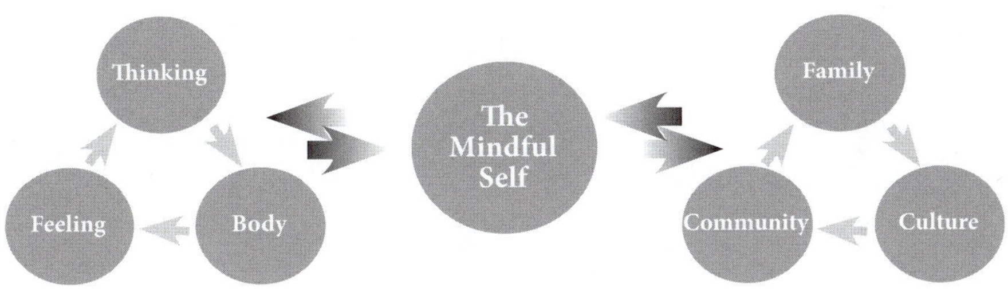

Figure 18.1
The Mindful Self

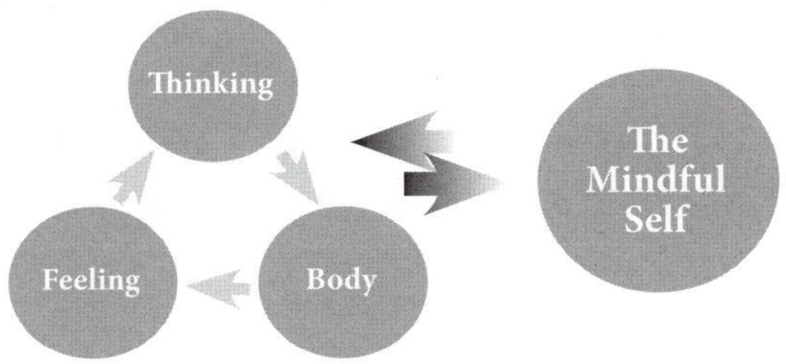

Figure 18.2
The Internal System and the Mindful Self

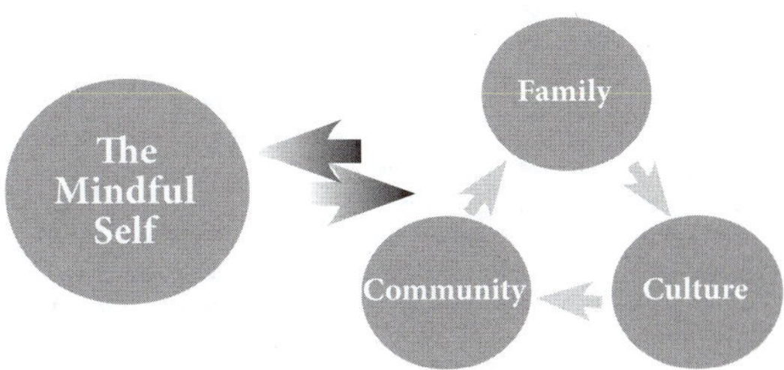

Figure 18.3
Relationships and the Mindful Self

Chapter 19

A Collegiate Children of Alcoholics/Addicts Psychoeducational Group

Mark Woodford, Juleen K. Buser, Linda Riccobono, and Rebecca Bartuska

Combined data from 2002 to 2007 indicate that at least 1 in 10 children in the United States live in homes with at least one substance-dependent or substance-abusing parent (Substance Abuse and Mental Health Services Administration, Office of Applied Studies, 2009). This represents more than 8.3 million children (or 11.9% of the total population of children younger than the age of 18). Moreover, estimates are that approximately one fourth of college students are adult children of alcoholics (ACOAs; Kelley et al., as cited in Kelley et al., 2007).

Some ACOA college students experience adaptive and/or problematic social and emotional effects related to their upbringing. A psychoeducational group counseling format provides an opportunity for them to learn about the possible social and emotional effects that having a substance-abusing or substance-dependent parent can have on their daily lives. The primary goal of this group is to help self-identified ACOA students (a) understand the influence of their family of origin on their choices related to their social and emotional lives and (b) begin to develop the self-knowledge and skills needed to become well-adjusted and well-functioning adults. This psychoeducational process involves six 90-minute group sessions and is considered a closed group, in that no new members should be admitted once the 6-week span of sessions has begun. Using this format, counselors can provide two 6-week group sessions each semester.

Group Plan

Session 1: Introductions and Understanding Addiction

- Begin by introducing yourself to the group. Provide information about your professional background and your reasons for wanting to have this particular group on campus.
- Review relevant ethical concerns related to group counseling.
- Have group members introduce themselves.
- Discuss and establish group rules and norms with the group members.
- Ice breaker activity
  - Provide group members with a stack of age- and content-appropriate magazines (choose magazines that you do not mind having destroyed).
  - Ask them to tear out pictures, words, or phrases that most represent who they are and who they want to be.
  - Ask them to talk about their choices with the group. (Save these cutouts in envelopes with students' names on them for the closing session.)
- Suggested process questions:
  - What did you learn about yourself?
  - What did you learn about others in the group?
  - What was the most challenging part?
  - How might this activity help this group process?
- Watch *What Is Addiction?* (20 minutes) from the HBO series *Addiction* (Home Box Office, 2007) and discuss group members' reactions. This segment includes a leading researcher talking with a group of family members about the environmental, behavioral, and genetic factors involved in addiction. The key point of this discussion is to have students discuss their thoughts and feelings about addiction.
- Establish a check-out ritual, summarizing some of the key content and process points from the group session and asking each group member to say one thing that he or she will remember from this first group meeting.

Session 2: Family of Origin and Family Roles

- Establish a check-in ritual, summarizing what was covered in the prior session, asking members to briefly restate and explain what they remember from the previous group, and asking group members to describe their current emotional state in terms of weather metaphors (e.g., "The weather in my world is partly cloudy with a chance of sun later on in the day," meaning that one feels slightly down at the moment but has hope for a brighter affect later on in the day).
- Watch *Lost Childhood: Growing Up in an Alcoholic Family* (30 minutes; Young Broadcasting of San Francisco, 2004) and discuss group members' reactions to this documentary that includes interviews

with children of alcoholics at a summer camp and follows two of them into young adulthood as they talk about the lessons they have learned.
- Provide group members with Handout 19.1 (Focus on Family Roles), which provides information about the roles that ACOAs may develop (Weigscheider, as cited in van Wormer & Davis, 2008) as adaptive strategies in a family in which one of the parents is abusing or dependent on alcohol or other drugs. The key point of this activity is to help group members understand family dynamics and choices about the roles individuals play in stabilizing family systems.
- Discuss the roles with the members. After the discussion, ask members for their thoughts and feelings about the roles and whether the roles are applicable to ACOAs.
- Do the check-out ritual established in Session 1.

Session 3: Families and Feelings

- Do the weather metaphor check-in ritual established in Session 2.
- Explain that this group session will focus on families and feelings.
- Do The Rubber Band Circle activity.
  - You will need an oversized stretchy band. Mark a section with a marker or tape.
  - Have each member place his or her hand on the rubber band.
  - Have the group rotate the band clockwise or counterclockwise.
  - Have you or a selected member say, "Stop."
  - The person with his or her hand on the marked area shares something with the group.
  - The group leader can define what "something" is before the activity starts (e.g., "Tell us something about yourself" or "Tell us something that went well this week or was difficult").
  - Discuss this activity as it relates to Claudia Black's (1981) notions about the family rule that ACOAs often learn in their family of origin: "Don't talk, don't trust, don't feel." Use Handout 19.2 (Families and Feelings) to process the activity.
- Suggested process questions:
  - What did you learn about yourself in this activity?
  - What was the most challenging part?
- Because of the potential shame and stigma associated with addiction, shame-based family messages are often transmitted from generation to generation. These messages can exacerbate common feelings of guilt, for example when one makes a mistake ("I made a mistake"), to feelings of shame ("I am a mistake"). Discuss with group members how shame becomes a potential magnifier of the basic feelings of guilt and embarrassment and can lead to feelings of self-doubt and self-loathing.
- Do the check-out ritual established in Session 1.

Session 4: Basic Psychological Needs

- Do the weather metaphor check-in ritual established in Session 2.
- Explain that this group session will focus on understanding basic needs.
- Begin by explaining Maslow's hierarchy of needs in terms of ACOA issues.
- Draw a picture of a pyramid that includes a base of *Basic Needs of Food, Water, Shelter, Safety, Health, Security, and Sex*; followed by a middle section that includes the *Basic Psychological Needs of Belonging, Power, Freedom, and Fun*; and a top reserved for *Self-Actualization and Fulfilling Your Unique Human Potential*.
- Discuss William Glasser's (1998) four basic psychological needs:
  - *Belonging*—fulfilled by loving, sharing, and cooperating with others
  - *Power*—fulfilled by achieving, accomplishing, and being recognized and respected
  - *Freedom*—fulfilled by making choices in our lives
  - *Fun*—fulfilled by laughing and playing
- The key point to this discussion is how substance abuse and addiction may cause sources of conflict with all of the needs listed above.
- Suggested process question: How might individuals respond to this conflict of needs within the family system?
  Unhealthy scenarios include
  - Avoidance—withdrawal, ignoring, denial
  - Confrontation—threats, aggression, anger
  Healthy scenarios include
  - Communication—understanding, respect, resolution
- Do the check-out ritual established in Session 1.

Session 5: Relationships and Communication

- Do the weather metaphor check-in ritual established in Session 2.
- Explain that this group session will focus on understanding relationships, specifically the tension between holding onto yourself and connecting to others.
- Draw a line with endpoints labeled *holding onto my sense of self* and *connecting to others*. Explain that we all live somewhere on this continuum and that there is a constant tension between these two emotional forces. Furthermore, explain that in reaction to emotionally unstable relationships with caregivers who abuse substances, ACOAs often choose one of two extremes (i.e., either they are compelled to be completely enmeshed with other people [and lose themselves in the process] or they choose to completely disengage from relationships when they begin to feel too much closeness in the relationship [choosing themselves over the relationship]). As you are explaining this, circle the corresponding endpoints. Explain that there is a middle ground called *differentiation* that allows one to hold onto

oneself while remaining open to connection with others. You can write *differentiation* slightly elevated in the middle of the continuum that has been drawn. Discuss with the group members what their personal tendencies are in relation to this dynamic. To which end of the continuum are they predisposed to act? You can divide the group into dyads to discuss this dynamic, asking them to talk about themselves and their extended families in relation to this process.

- Explain that healthy relationships require a level of communication of feelings. Remind them of the "Don't talk, don't trust, don't feel" rule. Discuss communication patterns in their families and have students examine their own style of communication in relationships. Have them provide a rationale for improving their communication in relationships.
- Time permitting, you can teach positive communication skills, such as using "I" statements. For example, you can provide a sample scenario that might result in hurt feelings. Then teach the group members how to communicate their feelings in this type of situation (e.g., "When you didn't introduce me to your friends yesterday, I felt sad and hurt. I would appreciate being acknowledged in situations like that in the future."). These scenarios can be provided by group members and can be rehearsed through the use of role playing.
- Do the check-out ritual established in Session 1.

Session 6: Closing

- Do the weather metaphor check-in ritual established in Session 2.
- Explain that this group session will focus on tying all of the loose ends together so that the group members will be able to communicate their own patterns in relation to their family rules and roles, emotional regulation, and self-care in relationships.
- As in the activity from Session 1, provide the group members with a stack of age- and content-appropriate magazines (again, choose magazines that you do not mind having destroyed).
- As before, ask them to tear out pictures, words, or phrases that most represent who they are and who they want to be.
- Ask them to talk about how these choices might have changed as a result of this group experience. Then return their initial cutouts to them for a return discussion.
- Suggested process questions:
  - What did you learn about yourself?
  - What did you learn about others in the group?
  - What was the most challenging part?
- In closing, emphasize to group members that they have a sense of personal agency and that they have choices related to their thoughts, feelings, and behaviors in the various naturally occurring contexts of their lives.

References

Black, C. (1981). *It will never happen to me.* Denver, CO: M.A.C. Printing.

Glasser, W. (1998). *Choice theory: A new psychology of personal freedom.* New York, NY: HarperCollins

Home Box Office. (2007). *What is addiction?* Available from http://www.hbo.com/addiction/thefilm/index.html?current=5

Kelley, M. L., French, A., Bountress, K., Keefe, H. A., Schroeder, V., Steer, K., . . . Guimienny, L. (2007). Parentification and family responsibility in the family of origin of adult children of alcoholics. *Addictive Behaviors, 32,* 675–685.

Substance Abuse and Mental Health Services Administration, Office of Applied Studies. (2009, April). *The NSDUH report: Children living with substance-dependent or substance-abusing parents: 2002 to 2007.* Rockville, MD: Author.

van Wormer, K., & Davis, D. R. (2008). *Addiction treatment: A strengths perspective* (2nd ed.). Pacific Grove, CA: Brooks/Cole.

Young Broadcasting of San Francisco. (2004). *Lost childhood: Growing up in an alcoholic family.* San Francisco, CA: Author.

Handout 19.1

Focus on Family Roles

Even though playing roles in families is not uncommon, when there are unusual stressors, roles can become more rigid. These roles can be adaptive and/or disruptive to social and emotional development. What role(s) have you played in your family of origin?

The Hero

Heroes tend to take on the role of being the overly responsible ones, the super-achievers who give it their all. They may believe that by being super-responsible, they can fix their family problems. At the very least, they may gain comfort in the thought that others may view their family in a favorable light because of their personal achievements. Heroes tend to be very well organized and can be counted on in times of need. Because these behaviors are tied into self-soothing and comfort in the face of anxiety, when stressors do increase, these once adaptive behaviors can become compulsive and interfere with life. Even though their achievements may make them popular, they may also feel very lonely. The hero's goal is to stop the pain; however, when heroes are not able to *earn* the nurturance and love they desire, they may be left with feelings of inadequacy. This dynamic of achieving to receive love can be a barrier to intimate relationships as an adult.

The Scapegoat

Whereas heroes draw attention toward achievements, the behaviors of scapegoats (e.g., delinquency, drug use, promiscuity) draw attention and blame to themselves as the ones responsible for their family's problems. Often seen as the rebels, they may engage in angry and hostile self-destructive behaviors that may mask feelings of hurt, fear, rejection, and shame and guilt. Because of these underlying feelings, their intimate relationships may remain superficial. The alternative to shallow relationships may be in trusting peer groups (the wrong crowd) in which needs for attachment and bonding may be met in a more concrete but risky way.

The Lost Child

These individuals withdraw from the drama of the family problems and fade into the background, growing increasingly isolated, lonely, scared, and confused; they are invisible to the family system. They may appear shy and have few friends because they have not been able to learn to share their opinions with others. A coping response to stress may be the adaptation of a super-flexible attitude that masks a loss of a sense of their social self. Consequently, a lack of effervescence on the outside may point to a deeply hurt child on the inside.

The Mascot

Mascots draw attention from the family problems by being a clown and a cut-up. Their humor may be highly valued because it often serves as a relief valve, redirecting the focus of the problems and breaking the tension in the household caused by caregivers' addictive behaviors. The adaptive strategy of being silly, telling jokes, and clowning around becomes the way in which mascots learn to gain acceptance and a sense of belonging around others. Translated into intimate relationships as an adult, these often superficial and distracting behaviors may inhibit the individual's ability to develop a deepening level of connection.

References

van Wormer, K., & Davis, D. R. (2008). *Addiction treatment: A strengths perspective* (2nd ed.). Pacific Grove, CA: Brooks/Cole.

Note. These descriptions of potential family roles are based on Weigscheider (as cited in van Wormer & Davis, 2008). Individuals may play any number of roles at various times within their family.

Handout 19.2

Families and Feelings Handout

Claudia Black (1981) wrote about a rule that is often found in families in which one or both of the primary caregivers exhibits substance abuse and/or addictive behaviors. This rule is "Don't talk, don't trust, don't feel."

Once the silence of following this rule has been broken, individuals growing up in these environments often describe similar feelings and experiences, such as the following:

- Never knowing what is going to happen next, leading to feelings of *anxiety and fear*
- A parent who could be happy or angry or cold or distant depending on the day, leading to feelings of *confusion and neglect*
- Parental fighting, leading to *fear and pain*
- Emotional abuse or name calling, leading to feelings of *hurt, sadness, guilt, and shame*
- Sexual abuse, leading to feelings of *betrayal and pain*
- Broken promises, leading to feelings of *anger and disappointment*
- Money problems, leading to *worry and neglect*
- Embarrassing behaviors, leading to feelings of *shame*
- Denial of problem(s), leading to feelings of *shame and secrecy*
- Broken homes, leading to feelings of *shame and guilt*

Because of the potential shame and stigma associated with addiction, shame-based family messages are often transmitted from generation to generation. These messages can exacerbate common feelings of guilt, for example when one makes a mistake ("I made a mistake"), to feelings of shame ("I am a mistake"). Shame can become a potential magnifier of the basic feelings of guilt and embarrassment and can lead to feelings of self-doubt and self-loathing.

References

Black, C. (1981). *It will never happen to me.* Denver, CO: M.A.C. Printing.

Substance Abuse Counseling With College Students

Edil Torres Rivera, Whitney A. Hendricks, and Perry Peace

A 2007 report of the National Center on Addiction and Substance Abuse at Columbia University indicated that close to half of all full-time college students engage in binge drinking and/or abuse prescription and illegal drugs. The study presented possible causes of the problem and barriers to resolving it, ranging from student resistance to a lack of responsibility among the administration. However, we believe that a model using psychoeducational groups to infuse liberatory or emancipatory principles is lacking in the literature on working with college students in substance abuse settings. Therefore, we introduce a theoretical framework and praxis that focuses on the following areas: (a) the theory and principles of liberation psychology as a process for reaching and providing alternatives to college students, (b) a psychoeducational model of group work with college students, and (c) roles of the college substance abuse counselor/group worker.

The National Center on Addiction and Substance Abuse at Columbia University (2007) report found that nearly 2 million full-time college students meet the medical criteria for substance abuse and dependence; this is 2.5 times the 8.5% of the general population who meet these same criteria. Other reports have indicated similar problems with alcohol and drug use among college students in general and gay, lesbian, and bisexual students in particular (Reed, Prado, Matsumoto, & Amaro, 2010). Thus, college counseling centers should make it a priority to call attention to this growing problem.

Professionals have made great strides in counseling college students in prevention and education with regard to the use and misuse of alcohol and drugs; however, binge drinking and drug abuse continue to be a problem (Carlson, Johnson, & Jacobs, 2010; Reed et al., 2010). Group work is one of the most popular modalities of treatment in college and university counseling centers, but it is difficult to determine if existing groups are for the treatment and prevention of alcohol and drug issues or for other issues (Kincade & Kalodner, 2004). Thus, we believe that a model based on liberation psychology that uses a psychoeducational modality could be a helpful approach to treatment and prevention among college students with substance abuse problems.

Martín Baró (as cited in Aron & Corne, 1994/1996) referred to *liberation psychology* as a psychology that has to begin with a new horizon, a new epistemology, and a new praxis. However, the essence of this type of psychology is creating critical consciousness and thus giving choices and creating liberation.

Based on the principles of liberation psychology, these three practical bases (new horizon, new epistemology, and new praxis) lead mental health professionals to three urgent tasks: (a) recovering historical memory, (b) de-ideologizing everyday experience and social reality, and (c) using the virtues of a people (Baró, as cited in Aron & Corne, 1994/1996).

Group Plan

Session 1: Introduction, Values Clarification, Rules, Expectations, Creating an Environment of Trust and Safety

- Review the purpose, expectations, and rules of the group. Give students the opportunity to add rules or delete them. Emphasize and explain the limits of confidentiality and boundaries, including university policies, from within the cultural context of the college students' community in a group setting and in particular the college or university.
- Introduce yourself to the students as the group leader. Ask the students if they have questions about you; this is done to establish rapport and trust and to increase students' comfort and safety talking about group issues.
- Instruct all group members to introduce themselves and share their expectations of the group. Ask students to identify some of the issues (themes) they would like to discuss.
- Values clarification exercise: This is the actual heart of the program in which group members investigate one another's values and beliefs. Discuss the meaning and distinction of tolerance and acceptance. Tolerance is the key.
- Learning how to respect other people's boundaries leads to tolerance. Some key concepts include the following: What is important to the students? Have the students make a list of things that are important to them (e.g., doing well in school, family, friends) and then rank

the items on their list. Have students make their lists on their own and then share them with the other group members without passing value judgments. Notice students' contradictions, if they have any, and help them to explore them.

- Explain the rules of dialogue. According to the Co-Intelligence Institute (2003),

> Dialogue can at times be truly magical, dissolving the boundaries between the world and us and opening up wellsprings of realization and resonant power. In those rare, deeply healing moments of dialogue in its most ideal form, we may experience the wholeness of who we are (beyond our isolated ego), listening and speaking to the wholeness of who we are (deep within and beyond the group around us). At those times it is almost as if wholeness is speaking and listening to itself through us, individually and collectively. Words become unnecessary; knowing is instantaneous, and meaning flows like a great river within and among us.
>
> These are moments of grace, whose frequency increases as we practice listening more deeply and exploring more openly with each other.

Here are some guidelines for dialogue in its most basic form:

1. We talk about what's really important to us.
2. We really listen to each other. We see how thoroughly we can understand each other's views and experience.
3. We say what's true for us without making each other wrong.
4. We see what we can learn together by exploring things together.
5. We avoid monopolizing the conversation. We make sure everyone has a chance to speak. (Co-Intelligence Institute, 2003)

Session 2: Prevention Versus Treatment, Understanding the History of Drugs in the United States, Understanding Systems and Social Factors in Substance Abuse

- View the series *Hooked: Illegal Drugs and How They Got That Way* (Yaroschuk, 2000). A search of YouTube will help you find portions of the series, or it can be purchased from the History Channel website (http://shop.history.com/detail.php?p=70337&v=history). The complete series contains two discs of 100 minutes each.
- Discuss group members' reactions to the video, such as what they found most interesting, what surprised them, and how it related to their lives.

Session 3: Culture and Family, Parental Patterns and Spirituality

- Help the students understand that it is vital to take into consideration an individual's family (and other social contexts) when exploring the development, maintenance, and treatment of substance use disorders.

- The family system is an important client context, in part because it is one of the interpersonal situations in which the problems occur. In some cases, the social context of family relationships may be a factor that becomes compelling for the maintenance of substance use problems; the specific nature of family interactions may foster the continuation of problematic use or abuse. In others, this context can facilitate improvement and recovery.
- Because in many cultures the issues of spirituality and substance abuse seem to be related, this session introduces the aspects of family, spirituality, treatment, and prevention of substance use (Conner, Anglin, Annon, & Longshore, 2009). This particular subject flows naturally into the next subject of change and social justice issues.

Session 4: When Do People Change? Understanding Educational, Individual, and Economic Factors

- This session is about change and how people change from a more existential and liberatory standpoint.
- The problematization process is a key point, and the bases of change and transformation go hand in hand with critical thinking and critical consciousness. A methodology based on Freire's (1970/2000) model of reflection → action → reflection followed by action → reflection → action is used and practiced.

Session 5: Understanding Relationship Issues, Dealing With Emotional and Honesty Issues

- Discuss with the group the notion that honesty with oneself is a basic psychological need. There is a premise that substance abuse may serve as a temporary coping mechanism to help individuals reduce anxiety and maintain honesty with themselves (Moustakas, 1966).
- Explain that according to Moustakas (1966) and Torres-Rivera, Wilbur, Phan, Maddux, and Roberts-Wilbur (2004), individuals merely want to live their lives their own way and express themselves directly in a way that is consistent with their own experiences.
- Important people in substance abusers' lives who have been influenced by majority culture ideas of acceptance or rejection (Torres-Rivera et al., 2004) may not listen to substance abusers' simple, honest expressions of feelings and life experiences.
- Consequently, as a way of coping with underlying and unexpressed emotions, substance abusers may hide and protect their feelings and experiences by using and deceiving others. Accordingly, substance abuse problems may also be seen as users' attempts to avoid self-deception by being dishonest with those who will not acknowledge the honest expression of their life experiences and emotions.
- Ask if any members defend substance abuse and resist attempts to change to cope with unexpressed life problems and emotions.

- Relate how some individuals may turn to substance abuse as a means of controlling unexpressed feelings and emotions. Ask whether this applies to anyone in the group and why.

Session 6: Getting to Know Oneself, Expression and Acceptance of Oneself

- Explain that the day's topic is honesty and how being dishonest with yourself and others fosters substance abuse.
- Ask members to rate how honest they are with people in general and what obstacles there are to being more honest.
- Ask members to rate and describe how honest they are with themselves and what obstacles there are to being more honest.
- Ask members to identify someone in their life with whom it was easy to be honest and to describe this experience.

Session 7: Addressing Issues of Sex and Violence

- In this session, the lack of tolerance and/or understanding is tied to violence as an outcome of the intolerance and misunderstanding. Violent behavior is examined, and the discussion focuses on how this behavior could be self-defeating.
- The goal is not about changing behavior but rather educating the students through sharing information and engaging in discussions. As a result, students will acquire greater understanding and knowledge to make their own choices.
- Ask questions such as the following: How strong and resilient are students at resisting being violent? What usually happens when they are about to become violent? Sometimes students need to walk away, and sometimes they feel they need to stand up for themselves.
- Ask the group if anyone has suggestions for how to deal with situations that involve violence. What are some other constructive ways to deal with violence?
- Instruct the group to reflect on their relationships with parents, friends, professors, and others. The goal once again is to help students be congruent with their feelings and their behaviors. Look for congruence and incongruence. What do students do to get people to like them? If they say that they do not do things to get people to like them, then why do they choose to do what they do? What do they do to attract people, and why do they want to be cool?
- Assess whether the consequences a student has to accept based on his or her choices are culturally fair. Act as an advocate for a student who is being treated differently because of race, ethnicity, gender, sexual orientation, disability, or socioeconomic status.

Session 8: Preparing to Deal With the Real World and Relapse Prevention

- This session is actually one of the most important ones, given that the idea is to prepare the students to face the real world in life terms.

- What has each group member taken from this group and perhaps specific group members? What has each group member learned about himself or herself and other group members throughout this entire process?
- What will each group member do with this new understanding and knowledge?
- Say goodbye to each student and share your connection and counseling relationship with each group member in the context of this group. By doing this, you acknowledge and solidify the work that each group member has contributed to the group and instill the belief that each student is a member of a community, in this case the group. Students achieve a sense of responsibility and community when they feel that their choices have an impact on themselves, their families, their school, and the community as a whole.

References

Aron, A., & Corne, S. (1996). *Writing for liberation psychology: Ignacio Martín-Baró.* Cambridge, MA: Harvard University Press. (Original work published 1994)

Carlson, S., Johnson, S., & Jacobs, P. (2010). Disinhibited characteristics and binge drinking among university student drinkers. *Addictive Behaviors, 35*(3), 242–251.

Co-Intelligence Institute. (2003). *Dialogue.* Retrieved from http://www.co-intelligence.org/P-dialogue.html

Conner, B., Anglin, M., Annon, J., & Longshore, D. (2009). Effect of religiosity and spirituality on drug treatment outcomes. *Journal of Behavioral Health Services & Research, 36*(2), 189–198.

Freire, P. (2000). *Pedagogy of the oppressed* (M. Bergman Ramos, Trans.). New York, NY: Continuum International. (Original work published 1970)

Kincade, E., & Kalodner, C. (2004). The use of groups in college and university counseling centers. In J. L. DeLucia-Waack, D. A. Gerrity, C. R. Kalodner, & M. T. Riva (Eds.), *Handbook of group counseling and psychotherapy* (pp. 366–377). Thousand Oaks, CA: Sage.

Moustakas, C. E. (1966). *Honesty, idiocy, and manipulation.* Unpublished manuscript, Merrill-Palmer Institute, Detroit, MI.

National Center on Addiction and Substance Abuse at Columbia University. (2007). *Wasting the best and the brightest: Substance abuse at America's colleges and universities.* Retrieved from http://www.casacolumbia.org/templates/publications_reports.aspx?keywords=college

Reed, E., Prado, G., Matsumoto, A., & Amaro, H. (2010). Alcohol and drug use and related consequences among gay, lesbian and bisexual college students: Role of experiencing violence, feeling safe on campus, and perceived stress. *Addictive Behaviors, 35*(2), 168–171.

Torres-Rivera, E., Wilbur, M. P., Phan, L. T., Maddux, C., & Roberts-Wilbur, J. (2004). Counseling Latinos with substance abuse problems. *Journal of Addictions & Offender Counseling, 25,* 26–44.
Yaroschuk, T. (Director). (2000). *Hooked: Illegal drugs and how they got that way* [Documentary]. United States: Arts and Entertainment Network.

Chapter 21

Group Programs for College Students: Combat Veterans

Eric Manley

Returning combat veterans face a unique set of mental health challenges as they begin the process of reorienting from their role as soldier back to their identities as spouses, parents, employees, and students. This chapter focuses on the unique challenges of veterans returning to colleges or universities.

War has significant effects on the personal well-being of armed combat veterans, who often return home with psychological disorders, debilitating injuries, and disease (Levy & Sidel, 2009). Veterans of wars, including such conflicts as World War II, the Vietnam War, the Persian Gulf War, and the wars in Iraq and Afghanistan, are all at high risk for posttraumatic stress disorder (PTSD), depression, and many related mood and anxiety disorders (Pietrzak, Johnson, Goldstein, Malley, & Southwick, 2009). It is also not uncommon for combat veterans to experience interpersonal and relationship difficulties in their transition to civilian life (Witvliet, Phipps, Feldman, & Beckham, 2004). Although research has been completed on the experiences of nonstudent veterans from World War II and the Vietnam War, the literature includes a limited number of studies regarding student veterans; more investigation of this population is needed (DiRamio, Ackerman, & Mitchell, 2008).

Many college student veterans do not have access to counseling or specific support resources on campus. In addition, veterans often face stigma and feelings of weakness as they sit face to face with a clinician. Veterans from the Iraq, Afghanistan, and Gulf wars are often faced with a myriad of adjustment difficulties without this critical support. Many of these students are challenged by a number of obstacles. For example, many student veterans have a wide range of experiences returning from active duty, and some branches of the military provide little to no mental health services to help them ease back into civilian or academic life (DiRamio et al., 2008). Campus mental health and academic support resources may help ease the burden of student veterans who have not gotten their emotional or psychological needs met by their service branch.

Group psychotherapy is an effective tool to help combat veterans struggling with mental health disorders. Murphy, Thompson, Murray, Rainey, and Uddo (2009) found that group work can be particularly helpful for students in general and especially combat veterans. For example, Yalom (1995) wrote about the power of groups to provide patients with hope that group therapy will make a difference in their lives and to allow them to meet others who have had similar experiences, thoughts, problems, and concerns.

Groups can help combat veterans learn to appropriately express their emotions and to understand that they are not isolated in their experiences; many veterans may gain insight into their style of interpersonal communication, thus improving relationships outside of the group (Dies, 2003). The role of the group leader is especially important because this person helps to build group cohesiveness, an essential component of group therapy, allowing members to show their vulnerability, to gain insight, to learn interpersonal and communication skills, and to create positive change in their lives (Yalom, 1995).

The group proposed here follows a brief therapy model. Brief therapy focuses upon the patient and therapist's endeavors to identify the problems that precipitated therapy and to seek an immediate resolution to the patient's issues (Hoyt, 2003). Brief therapy also includes establishing obtainable and concrete goals and providing the client with direct help with a specific concern (Hoyt, 2003). Brief therapy advocates making the most out of each session, with a focus on accessing strength, resources, and healing in a direct fashion. This form of therapy appears to have a bright future, as it is effective and is likely to be compatible with the demands of managed care (Hoyt, 2003). This group is planned for eight sessions and centers on the challenges of being both a veteran and a college student.

Group Plan

Session 1: Introduction to the Group

- Introduce yourself to the group and provide members with information about your professional training.
- Discuss ethical expectations and guidelines for group participation.
- Ask participants to introduce themselves to the group and identify a goal for group therapy.
- Use the Miracle Question ("If you woke up tomorrow and your problems about the war were all gone, how would life be different?") to help elicit goals.
- Ask the members to rate on a scale of 1 to 10 how close they are to achieving this goal.
- Ask the group members to provide an overview of their military background.

Session 2: Unique Problems of College Student Veterans

- Prior to the group meeting, familiarize yourself with institutional services specifically for veterans and be aware of other resources available on campus, such as career counseling, individual counseling, and academic help.
- Allow group members to discuss their experiences with and the quality of help resources offered by their particular branch of service before returning to the United States.
- Ask the group members to discuss what kind of personal challenges they have faced since transitioning to college.
- Ask the group members to discuss academic difficulties they have or may have experienced upon returning to college.
- Allow the group members to discuss the often frustrating bureaucratic barriers they may have experienced since returning to school.
- Encourage the group members to discuss their feelings about returning to college with traditional-age college students without a military background.

Session 3: Combat Stress and PTSD

- Provide group members with psychoeducation using Handout 21.1 regarding the signs and symptoms of PTSD as well as current treatment modalities, especially the importance of talking about the traumatic event(s).
- Ask the group members to discuss their reactions to the description of PTSD.
- Ask group members to discuss how combat-related stress and PTSD have negatively affected their day-to-day lives.
- Ask the group members to describe their coping style when they experience symptoms of PTSD.
- Track progress by asking members to compare their ratings on a scale of 1 to 10 (how close to their goal) with ratings from Session 1. What accounted for any changes?

Session 4: Combat Stress and PTSD (Continued)

- Ask group members to recall particularly traumatic combat experiences.
- Encourage group members to explore their emotional reactions to the trauma in as much detail as possible.
- Allow members to identify and discuss intrusive thoughts and flashbacks, and ask what they have done in the past to help cope with these.
- Encourage group members to seek out individual counseling when needed, and encourage them to be open to recalling traumatic events.

Session 5: Stress Management

- Have group members identify recurring or common stressors in their lives.

- Have members share with one another how they cope with stress.
- Demonstrate and train group members to use effective means of coping with stressors, such as deep breathing and muscle relaxation.
- Provide instruction about relaxation techniques.

Session 6: Anger Management

- Encourage group members to describe and identify targets, situations, and triggers that typically create angry outbursts.
- Have group members discuss the negative ways in which anger has affected their personal lives.
- Explain the difference between assertiveness and anger/aggression, and discuss examples of assertiveness and aggression management.
- Encourage group members to identify how they would like to manage angry outbursts in the future.

Session 7: Interpersonal Issues and Relationships

- Ask the group members to acknowledge and discuss any current relationship difficulties with spouses, significant others, children, parents, or others.
- Encourage group members to discuss positive aspects of their relationships as well.
- Ask group members to discuss a behavior that they would like to change that may improve the relationship.
- Use some group time to educate group members about family counseling and couples counseling and how the members may benefit from those therapeutic modalities.
- Make the group members aware of family and couples counseling resources on campus.

Session 8: Group Wrap-Up and Termination, and Identification of Community Resources

- Ask group members to identify something that they learned about themselves and about managing psychological issues on campus.
- Use the rating scale again to rate progress toward the goal. Discuss and share coping mechanisms and what specific changes got them closer.
- Ask group members to discuss what was helpful about the group and how they will use what they learned from the group experience.
- Ask for feedback regarding how to make the group more effective in the future.
- Ask group members to identify university-based support resources they plan to use, such as housing, counseling, financial aid, and advising.
- Provide the group members with a list of university and community resources.

References

Dies, R. (2003). Group psychotherapies. In A. S. Gurman & S. Messer (Eds.), *Essential psychotherapies* (pp. 515–550). New York, NY: Guilford Press.

DiRamio, D., Ackerman, R., & Mitchell, R. (2008). From combat to campus: Voices of student-veterans. *NASPA Journal, 45*(1), 73–102.

Hoyt, M. (2003). Brief psychotherapy. In A. S. Gurman & S. Messer (Eds.), *Essential psychotherapies* (pp. 350-359). New York, NY: Guilford Press.

Levy, S., & Sidel, V. (2009). Health effects of combat: A life-course perspective. *Annual Review of Public Health, 30,* 123–136.

Murphy, R., Thompson, K., Murray, M., Rainey, Q., & Uddo, M. (2009). Effects of motivation enhancement intervention on veterans' engagement in PTSD treatment. *Psychological Services, 6,* 264–278.

Pietrzak, R., Johnson, D., Goldstein, M., Malley, J., & Southwick, S. (2009). Psychological resilience and post deployment social support protect against traumatic stress and depressive symptoms in soldiers returning from Operations Enduring Freedom and Iraqi Freedom. *Depression and Anxiety, 26,* 745–751.

Witvliet, C., Phipps, K., Feldman, M., & Beckham, J. (2004). Posttraumatic mental and physical health correlates of forgiveness and religious coping in military veterans. *Journal of Traumatic Stress, 17,* 269–273.

Yalom, I. (1995). *The theory and practice of group psychotherapy.* New York, NY: Basic Books.

Handout 21.1

Posttraumatic Stress Disorder (PTSD): Causes, Symptoms, and Treatment

PTSD is sometimes diagnosed when an individual experiences a traumatic and overwhelming event. Examples of trauma include combat, car accidents, natural disasters, physical or sexual assault, sudden violence, and the onset of a serious illness.

In most cases, death or threat of death occurs.

Physical Symptoms

- Fatigue, insomnia, changes in appetite, headaches, upset stomach, chronic feelings of tension, muscle soreness, and digestion problems.

Cognitive Symptoms

- Problems focusing or concentrating, intrusive thoughts or intrusive flashbacks to the events, problems with decision making, and memory disturbances.

Emotional Symptoms

- Feelings of helplessness, feelings of worthlessness, hypervigilance, anxiety and feeling unsafe, nightmares, depression, moodiness, guilt, anger, feeling afraid of being alone, crying, and feelings of isolation from others.

Strategies for Coping

- Familiarize yourself with resources on campus that may benefit you as a veteran returning student, such as advising services, counseling, and learning centers.
- Discuss and recall the traumatic event in a safe space or with people you trust.
- Allow yourself to be comfortable with your emotional reactions to the event. Sometimes you may feel like crying, being alone, or being with others. Allow yourself to feel what you need to feel.
- Engage in physical activity on a frequent basis, such as walking, weightlifting, swimming, and/or other forms of aerobic exercise.
- Effectively manage your time, and stick to your schedule as much as possible. Make sure to add in time to relax.
- Reach out for help. Join a support group. Seek out individual therapy.
- Ask friends and family for support.
- Distract yourself when under distress, such as through reading, watching a film, talking with an old friend, or playing video games.
- Take 15 minutes every day to write in a journal about your thoughts, feelings, and experiences for the day.

- Avoid using alcohol or recreational drugs to cope with your feelings.
- Take medication exactly how it is prescribed by your physician.
- Monitor yourself for suicidal thoughts and plans. If you find that you are suicidal, contact the university counseling center or police department, call 911, and/or report to the nearest emergency room.
- Make sure to follow up with a counselor after a psychological or an emotional crisis.
- Learn to relax by using deep-breathing techniques or deep muscle relaxation techniques. Practice this strategy everyday.
- Investigate new and emerging treatments for PTSD, such as eye-movement desensitization and reprocessing.

Chapter 22

A Psychoeducational Group for Student Athletes With Performance Anxiety

Jason Braun

Whether it is giving an important speech, taking a crucial exam, or competing in a critical game or match, everyone has experienced some level of stress and anxiety related to performance. The anxiety–performance relationship seems axiomatic to the human experience. The existence of a relationship between stress, anxiety, or the interrelated concept of arousal and performance has been the subject of research for more than a century (Yerkes & Dodson, 1908), and this research has offered numerous models of the anxiety–performance relationship (Zaichkowsky & Takenaka, 1993). However, the exact nature of this relationship has remained largely elusive. Some researchers in sport psychology believe this elusiveness exists at least in part because performance or competitive anxiety is a complex construct involving somatic and cognitive components (Davidson & Schwartz, 1976), with each component impacting performance differently. Cognitive anxiety is characterized by the mental aspects of anxiety and includes negative expectations of success, negative self-evaluations, and worry. It has a negative linear relationship to performance: As cognitive anxiety increases, performance decreases (Burton, 1988). The somatic component is "the physiological or affective component of anxiety that is directly related to autonomic arousal" (Burton, 1988, p. 46). Somatic anxiety generally adheres to a curvilinear relationship with the performance of complex tasks (Gallucci, 2008). Often called the inverted-U curve (Yerkes & Dodson, 1908), this relationship states that increasing somatic anxiety or arousal is facilitative to performance, but only to a point—an experience athletes may label as being "psyched up" for a competition. However, once this peak level of anxiety or arousal is surpassed—if athletes become too psyched up—performance begins to decline (Graydon, 2002).

Although some research has examined the use of a single mode of treatment for competitive performance anxiety (e.g., Cumming, Olphin, & Law, 2007; Maynard, Hemmings, & Warwick-Evans, 1995; Maynard, Smith, & Warwick-Evans, 1995), the sport psychology intervention literature has predominantly examined the use of multimodal interventions that address both cognitive and somatic aspects of performance (e.g., Annesi, 1998; Hanton & Jones, 1999; Kendall, Hrycaiko, Martin, & Kendall, 1990; Patrick & Hrycaiko, 1998; Savoy, 1993). The intervention outlined in this chapter adapts these same or similar strategies into a psychoeducational group format for college student athletes. To be clear, the goal of this group is to facilitate athletes' development of anxiety control skills. As Savoy (1993) suggested, this typically involves reducing arousal/activation, as most athletes are more prone to becoming overstimulated rather than understimulated in competitive situations. Therefore, interventions focused on reducing anxiety and/or mitigating the debilitative effects of anxiety are used in the structured group outlined here.

Group Plan

Session 1: Group Introduction

- Introduce yourself and discuss your professional background.
- Introduce the general format of the group, including the five hour-long session structure and the objectives of the group.
  - Specifically inform student athletes that this program will *not* focus on winning or otherwise improving their individual or team results but rather on teaching them strategies to help them better address the anxiety that may be keeping them from performing at their best in any given moment.
- Get an introduction from the group members (this may not be necessary if the group is made up of teammates and/or male and female team members from the same sport).
- Discuss ethical issues for groups, and establish group rules collaboratively.
- As an ice breaker or bonding activity, facilitate a discussion exploring what the student athletes love (or loved) about *playing* their particular sport, attempting to focus the discussion on their physical and/or psychological experiences (e.g., the feel of the water for swimmers). Make sure to elicit feedback and related examples to build group cohesion and promote interaction among the student athletes.
- After a number of positive experiences have been elicited and discussed, shift discussion to exploring what, if anything, is different about their experience of their sport *in competition*.
  - Use examples from this discussion to highlight the role of perception in anxiety (i.e., the physical act of playing the sport remains the same, only the meaning of the play changes).

- Introduce the performance anxiety concept, offering a definition of *performance anxiety*, such as the following definition that I use: the heightened physical and psychological arousal brought on by real or perceived threat that may inhibit or impair performance.
- Note the existence of both cognitive and somatic aspects of performance anxiety and elaborate briefly on them.
    - Reiterate the role of perception as an example of the cognitive component of anxiety, and use already generated examples from earlier discussion or elicit or offer additional examples (e.g., shooting a free throw in practice vs. shooting a free throw to win a championship game).
    - Discuss the fight–flight response of the sympathetic nervous system in response to threat/stress, eliciting examples of physical symptoms of anxiety from the group.
    - Discuss the inverted-U curve and how it describes the relationship between physical arousal or anxiety symptoms and performance.
- Discuss the idea of an optimal level of anxiety or arousal, using the peak of the inverted-U curve to graphically depict this concept and noting that this optimal level exists for both somatic and cognitive anxiety. State that optimal levels are unique to each student athlete.
- Summarize (or ask members of the group to summarize) the concepts of performance anxiety, the inverted-U curve, and optimal levels of anxiety/arousal.
- Reemphasize that the goal of the group is to learn to manage anxiety/arousal, not get rid of it, and let the student athletes know that the remaining sessions will focus on various ways to help them achieve this goal.
- For homework, ask student athletes to come to the next session with a personal definition of success and/or personal goals regarding their sport.

Session 2: Physical and Psychological Skills Development

- Review several volunteered personal definitions of success or goals, noting their interpersonal or external focus.
- Discuss process- or performance-oriented goals versus outcome or results goals, and note how focusing on aspects of performance under the students' own control can help reduce anxiety.
- Broaden the discussion of focusing on controllable elements of performance as they relate to anxiety, including noting the importance of practice, being and feeling physically prepared to meet challenges of competition.
    - As practice is a familiar concept for athletes, present the rest of the skills and strategies as ways to physically and psychologically prepare to perform at their best, and encourage the student athletes to practice these skills regularly.

- Introduce relaxation and its impact on performance anxiety/arousal.
- Facilitate the group practicing a structured breathing exercise using Handout 22.1.
- For homework, ask group members to practice this breathing exercise three times per day for 3 to 5 minutes each time and notice any physical and/or emotional effects as well as any difficulties they may have during the exercise.
  - Have student athletes write down (in journals provided) their observations during each practice session for discussion during the next session.

Note: If you have more time and want to present more relaxation strategies, see Gallucci (2008) for a description of various well-researched relaxation strategies and Maynard, Hemmings, and Warwick-Evans (1995) for a specific 8-week applied relaxation technique for use with athletes.

Session 3: Skills Development (Continued)

- Facilitate discussion of group members' experiences with the relaxation exercise, elicit feedback and suggestions from other group members, and provide needed trouble shooting regarding specific questions or concerns.
- Introduce mental imagery and its impact on performance anxiety/arousal; see White and Hardy (1998) for a sample definition of imagery used with athletes.
- Facilitate and process the group practicing at least two brief non-sport-specific imagery scripts that offer the chance to experience differing physiological experiences during imagery (examples include running energetically on the beach and walking calmly by a gently flowing stream). Guide group members to be aware of and focus on physical sensations and situational and context cues (response and stimulus propositions; Lang, 1979) in the imagery as a way to train them in how to make their self-created, sport-specific imagery scripts more effective.
  - Remember to begin with a few minutes of relaxation (using the technique learned previously) before beginning the imagery script.
  - Emphasize the importance of details/vividness (engaging as many senses as possible), and have group members play with internal (looking out of your own eyes) versus external (watching yourself from afar) perspectives during these practice sessions to find what works best for them.
- For homework, ask student athletes to compose (in their journals) their own coping imagery scripts (Cumming et al., 2007) that include both activating/arousing imagery (specific mention of physical sensations they typically experience prior to or during competitions) and positive interpretations of this heightened activation/arousal and images of themselves successfully coping with the challenging competitive situation (for a generic example of a coping imagery script, see the appendix of Cumming et al., 2007).

- Make sure student athletes' scripts focus on what they want to have happen versus what they want to avoid ("You feel under control" vs. "You are not freaking out"). Encourage them to explore multiple scenarios, as competitions are often multifaceted and unpredictable.
- Also encourage group members to continue practicing relaxation technique(s), making any modifications they wish based on discussion and feedback received during this session. Ask them to bring any further observations and/or questions to future sessions for discussion.

Session 4: Skills Development (Continued)

- Ask for volunteers to share the coping imagery scripts they composed, elicit feedback and suggestions from other group members based on what was discussed in previous sessions, and provide trouble shooting or further guidance as needed to address questions or concerns from the group.
- Introduce self-talk and its impact on performance anxiety.
- Elicit a few examples (positive or negative) of self-talk from the group, using any opportunities to clarify the difference between thoughts and feelings.
- If group members are struggling to come up with examples, you may choose to offer some initial examples or ask group members to imagine a recent experience with performance anxiety and then work with volunteers to uncover examples of negative self-talk.
- Facilitate the group working through the process of countering several examples of negative self-talk (the use of a dry erase board or chalkboard can facilitate this exercise, or you might have student athletes write these examples in their journals).
- For homework, ask group members to write down (in their journals) examples of negative self-talk they experience over the course of the following week or examples of such self-talk they are aware of having experienced in the past related to their sport. Also have them write down their attempts to counter these thoughts.
  - Handout 22.2 can be used to introduce the concept of self-talk and guide this homework assignment.
- Continue to encourage student athletes to practice relaxation regularly. Discuss options for group members to record their coping imagery scripts (either by themselves or by someone else whose voice they find pleasing) with any modifications they wish based on the discussion and feedback received during this session (and future sessions). Have them begin to use these recordings along with the relaxation technique at least three times per week.

Session 5: Skills Development Completion and Wrap-Up

- Process several examples of negative self-talk and positive counter-statements offered by volunteers from the group, eliciting feedback and suggestions from group members, and provide trouble shooting and further guidance as needed to address questions or concerns from the group.

- Explore for any patterns or themes group members may notice in their negative self-talk. Discuss possible positive self-talk statements student athletes might use before and during competitions to rationalize their thoughts and feelings into a positive state, suggesting that each group member write down on note cards at least three positive statements for reference prior to competing.
  - Explain that self-talk can be used for prevention as well as remediation.
- Summarize the various strategies discussed in the group, and reemphasize the importance of students practicing these skills regularly in order to continue developing their ability to better manage their performance anxiety.
- Facilitate a discussion about student athletes' current rituals prior to and during competitions and how, if at all, group members believe these rituals impact their anxiety levels. Elicit specific examples and note which strategies, if any, discussed in the group are included.
- Discuss how group members might incorporate or better integrate some or all of these strategies into their routines as a way to systematically enhance their ability to manage their performance anxiety and give themselves the best chance to perform optimally. Ask for specific examples, and encourage student athletes to write down these rituals or routines and how they will use them in the future.
  - For groups that include members from the same team, discuss any existing team rituals (e.g., huddling up before or after plays) and the possibility of developing or enhancing team routines to better manage anxiety and improve performance.
- Ask group members to share at least one thing they learned from the group, including from each other, and to note their confidence in their ability to use and benefit from what they have learned.

References

Annesi, J. J. (1998). Applications of the individual zones of optimal functioning model for the multimodal treatment of precompetitive anxiety. *The Sport Psychologist, 12,* 300–316.

Burton, D. (1988). Do anxious swimmers swim slower? Reexamining the elusive anxiety-performance relationship. *Journal of Sport & Exercise Psychology, 10,* 45–61.

Cumming, J., Olphin, T., & Law, M. (2007). Self-reported psychological states and physiological responses to different types of motivational general imagery. *Journal of Sport & Exercise Psychology, 29,* 629–644.

Davidson, R. J., & Schwartz, G. E. (1976). The psychobiology of relaxation and related states: A multiprocess theory. In D. I. Mostofsky (Ed.), *Behavior control and modification of physiological activity* (pp. 399–422). Englewood Cliffs, NJ: Prentice Hall.

Gallucci, N. T. (2008). *Sport psychology: Performance enhancement, performance inhibition, individuals and teams.* New York, NY: Psychology Press.

Graydon, J. (2002). Stress and anxiety in sport. *The Psychologist, 15,* 408–410.

Hanton, S., & Jones, G. (1999). The effect of a multimodal intervention program on performers: Training the butterflies to fly in formation. *The Sport Psychologist, 13,* 22–41.

Kendall, G., Hrycaiko, D., Martin, G. L., & Kendall, T. (1990). The effects of an imagery rehearsal, relaxation, and self-talk package on basketball game performance. *Journal of Sport & Exercise Psychology, 12,* 157–166.

Lang, P. J. (1979). A bio-informational theory of emotional imagery. *Psychophysiology, 16,* 495–512.

Maynard, I. W., Hemmings, B., & Warwick-Evans, L. (1995). The effects of a somatic intervention strategy on competitive state anxiety and performance in semi-professional soccer players. *The Sport Psychologist, 9,* 51–64.

Maynard, I. W., Smith, M. J., & Warwick-Evans, L. (1995). The effects of a cognitive intervention strategy on competitive state anxiety and performance in semi-professional soccer players. *Journal of Sport & Exercise Psychology, 17,* 428–446.

Patrick, T. D., & Hrycaiko, D. W. (1998). Effects of a mental training package on an endurance performance. *The Sport Psychologist, 12,* 283–299.

Savoy, C. (1993). A yearly mental training program for a college basketball player. *The Sport Psychologist, 7,* 173–190.

White, A., & Hardy, L. (1998). An in-depth analysis of the uses of imagery by high-level slalom canoeists and artistic gymnasts. *The Sport Psychologist, 12,* 387–403.

Yerkes, R. M., & Dodson, J. D. (1908). The relation of strength of stimulus to rapidity of habit formation. *Journal of Comparative and Neurological Psychology, 18,* 459–482.

Zaichkowsky, L., & Takenaka, K. (1993). Optimizing arousal level. In R. N. Singer, M. Murphey, & L. K. Tennant (Eds.), *Handbook of research on sport psychology* (pp. 511–527). New York, NY: Macmillan.

Handout 22.1

Structured Breathing Exercise

1. Find a comfortable position and begin to pay attention to your breath.
2. Breathe in slowly and deeply through your nose so that you notice your stomach/abdomen expanding with each inhale (your chest will move slightly as well).
3. When you have taken in a comfortably full breath, you may choose to pause briefly or immediately begin to exhale slowly through your nose or mouth, finding a rhythm that feels right to you.
4. Focus on exhaling fully, and allow your whole body to let go as you release your breath. You might visualize your arms and legs going limp or feel your body become heavier with each exhale.
5. Continue finding a rhythm that feels right to you, maintaining a smooth transition from inhale to exhale without gulping in air or letting it all out at once. If you need help slowing your breath down, try counting to 4 with each inhale and exhale.
6. Once you have found your rhythm, begin counting down from 10 to 1, saying the number softly to yourself with each exhale as you focus on letting go. If you prefer, feel free to count from 1 to 10.
7. Complete two or three sets of 10 abdominal breaths while remaining focused on the rhythm of your breath and letting go with each exhale.

Find regular time(s) in your day to complete this exercise, and with practice you will learn to quickly address the physiological symptoms of anxiety and panic.

Note. Adapted from exercises found in *The Anxiety and Phobia Workbook*, by E. J. Bourne, 2005, Oakland, CA: New Harbinger.

Handout 22.2

Self-Talk

Self-talk is the continual stream of images and internal monologue running through our minds.

The ABCs of Self-Talk

A—*Activating Event:* something that happens, internally (e.g., emotion, memory, or physical pain) or externally (e.g., events, actions of others, or our own behavior).

B—*Belief:* our interpretations and thoughts about what is happening and/or about ourselves, our *perception* of reality. This is what is experienced as self-talk, and it can be positive/rational or negative/irrational.

C—*Consequence:* emotional, physical, mental and behavioral responses to the activation of our beliefs.

$$A \to B \to C$$

When we feel anxious or overly aroused (C) before or during a performance situation (A) when there is no objective danger, our perception of this event or how we are talking to ourselves about it (B) can be described as negative or irrational.

Learning to identify our negative self-talk in such situations, dispute its validity, and counter it with more positive or realistic self-talk allows us to feel a more appropriate and more manageable level of emotional arousal (e.g., anxiety $\to$ excitement, challenge, and/or concern).

Countering Negative Self-Talk

Write down examples of negative self-talk (what you "say" to yourself) related to anxiety you feel before and/or during competitive situations. Remember that self-talk consists of thoughts, not feelings. Try to focus on writing down *the thoughts* that lead to your feelings of anxiety (e.g., "If I miss this shot, we will lose this game and it will be all my fault," "If I lose this race, I failed/I'm a failure").

If you are having trouble coming up with examples of negative self-talk (e.g., thoughts/images), first notice when you are actually experiencing performance anxiety and then try to relax and *slow down* using a previously learned relaxation technique. Once you are more relaxed, ask yourself, "What am I telling myself to make me feel this way?" or "What is going through my mind?" Similarly, you can think back to past experiences when you felt performance anxiety (even use imagery to make the experience more real and present) and then ask yourself what negative self-talk was present during this time.

Questioning your negative thoughts can help you construct positive counterstatements. Such questions include the following:

- What is the evidence for or against this thought?

Note: Often a more balanced and realistic statement can be composed by combining evidence for and against the initial negative thought.

- Is this statement true for me, for all people, all of the time?
- Is this thinking helpful? (Consider the costs/benefits)

The following are additional questions that can be helpful:

- If my teammate had this thought, what would I tell him or her?
- If my teammate or another person who cares about me knew I was thinking this thought, what would he or she say?
- When I am not feeling this anxious, do I think about this type of situation any differently?
- When I have felt this anxious in the past, what did I think about that helped me feel less anxious?

Divide your paper in half and write your negative self-talk on one side and your positive counterstatements on the other. For example:

Negative Self-Talk	*Positive Counterstatement*
If I miss this shot, we will lose this game and it will be my fault.	I have practiced and made this shot thousands of times, and I know I am capable of making it. If I do miss this time, my team and I will be very disappointed, but we all know that many factors determine the outcome of a game, and we win and lose as a team. Sure, we'll be upset if I miss and we end up losing this game, but my teammates and I will know that I did the best I could.
If I lose this race, I failed.	I have worked hard to be mentally and physically prepared for this race, and I want to win. I can only control how well I perform. Although that does not guarantee victory, it does give me the best chance to win, and that's all I can ask of myself. If I know I did my best, then I will consider this a successful race, win or lose.

Note. Adapted from *The Anxiety and Phobia Workbook*, by E. J. Bourne, 2005, Oakland, CA: New Harbinger; *Overcoming Performance Anxiety*, by R. Farnbach and E. Farnbach, 2001, New York, NY: Simon & Schuster; and *Mind Over Mood*, by D. Greenberger and C. A. Padesky, 1995, New York, NY: Guilford Press.

A Psychoeducational Group Intervention for Childhood Emotional Abuse

Trevor J. Buser

Childhood emotional abuse refers to hostile nonphysical behaviors (e.g., verbal attacks) that are directed toward a child by an adult and that endanger the child's psychological and/or physical well-being (Esteban, 2006; Keashly & Harvey, 2005; McGee & Wolfe, 1991). Common examples of childhood emotional abuse within the wider cultural milieu of North America include humiliation, rejection, derogation, and intimidation of children by adults (Alloy, Abramson, Smith, Gibb, & Neeren, 2006; Gibb, Abramson, & Alloy, 2004; Nicholas & Bieber, 1997). Research suggests that a history of emotional abuse is surprisingly prevalent among college students: For example, Paivio and McCulloch (2004) found that 44% of college students ($N = 100$; M age = 21) reported a history of emotional abuse. By contrast, 23% of the sample reported a history of physical abuse and 20% reported a history of sexual abuse.

Emotional abuse is most commonly understood as a pattern of behaviors over time rather than an isolated event (Glaser & Prior, 1997; Horton & Cruise, 2001; Twaite & Rodriguez-Srednicki, 2004). As Horton and Cruise observed, virtually all parents verbally insult their children on rare occasions. However, when nonphysical forms of aggression become repetitive in the parent–child relationship—or, sadly, the norm for interpersonal exchanges—then the frame of childhood emotional abuse is well applied (Hamarman & Bernet, 2000; Romeo, 2000).

The damaging nature of emotional abuse is perhaps best seen in the literature on the pessimistic explanatory style. *Explanatory style* is a cognitive characteristic that refers to an individual's habitual mode of understanding the causes of events (McKeever, McWhirter, & Huff, 2006; Peterson & Park, 2007; Quinless & Nelson, 1988). Someone with a pessimistic explanatory style views the causes of negative events as stable (vs. unstable, or transient) in duration; global (vs. specific, or circumscribed) in their generalization to various aspects of life; and internal (vs. external) to the person (Abela, 2001; Peterson & Park, 2007). By contrast, someone with an optimistic explanatory style attributes negative events to unstable (i.e., transient), specific (i.e., circumscribed), and external causes (Abela, 2001; Peterson & Park, 2007). Numerous studies have found a positive correlation between a pessimistic explanatory style and emotional abuse (e.g., Gibb & Abela, 2008; Hankin, 2005).

In view of these results, identifying and altering a pessimistic explanatory style may be an important element in the treatment of emotionally abused clients. If these clients manifest a pessimistic explanatory style, it may be beneficial for counselors to assist in reforming these cognitions as they are presented in the discussion of specific negative events. For example, a counselor may challenge a client's internal causal explanations by highlighting external, systemic variables (e.g., lack of procedural fairness in a work environment or discrimination by a teacher or employer) that potentially contribute to negative events.

Over the course of counseling, clients may develop skill in identifying and reformulating their own explanatory styles. Positive treatment outcomes could accompany clients' shifts toward an optimistic explanatory style. Along this line, studies have shown that a pessimistic explanatory style can be altered through psychotherapeutic intervention (Hamilton & Abramson, 1983; Persons & Rao, 1985).

The following group plan is psychoeducational in nature. The purpose is to educate students about the nature of childhood emotional abuse, its adverse psychological correlates, and treatment directions.

Group Plan

Session 1: Recognizing Emotional Abuse

- Introductions, including each member's name, year in college, and background.
- Leader states clearly the purpose of the group and the focus of the day's session, which is understanding the defining characteristics of emotional abuse.
- *Movement Exercise:* Leader notes that he or she intends to share research on the prevalence of emotional abuse. Members are asked to stand in different areas of the room depending on their guesses about the prevalence of emotionally abusive experiences among college students. For example, if they would guess that 0%–15% of college students report a history of emotional abuse, they are directed to stand in one corner of the room. Other areas of the room would be designated for prevalence rates of 15%–30% and 30%–45%. Members are asked to share with others at their meeting spot about their reason for choosing that particular prevalence rate.

- Leader asks members to join as one large group and share reasons for choosing different prevalence rates for emotional abuse. Leader discusses research (see the literature review) indicating that 44% of college students report a history of childhood emotional abuse (Paivio & McCulloch, 2004).
- *Triads Exercise:* Group members split into groups of three and discuss the following questions: How would you define emotional abuse? What's the difference between emotional abuse and physical or sexual abuse?
  - After 5 minutes, members come together and share responses from the triads with the larger group. Leader provides copies of Handout 23.1 and discusses the definition of emotional abuse and its unique aspects (viz., its nonphysical form).
- *Mini-Lecture Exercise:* Leader presents information from Handout 23.1, which suggests that most theorists conceptualize emotional abuse as a pattern of behaviors rather than an isolated event. Leader provides an example of an instance of verbal emotional abuse (e.g., "You are a worthless, stupid child!") and an example of an instance of nonverbal emotional abuse (e.g., the solitary confinement of a child for extended periods).
- *Brainstorm Exercise:* In small groups of four, members brainstorm two mild examples of emotional abuse and two severe examples of emotional abuse. For verbal instances of emotional abuse, members are encouraged to write remarks in quotation marks.
  - Members rejoin as one large group and share their ideas with the larger group.
- *Closing Round Exercise:* Leader makes a round with the group, inviting each member to finish the following sentence: "I would guess that the effect of emotional abuse on children is . . . " Leader notes that, during the next session, research will be presented on the negative outcomes associated with emotional abuse.

Session 2: What's Linked With Emotional Abuse?

- Leader states clearly the focus of the day's session, which is understanding the psychological difficulties associated with emotional abuse.
- *Dyad Exercise:* Group members split into pairs and finish the following sentence: "After a lengthy history of facing emotional abuse from parents, I'm guessing the impact on a child would be . . . " Members are encouraged to come up with several possible responses.
  - After 5 minutes, members come together in group and share their responses.
- *Mini-Lecture Exercise:* Leader provides a copy of Handout 23.2 for all participants and presents information from Section I. In order to stimulate discussion, leader defines each condition noted on Handout 23.2 or asks members to define terms. Leader facilitates discussion of questions listed under Section I.

- *Individual Written Exercise:* Leader provides a list of five negative events and asks members to imagine that each event has happened to them. Members are instructed to write what the *cause* of the negative event might be, if it were to happen to them. Leader may generate a list of five negative events or use the following: (a) You're too tired to stay awake in class, (b) you lose your job, (c) a friend says that he or she never wants to speak with you again, (d) you don't have enough money to cover your bills for the month, (e) you fail a major project in a class (adapted from Dykema, Bergbower, Doctora, & Peterson, 1996).
- *Mini-Lecture Exercise:* Leader directs attention to Section II on Handout 23.2 and presents the definition of *explanatory style*. Leader provides examples of each type, using one of the negative events from the written exercise. Leader states that emotional abuse is consistently related with a pessimistic explanatory style, the focus of discussion for next week. Leader then asks members to take the five causes from the previous exercise and apply an explanatory style to each and then discuss this within groups or dyads.
- *Closing Round Exercise:* Leader makes a round with the group, inviting each member to answer the following question: What surprised you in today's session?

Session 3: Our Thinking *May Be Related to* Early Family Messages

- Leader states clearly the focus of the day's session, which is exploring explanatory style as one example of the potentially damaging nature of childhood emotional abuse.
- *Mini-Lecture Exercise:* Leader briefly summarizes the difference between pessimistic and optimistic explanatory styles. Leader directs members' attention to Handout 23.3, Section I, and presents research linking a pessimistic explanatory style with emotional abuse but not physical or sexual abuse.
- *Triad Exercise:* In groups of three, members are asked to develop initial responses to the following questions: Why do you suppose a pessimistic explanatory style has been linked consistently with emotional abuse but not with sexual or physical abuse? What is it about emotional abuse that might make it a consistent contributor to a pessimistic explanatory style?
  - After 5 minutes, members come together in the group and share their responses.
- *Mini-Lecture Exercise:* Leader directs members' attention to Handout 23.3, Section II, and describes theory about the particularly damaging nature of emotional abuse.
- *Large-Group Discussion:* Leader facilitates discussion of questions listed on Handout 23.3, Section II.
- *Closing Round Exercise:* Leader makes a round with the group, inviting each member to complete the following sentence: "Having learned more about the potentially negative effects of emotional abuse, I hope to . . ."

Session 4: Next Steps

- Leader states clearly the focus of the day's session, which is summarizing information learned in the psychoeducational group, exploring shifts toward an optimistic explanatory style, and discussing local referral options.
- *Mini-Lecture Exercise:* Leader discusses the fact that psychotherapy facilitates shifts from pessimistic explanatory styles toward optimistic styles (Hamilton & Abramson, 1983; Persons & Rao, 1985). Leader notes that such shifts may be one means of remedying long-term effects of emotional abuse. Leader provides a concrete example of modifying a pessimistic explanation into optimistic alternatives.
- *Poster Board Movement Exercise:* Around the room, leader posts four poster boards, each of which has one negative event written at the top, followed by a pessimistic interpretation of the cause of the event. Leader provides markers to members and asks them to walk by and read each poster board. Members are instructed to write an alternative interpretation of the negative event on each poster board that captures at least one feature of the optimistic explanatory style (e.g., shifting from an internal cause to an external cause).
  - After 5–10 minutes, members come together and share responses. Leader places poster boards in the middle of the group circle during discussion.
- *Dyads Exercise:* Group members split into pairs and answer the following questions: What were the most important pieces of information gained from this 4-week group experience? What other questions about emotional abuse remain for you?
  - After 5 minutes, members come together in a group and share their responses.
- *Closing Summary and Referral Information:* Leader summarizes aspects of the group not mentioned by members during the previous exercise. Leader distributes a list of local referral options for members interested in additional counseling services.

References

Abela, J. (2001). The hopelessness theory of depression: A test of the diathesis-stress and causal mediation components in third and seventh grade children. *Journal of Abnormal Child Psychology, 29,* 241–254.

Alloy, L., Abramson, L., Smith, J., Gibb, B., & Neeren, A. (2006). Role of parenting and maltreatment histories in unipolar and bipolar mood disorders: Mediation by cognitive vulnerability to depression. *Clinical Child and Family Psychology Review, 9,* 23–64.

Dykema, J., Bergbower, K., Doctora, J. D., & Peterson, C. (1996). An attributional style questionnaire for general use. *Journal of Psychoeducational Assessment, 14,* 100–108.

Esteban, E. (2006). Parental verbal abuse: Culture-specific coping behavior of college students in the Philippines. *Child Psychiatry & Human Development, 36,* 243–259.

Gibb, B. E., & Abela, J. R. (2008). Emotional abuse, verbal victimizations, and the development of children's negative inferential styles and depressive symptoms. *Cognitive Therapy and Research, 32,* 161–176.

Gibb, B., Abramson, L., & Alloy, L. (2004). Emotional maltreatment from parents, verbal peer victimization, and cognitive vulnerability to depression. *Cognitive Therapy and Research, 28,* 1–21.

Glaser, D., & Prior, V. (1997). Is the term child protection applicable to emotional abuse? *Child Abuse Review, 6,* 315–329.

Hamarman, S., & Bernet, W. (2000). Evaluating and reporting emotional abuse in children: Parent-based, action-based focus aids in clinical decision-making. *Journal of the American Academy of Child and Adolescent Psychology, 39,* 928–930.

Hamilton, E., & Abramson, L. (1983). Cognitive patterns and major depressive disorder: A longitudinal study in a hospital setting. *Journal of Abnormal Psychology, 92,* 173–184.

Hankin, B. (2005). Childhood maltreatment and psychopathology: Prospective tests of attachment, cognitive vulnerability, and stress as mediating processes. *Cognitive Therapy and Research, 29,* 645–671.

Horton, C. B., & Cruise, T. K. (2001). *Child abuse and neglect: The school's response.* New York, NY: Guilford Press.

Keashly, L., & Harvey, S. (2005). Emotional abuse in the workplace. In S. Fox & P. Spector (Eds.), *Counterproductive work behavior: Investigations of actors and targets* (pp. 201–235). Washington, DC: American Psychological Association.

McGee, R., & Wolfe, D. (1991). Psychological maltreatment: Toward an operational definition. *Development and Psychopathology, 3,* 3–18.

McKeever, V. M., McWhirter, B. T., & Huff, M. E. (2006). Relationship between attribution style, child abuse history, and PTSD symptom severity in Vietnam veterans. *Cognitive Therapy and Research, 30,* 123–133.

Nicholas, K., & Bieber, S. (1997). Assessment of perceived parenting behaviors: The Exposure to Abusive and Supportive Environments Parenting Inventory (EASE-PI). *Journal of Family Violence, 12,* 275–291.

Paivio, S., & McCulloch, C. (2004). Alexithymia as a mediator between childhood trauma and self-injurious behaviors. *Child Abuse & Neglect, 28,* 339–354.

Persons, J., & Rao, P. (1985). Longitudinal study of cognitions, life events, and depression in psychiatric inpatients. *Journal of Abnormal Psychology, 94,* 51–63.

Peterson, C., & Park, N. (2007). Explanatory style and emotion regulation. In J. J. Gross (Ed.), *Handbook of emotion regulation* (pp. 159–179). New York, NY: Guilford Press.

Quinless, F. W., & Nelson, M. M. (1988). Development of a measure of learned helplessness. *Nursing Research, 37,* 11–15.

Romeo, F. F. (2000). The educator's role in reporting the emotional abuse of children. *Journal of Instructional Psychology, 27,* 183–186.

Twaite, J. A., & Rodriguez-Srednicki, O. (2004). Understanding and reporting child abuse: Legal and psychological perspective. *Journal of Psychiatry and Law, 32,* 443–481.

Handout 23.1

Recognizing Emotional Abuse

Definition of *childhood emotional abuse*

- Hostile *nonphysical* behaviors (e.g., verbal attacks) that are directed toward a child by an adult and that endanger the child's psychological and/or physical well-being

Unique characteristic

- *Nonphysical* aggression

Two main types

- Verbal attacks (e.g., "You're a stupid, worthless kid!")
- Nonverbal, nonphysical aggression (e.g., the solitary confinement of a child for an extended period)

Pattern of behavior

- Don't all parents verbally insult their children on rare occasions? (Many parents verbally insult their children on occasion, but it is not a pattern or common occurrence.)
- Emotional abuse: when nonphysical aggression becomes repetitive in the child–parent/guardian relationship

Handout 23.2

What's Linked With Emotional Abuse?

Section I

When two things are positively related, this means that as one of them increases, the other also usually tends to increase.

Research has shown that emotional abuse is positively associated with

- Elevated anxiety
- Depression
- Self-criticism
- Insecure attachment style
- Nonsuicidal self-injurious behaviors (e.g., cutting)

Discussion Questions

Which of these outcomes fits most closely with your expectations about the outcomes of emotional abuse?

Which of these outcomes surprises you? Is there another outcome you expected to see listed here?

Section II

Definition of *explanatory style*

- An individual's typical way of understanding or interpreting the *causes* of events.

Pessimistic explanatory style

- Views the *causes* of negative events as *stable* (vs. unstable, or transient) in duration, *global* (vs. specific, or circumscribed) in their generalization to various aspects of life, and *internal* (vs. external) to the person.

Optimistic explanatory style

- Views the *causes* of negative events as *unstable* (i.e., transient), *specific* (i.e., circumscribed), and *external* to the person.

Handout 23.3

Our *Thinking* May Be Related to *Early Family Messages*

Section I

Research on Pessimistic Explanatory Style

- Research has consistently found that individuals with a pessimistic explanatory style also tend to report a history of childhood emotional abuse (Gibb & Abela, 2008; Gibb, Alloy, Abramson, & Marx, 2003; Gibb et al., 2001; Hankin, 2005; Steinberg, Gibb, Alloy, & Abramson, 2003).
- However, research has not consistently documented a connection between a pessimistic explanatory style and childhood physical or sexual abuse (Gibb, 2002; Gibb et al., 2001, 2003; Hankin, 2005).

Triad Discussion

- Why do you think a pessimistic explanatory style has been linked consistently with emotional abuse but not sexual or physical abuse?
- What is it about emotional abuse that might make it a more consistent contributor to a pessimistic explanatory style?

Section II

Theory on Pessimistic Explanatory Style

- Unlike physical and sexual abuse, emotional abuse is typified by hostile verbal communications from a parent to a child.
- These communications often convey stable, global, and internal explanations for negative events (e.g., "You are a worthless child, and our problems are your fault").
- Over time, the emotionally abused child may adopt these explanations, assuming a pessimistic explanatory style marked by stable, global, and internal explanations (Rose & Abramson, 1992).

Discussion Questions

- Which aspects of this theory do you agree with? Which aspects do you disagree with?
- What defenses would a child have against adopting such pessimistic explanations from parents/guardians?
- How would you help a child who faced repetitive negative messages from his or her family?

References

Gibb, B. (2002). Childhood maltreatment and negative cognitive styles: A quantitative and qualitative review. *Clinical Psychology Review, 22,* 223–246.

Gibb, B. E., & Abela, J. R. (2008). Emotional abuse, verbal victimizations, and the development of children's negative inferential styles and depressive symptoms. *Cognitive Therapy and Research, 32,* 161–176.

Gibb, B., Alloy, L., Abramson, L., & Marx, B. (2003). Childhood maltreatment and maltreatment-specific inferences: A test of Rose and Abramson's (1992) extension of the hopelessness theory. *Cognition and Emotion, 17,* 917–931.

Gibb, B., Alloy, L., Abramson, L., Rose, D., Whitehouse, W., Donovan, P., . . . Tierney, S. (2001). History of childhood maltreatment, negative cognitive styles, and episodes of depression in adulthood. *Cognitive Therapy and Research, 25,* 425–446.

Hankin, B. (2005). Childhood maltreatment and psychopathology: Prospective tests of attachment, cognitive vulnerability, and stress as mediating processes. *Cognitive Therapy and Research, 29,* 645–671.

Rose, D., & Abramson, L. (1992). Developmental predictors of depressive cognitive style: Research and theory. In D. Cicchetti & S. Toth (Eds.), *Rochester symposium of developmental psychopathology* (Vol. 4, pp. 323–349). Rochester, NY: University of Rochester Press.

Steinberg, J., Gibb, B., Alloy, L., & Abramson, L. (2003). Childhood emotional maltreatment, cognitive vulnerability to depression, and self-referent information processing in adulthood: Reciprocal relations. *Journal of Cognitive Psychotherapy, 17,* 347–358.

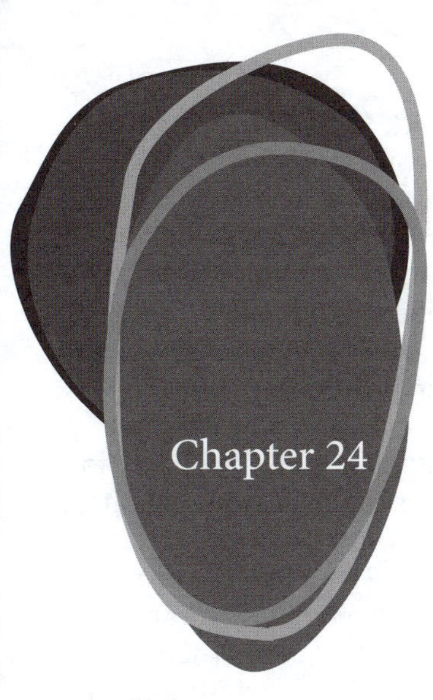

Group Work for Self-Injuring Clients

Trevor J. Buser

Nonsuicidal self-injury (NSSI) refers to the direct damaging of one's own bodily tissue without the intent to die and without social sanction (Favazza, 1998). Common methods of NSSI include cutting, burning, hitting, hair pulling, obstructing the healing of wounds, and severe scratching (Klonsky, 2007; Lloyd-Richardson, Perrine, Dierker, & Kelley, 2007). Research suggests that college students are at particular risk for engaging in this behavior: Prevalence rates of NSSI tend to be significantly higher among adolescents and young adults compared to older populations (Aizenman & Jensen, 2007; Briere & Gil, 1998; Lloyd-Richardson et al., 2007; Paivio & McCulloch, 2004). In view of these findings, there exists a strong warrant for implementing counseling interventions designed to assist self-injurers in college settings. This chapter describes a group counseling intervention for individuals who engage in cutting and other nonsuicidal self-injurious behaviors. First attention is given to the relevant literature on NSSI. Subsequently a brief description of the group intervention is provided and a detailed session-by-session plan is presented.

Numerous studies suggest that NSSI serves meaningful functions for self-injurers (Andover, Pepper, & Gibb, 2007; Briere & Gil, 1998; Hilt, Cha, & Nolen-Hoeksema, 2008; Nock & Prinstein, 2004). Klonsky (2007) reviewed the extant research on functions of NSSI. His findings indicated that the majority of self-injurers identified affect regulation as a function of NSSI. That is, NSSI functioned as a means of lessening negative affect (e.g., anxiety, anger, sadness) or generating positive affect (e.g., a sense of calm or peacefulness). Another prominent function of NSSI, according to Klonsky's review, was self-punishment. This function refers to the use of NSSI as a means of expressing anger or blame toward the self (Klonsky, 2007). Along this line,

Glassman, Weierich, Hooley, Deliberto, and Nock (2007) documented a positive association between NSSI and the cognitive variable of self-criticism. Furthermore, findings have suggested that self-injurers may engage in NSSI as a means of influencing social interactions (Nock & Prinstein, 2004). For instance, self-injurers might use NSSI as a way to avoid negative exchanges with others (e.g., avoiding punishment) or obtain positive exchanges with others (e.g., increasing attention). These social functions have also been documented in research on NSSI (Nock & Prinstein, 2004).

Given that by definition NSSI does not involve the intent to die, many self-injurers might balk at the notion that NSSI carries the potential for serious injury. Empirical findings, however, suggest that self-injurers often underestimate the lethality of self-injurious behaviors. For example, Whitlock, Eckenrode, and Silverman (2006) found that 21% of self-injurers in a college sample (N = 2,875; 56% female; 73% between ages 18 and 24) reported the experience, on at least one occasion, of injuring themselves more severely than expected. Similarly, in research by Briere and Gil (1998), 34% of self-injurers reported that most of the time they did not feel in control of their self-injurious behaviors.

The following group plan outlines various interventions for those who engage in self-injury. The format facilitates insight, provides information, and aims to help students reduce the occurrences of these behaviors.

It should be noted that some authors (e.g., Walsh, 2006) have voiced concerns about the use of group work for self-injurers, given that members could be triggered to self-injure as a result of hearing the explicit details of the self-injury of others. In general, however, group work has been recognized as an important therapeutic approach for self-injurers, provided that sessions focus on a functional analysis of this behavior, encourage the development of adaptive coping skills, and refrain from detailed discussions of incidents of self-injury in members' lives (Toste & Heath, 2010).

Group Plan

Session 1: Answering the "Why" Question: Functions of NSSI

- Introductions, including each member's name, year in college, and background.
- Provide a brief overview of the group purpose, rules, and confidentiality issues.
- State clearly the focus of the day's session, which is understanding and exploring the functions or purposes underlying the use of NSSI.
- *Dyads Exercise:* Split the group into pairs and have each member pose three warm-up, introductory questions to his or her partner (e.g., "Where is your hometown?" "What do you enjoy most about life at college?" "How do you handle or cope with stress at college?").
- After the dyads work, bring the group together and ask each member to report on his or her partner's responses, thereby introducing the person to the group.

- *Rounds Exercise:* Make a round with the group, inviting each member to finish the following sentence: "When I harm myself, I think the purpose behind this act is to . . ."
- *Psychoeducational Exercise:* Provide a copy of Handout 24.1 to all participants and present the main points.
- *Rounds Exercise:* Make a round with the group, asking each member to identify and discuss one function from Handout 24.1 that matches his or her own experience most closely. Bridge similarities between members.
- Additional discussion questions, time permitting, are provided on Handout 24.1.
- Summarize the functions identified by the participants. Highlight the fact that, in many cases, NSSI appears to be a meaningful behavior. You may comment on the possibility of finding more effective ways to reach similar goals.
- *Closing Round Exercise:* Make a round with the group, inviting each member to finish the following sentence: "My goal for this group experience is to . . ."

Session 2: What's Linked With Cutting?

- State clearly the focus of the day's session, which is understanding other psychological difficulties associated with cutting (and other forms of NSSI).
- *Dyads Exercise:* Have group members split into pairs and finish the following sentence: "Besides cutting (or another form of NSSI), my biggest struggle or difficulty seems to be . . ." After 5 minutes, have the members come together in the group and share their own responses, if they are comfortable doing so.
- *Psychoeducational Exercise:* Provide a copy of Handout 24.2 to all participants and present the main points. Define each condition noted on Handout 24.2, or ask members to define the terms as best they can.
- *"Tag" Group Discussion Exercise:* After a member answers the question, this person chooses who will answer next. The question is: "Which of these difficulties seems to match your experience most closely? Tell us about the experience of this difficulty."
- Follow-up questions, time permitting, are provided on Handout 24.2.
- *Closing Round Exercise:* Make a round with the group, inviting each member to finish the following sentence: "If I could suggest one positive way of coping with life's challenges to others in this group, I would recommend . . ."

Session 3: Is Cutting Hazardous to My Health?

- State clearly the focus of the day's session, which is discussing the risks associated with cutting (and other forms of NSSI).
- *Rounds Exercise:* Make a round with the group, asking each member to answer the following question: "On a scale of 0 to 10, with 0 meaning no risk or danger at all and 10 being the most dangerous,

risky behavior imaginable, how would you rate your cutting (or other forms of NSSI)?"

- *Group Discussion:* Follow up by asking members to elaborate on their responses. For example, you might ask the two members who had the most divergent responses to share in more detail.
- *Psychoeducational Exercise:* Provide a copy of Handout 24.3 to all participants and present the main points.
- *Free Association Exercise:* Present the group with a stack of blank sheets and a bowl of tape, pens, pencils, and colored markers. Inform the members that they have 5–7 minutes to free associate in response to the information on Handout 24.3, drawing, journaling a reaction (e.g., expressing their disagreement with the research), or making something by folding and/or taping the paper.
  - After 5–7 minutes, invite members to share their reactions with the larger group.
- Follow-up questions, time permitting, are provided on Handout 24.3.
- *Closing Round Exercise:* Make a round with the group, inviting each member to finish the following sentence: "One thing that surprised me today was . . ."

Sessions 4–6: Reducing the Frequency of NSSI

- State clearly the focus of these sessions, which is integrating information learned in earlier sessions, identifying the goals of members, anticipating obstacles to achieving these goals, exploring means of reaching the goals, and supporting one another toward change.
- Each session may begin with a Rounds Exercise: Make a round with the group, asking each member to complete a sentence (e.g., "In earlier sessions, I was most struck by . . ." "When I think about my own use of cutting, I would like to . . ." "A success that I had last week was . . .").
- The middle phase of these sessions is devoted to articulating and working on members' goals. For example, if affect regulation is a meaningful goal for many members, then you may consider the introduction and practice of stress reduction techniques (e.g., progressive muscle relaxation).
- Closing: Bring repeated attention to members' goals, monitor progress toward goals, and help members anticipate obstacles. The closing phase may be directed toward discussing concrete goals for the week ahead and highlighting positive developments.

References

Aizenman, M., & Jensen, M. (2007). Speaking through the body: The incidence of self-injury, piercing, and tattooing among college students. *Journal of College Counseling, 10,* 27–43.

Andover, M., Pepper, C., & Gibb, B. (2007). Self-mutilation and coping strategies in a college sample. *Suicide and Life-Threatening Behavior, 37,* 238–243.

Briere, J., & Gil, E. (1998). Self-mutilation in clinical and general population samples: Prevalence, correlates, and functions. *American Journal of Orthopsychiatry, 68,* 609–620.

Favazza, A. (1998). The coming of age of self-mutilation. *Journal of Nervous and Mental Disease, 186,* 259–268.

Glassman, L., Weierich, M., Hooley, J., Deliberto, T., & Nock, M. (2007). Child maltreatment, non-suicidal self-injury, and the mediating role of self-criticism. *Behaviour Research and Therapy, 45,* 2483–2490.

Hilt, L., Cha, C., & Nolen-Hoeksema, S. (2008). Nonsuicidal self-injury in young adolescent girls: Moderators of the distress-function relationship. *Journal of Consulting and Clinical Psychology, 76,* 63–71.

Klonsky, E. (2007). The functions of deliberate self-injury: A review of the evidence. *Clinical Psychology Review, 27,* 226–239.

Lloyd-Richardson, E., Perrine, N., Dierker, L., & Kelley, M. (2007). Characteristics and functions of non-suicidal self-injury in a community sample of adolescents. *Psychological Medicine, 37,* 1183–1192.

Nock, M., & Prinstein, M. (2004). A functional approach to the assessment of self-mutilative behavior. *Journal of Consulting and Clinical Psychology, 72,* 885–890.

Paivio, S., & McCulloch, C. (2004). Alexithymia as a mediator between childhood trauma and self-injurious behaviors. *Child Abuse & Neglect, 28,* 339–354.

Toste, J. R., & Heath, N. L. (2010). School response to non-suicidal self-injury. *The Prevention Researcher, 17,* 14–17.

Walsh, B. (2006). *Treating self-injury: A practical guide.* New York, NY: Guilford Press.

Whitlock, J., Eckenrode, J., & Silverman, D. (2006). Self-injurious behaviors in a college population. *Pediatrics, 117,* 1939–1948.

Handout 24.1

Functions of Cutting and Other Forms of Nonsuicidal Self-Injury (NSSI)

In research studies, self-injurers have reported using cutting and other forms of NSSI for the following purposes or functions:

1. Affect Regulation
   - Way to lessen difficult, painful feelings (e.g., anger or sadness)
   - Way to increase positive, satisfying feelings (e.g., sense of calm or peace)
2. Self-Punishment
   - Way to express anger or blame toward the self
3. Social Change
   - Way to avoid negative interactions with others (e.g., avoid punishment)
   - Way to obtain positive interactions with others (e.g., increase the concern of others)

Discussion Questions

Which function matches your experience most closely?

Are there any other functions or purposes of cutting (or other forms of NSSI) that are not addressed in this handout?

Handout 24.2

What's Linked With Cutting and Other Forms of Nonsuicidal Self-Injury (NSSI)?

When two things are positively related, this means that as one of them increases, the other also usually tends to increase.

Research has shown that NSSI is positively related with

- Elevated anxiety
- Depression
- Difficulty talking about emotions
- Low self-esteem
- A self-critical style
- Disordered eating
- A history of childhood maltreatment (neglect, emotional, physical, and/or sexual abuse by an adult)

Discussion Questions

Which of these difficulties linked with NSSI resonates with your own personal experience? What is that experience like for you? For example, when do you tend to notice it most? How does your body feel as you face it? How long have you faced this challenging issue?

Are there other major difficulties that you face but that are not covered on this handout?

Why do you suppose cutting (or other forms of NSSI) might be positively related to these difficulties? Does cutting help this issue, or give expression to it, in some way?

Handout 24.3

Is Nonsuicidal Self-Injury (NSSI) Hazardous to My Health?

Research studies based on the responses of self-injurers have found that

- 21% of self-injurers in college have had the experience, on at least one occasion, of injuring themselves more severely than expected (Whitlock, Eckenrode, & Silverman, 2006)
- 34% of self-injurers feel that, most of the time, they are not in control of their self-injurious behaviors (Briere & Gil, 1998)

Discussion Questions

What reasons lead you to believe that cutting (or other forms of NSSI) might be more dangerous than you initially thought? What reasons lead you to believe that cutting is not very dangerous at all? What is your opinion?

What thoughts do you have about the mix of cutting (or other forms of NSSI) with alcohol or drugs? What concerns would you have about a person cutting while drinking or using drugs?

References

Briere, J., & Gil, E. (1998). Self-mutilation in clinical and general population samples: Prevalence, correlates, and functions. *American Journal of Orthopsychiatry, 68,* 609–620.

Whitlock, J., Eckenrode, J., & Silverman, D. (2006). Self-injurious behaviors in a college population. *Pediatrics, 117,* 1939–1948.

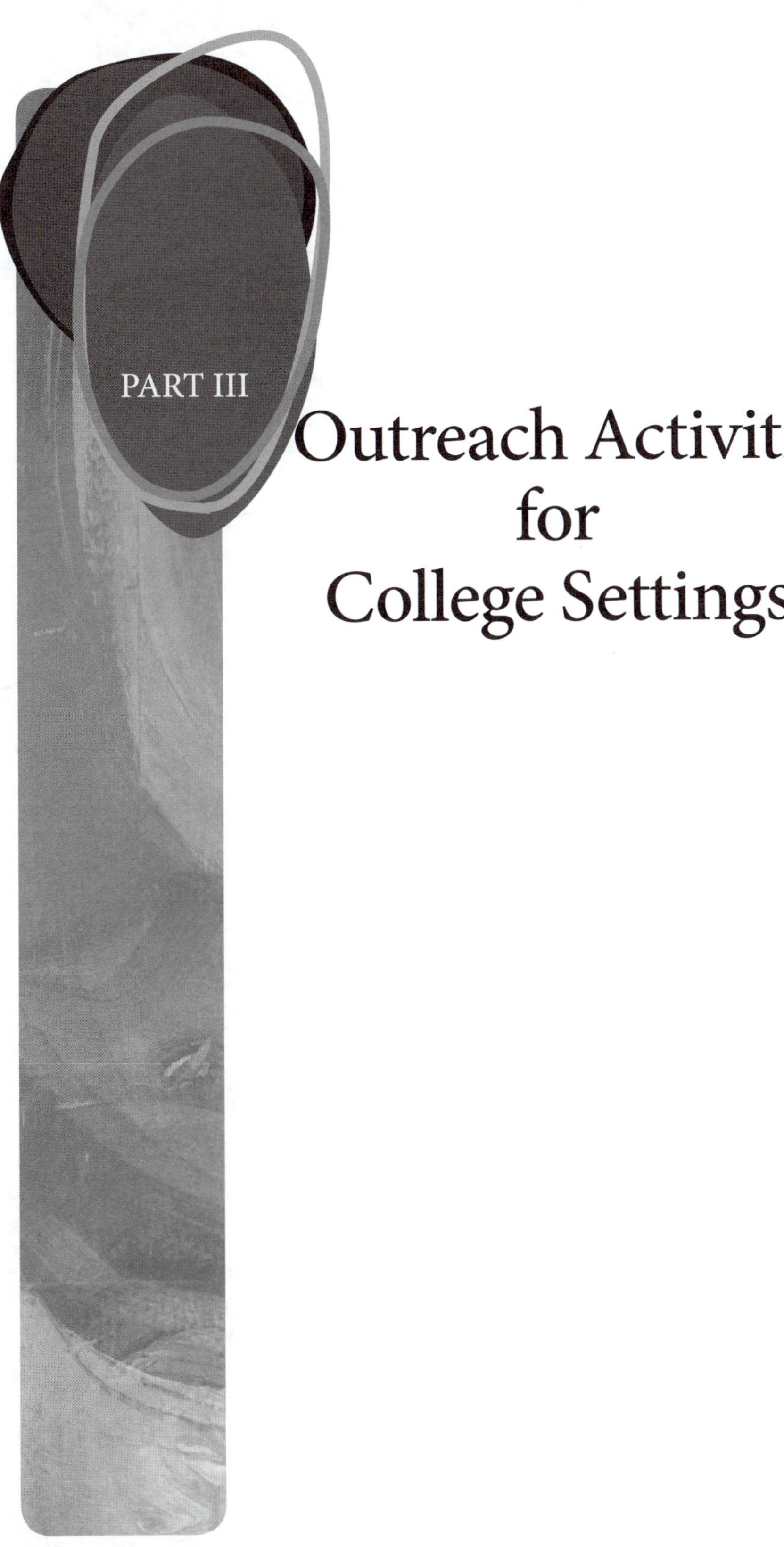

Outreach Activities
for
College Settings

Chapter 25

Freshman Orientation: The Counseling Center

S. Lenoir Gillam and Dan Rose

In institutions of higher learning, freshman orientation is a typical component of the traditional student's induction into college. Among the many advantages of this kind of programming are that students have the opportunity to become acclimated to the university environment, learn about academic and support services available to enhance student success, receive advising and register for classes, facilitate social connections with peers, and foster a sense of community on campus. Although these benefits of freshman orientation sessions are likely to be realized, a comprehensive, developmental set of services that extends beyond initial campus visits and includes parents, university personnel, and other students can have a longer-lasting impact on students.

Key components of a comprehensive outreach program focusing on freshman orientation can be organized around issues pertaining to planning, program delivery, and evaluation. Considerations of each stage are addressed in subsequent sections, and the role of the counseling center in the orientation process is also addressed in further detail.

Planning

Preparing for a comprehensive orientation session includes identifying both general academic and support services available on campus and those interventions specific to the needs of the population of each institution. It also involves identifying the social and cultural components of the university that should be highlighted. The first step should involve conducting a needs assessment to make decisions about the short- and long-range components to include in the outreach program (American School Counselor Association, 2003). Faculty, staff, administrators, student government leaders, current and prospective students, alumni, and community stakeholders should all be consulted when making these decisions.

In addition to ensuring that important content and experiences are included in the freshman orientation, involving all relevant parties in the assessment process is also likely to have a positive impact on processes that affect the overall well-being of campus functioning (e.g., campus safety, crisis intervention). In other words, bringing people together provides opportunities for strategic planning not only for orientation but also for other important campus events and practices, fostering communication and shared responsibility across units on campus (Archer & Cooper, 1999).

When planning a freshman orientation, organizers need to consider the importance of a multimodal, multidisciplinary, comprehensive approach that extends beyond the timeframe of a single-session meeting(or another variant of a short-term program). Brief therapy may be appropriate for addressing a number of mental health problems when one is providing direct counseling services to clients (Cooper & Archer, 1999). However, a brief outreach program is not likely to make as lasting an impact as a more comprehensive program in which students receive ongoing interventions targeting academic and support services at various times throughout their college years, as their needs are likely to change over time. Reexposing students to orientation content and process at different periods can serve as reinforcement as opposed to simply being redundant.

Program Delivery

Once a well-conceptualized plan is prepared for delivery, a comprehensive outreach program includes both short- and long-term interventions provided by counseling center staff members. Evaluation should include both a formative and a summative assessment of the program.

Short-Term Outreach

Short-term interventions involve content and processes that are addressed in the initial orientation outreach session (e.g., a workshop during a freshman visitation weekend). In contrast, long-term interventions include ongoing programming throughout the course of the college students' years that serves to (a) introduce new material or services that have been developed or discovered since the initial outreach session (e.g., changes to crisis intervention plans) or that are developmentally relevant (e.g., career-related services as students prepare for academic or career options after graduation), (b) reinforce previously learned information, (c) introduce new information relevant to the students' developing needs, and/or (d) promote the visibility of the counseling center.

Long-Term Outreach

Although outreach at the initial orientation session can provide freshmen with content and processes that assist them in beginning college, implementing a long-range set of services can help to reinforce information, offer ongoing support, and promote the continued visibility of the counseling center. A one-shot approach to service delivery and an absence of multiple interventions over time may prove to lack a lasting impact.

Sample Outreach Session

Although this chapter advocates for a comprehensive, ongoing set of services targeting the needs of college freshmen, the following outline highlights a sample presentation to be conducted during an initial freshman orientation experience held prior to the commencement of a student's freshman year (e.g., freshman visitation weekend). It is important to note that given the involvement of numerous departments on campus in the coordination and delivery of freshman orientation content, it is recommended that counseling center staff members consult with other campus personnel to reduce redundancy in content across sessions. The session outlined here is intended to (a) provide an overview of the counseling center, (b) identify services available for students, (c) distinguish counseling services from other academic support services on campus, and (d) introduce the campus safety plan.

Group Outreach Plan

1. Introduce yourself and welcome students to the session. If the number of attendees is small (e.g., if the outreach is being delivered in a breakout session) and time is structured to allow for student introductions, then students may engage in brief introductions. Otherwise, a brief icebreaker can be used.
2. Provide an overview of the counseling center, identify services available to students, distinguish counseling center services from other health or academic support services on campus, and introduce the campus safety plan.
3. Provide an overview of the counseling center's mission. Discuss how the center fits into the organizational structure of the university. Normalize the counseling process and the comprehensive set of services available (e.g., from crisis intervention to development of assets and wellness).
4. Discuss, at a minimum, the following services: individual counseling, group counseling, consultation, outreach, testing, crisis intervention, and referral.
   - Discuss personal counseling (including interpersonal and intrapersonal issues) and the holistic nature of career counseling.
   - Address academic issues and how some may relate to counseling/assessment (e.g., psychological testing). State that other academic services are provided by different departments on campus (e.g., services for students with disabilities, advising).

- Provide an overview of how to access services
- Provide contact information
- Provide location
- Discuss how to schedule appointments
- Provide website information
- Share examples of common concerns and issues that might prompt students to seek services, including both overt and subtle characteristics that may be associated with psychological distress (e.g., adjustment difficulties, anxiety or depression, safety concerns, grief/loss, relationship concerns)
- Discuss early intervention

5. Help clarify differences among departments on campus:
   - Counseling center
   - Student health center
   - Career center (Career Planning and Placement Office)
   - Advising centers
   - Office of Disability Services
6. Review campus safety and discuss the campus-wide crisis intervention plan, University Police Department, and other services/departments (e.g., Judicial Affairs).
7. Share contact information and/or websites specific to university academic and support offices (e.g., the counseling center, Office of Disability Services, health center, career center) that have not already been provided in the workshop.
8. Review and summarize the session, ask for questions, and distribute Handout 25.1.

References

American School Counselor Association. (2003). *The ASCA national model: A framework for school counseling programs.* Alexandria, VA: Author.

Archer, J., Jr., & Cooper, S. (1999). An initiator-catalyst approach to college counseling outreach. *Journal of College Counseling, 2,* 76–88.

Cooper, S., & Archer, J., Jr. (1999). Brief therapy in college counseling and mental health. *Journal of American College Health, 48,* 21–28.

Handout 25.1

Sample Freshman Orientation Outreach Survey

- I have had counseling/psychotherapy in the past. ☐ Yes ☐ No
  a. If yes, for what reason?
  b. How long?
- I have had a psychological evaluation and/or learning disability testing in the past. ☐ Yes ☐ No
  a. If yes, when?
  b. What was the diagnosis?
- I struggle with the following issues:

  anxiety, depression, homesickness, anger, fighting with friends/roommates, trouble concentrating, test anxiety, learning disability, and/or other. (*Please circle all that apply*)
- My biggest fear about coming to college is:
- I would describe my parents as: uncaring, supportive, involved, too involved
- My greatest strengths are:
- My greatest weaknesses are:
- School has always been: easy, okay, difficult, very difficult
- Based on the information I've just been given in this session, I would use the counseling center resources. ☐ Yes ☐ No
  a. If yes, which ones?
  b. If no, why not?
- Did some counseling center resources need a better explanation? If yes, which ones?

Are there resources you wish the counseling center provided that we did not mention?

____

____

____

____

**If you are interested in setting up a counseling appointment,
please feel free to call the center.**

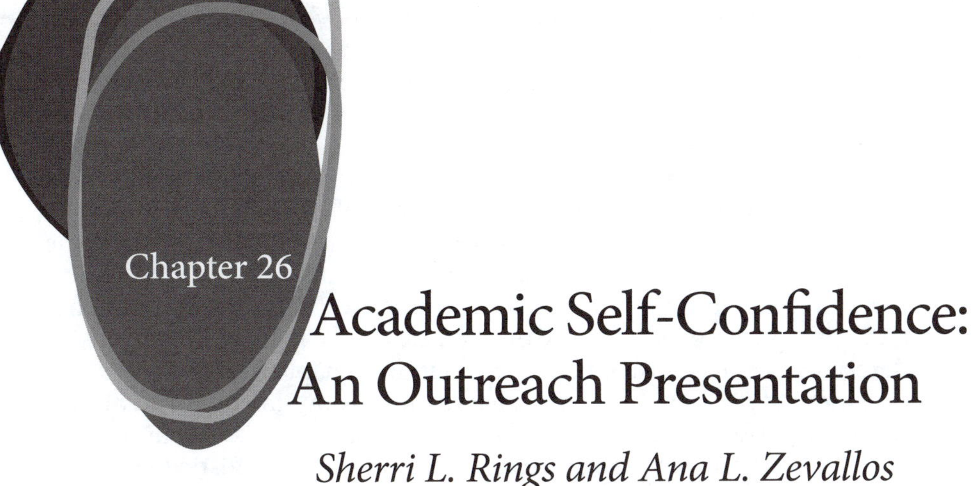

Chapter 26

Academic Self-Confidence: An Outreach Presentation

Sherri L. Rings and Ana L. Zevallos

Students' previous academic experiences can affect their academic performance in college. Whereas students with positive past experiences may have increased academic self-confidence, students who have struggled academically may have low academic self-confidence or may not understand what it takes to succeed in college. Bandura (1986) referred to situation-specific self-confidence as *self-efficacy*—the strength of an individual's belief that he or she can perform a specific task successfully. Thus, *academic self-efficacy* refers to a student's belief in his or her ability to perform academic tasks. Students obtain self-efficacy information from four sources: (a) previously performing a task successfully (the most powerful source of self-efficacy); (b) watching others model successful task performance; (c) receiving verbal persuasion from others; and (d) paying attention to their physiological reactions or states before, during, and after a task (Bandura, 1986). According to Bandura (1997), people with high self-efficacy are more likely to have high aspirations, think long-term, set challenging goals, and commit to meeting those goals. Furthermore, they visualize successful outcomes rather than focusing on personal deficiencies or what could go wrong.

Several studies have demonstrated the potential benefits of self-efficacy for college students. In a meta-analysis of 109 studies, Robbins et al. (2004) examined the relationship between psychosocial and study skill factors and college outcomes (grade point average [GPA] and retention). The psychosocial and study skill factors examined were achievement motivation, academic goals, institutional commitment, perceived social support, social involvement, academic self-efficacy, general self-concept, academic-related skills, and contextual influences. Robbins et al. found that academic self-efficacy was the strongest predictor of college GPA and the second strongest predictor of retention. The strongest predictor of retention was academic skills. They concluded that academic self-efficacy beliefs account for variance in GPA and retention over and above that accounted for by high school performance and standardized test scores.

Students with low academic efficacy may come to expect academic disappointment and could develop a pattern of negative perceptions (cognitive distortions) or self-talk that further undermines their chances of academic success. Several authors have discussed the ways in which cognitive distortions can negatively impact self-confidence, self-esteem, mood, and other factors (e.g., Beck, 1976; Burns, 1980; McKay & Fanning, 1992). However, learning to identify and challenge cognitive distortions can result in more accurate self-perceptions, enhanced self-confidence, and other positive outcomes. Common types of cognitive distortions are described in the outreach presentation in this chapter.

Bandura (1995, 1997) asserted that reasonably optimistic efficacy beliefs facilitate performance, whereas realistic efficacy beliefs can undermine performance. However, some research indicates that realistic beliefs may better predict performance. In his review of several cross-cultural studies, Klassen (2004) found that people from individualist (Western) cultures typically rate their efficacy beliefs higher than those from collectivist (non-Western) cultures, even though the collectivists' beliefs are equally or more predictive of performance. He concluded that for students from non-Western cultures, realistic efficacy beliefs are functional and may be due to cultural influences rather than a lack of confidence.

Furthermore, Svanum and Bigatti (2006) found that students with lower cumulative GPAs tended to be more optimistic than students with higher cumulative GPAs when predicting their grades in an undergraduate psychology course; however, they were less able to translate their optimism into course success. These authors suggested that helping lower achieving students develop informed optimism—encouraging optimism while also helping students develop study skills—might increase students' chances of academic success. Similarly, Weisberg, Owen, Jenkins, and Harburg (2003) suggested that compared to their unrealistically optimistic classmates, students with more realistic expectations regarding test grades and their chance of earning a degree might be more likely to engage in positive academic behaviors such as attending class or using helpful college services and resources.

A detailed outline of an academic self-confidence outreach presentation follows. The goals of the presentation are to help students (a) recognize what academic self-confidence is, (b) identify and challenge cognitive distortions and negative self-talk, (c) develop effective study and test-taking strategies, and (d) learn about campus support services.

Group Outreach Plan

1. Introduce yourself and give your qualifications. Note that the presentation will provide students with an introduction to the topic and that student participation is encouraged.

2. Ask students the following: What is academic self-confidence? How do you know if you have it? Supplement their answers if necessary.

3. Review the indicators of academic self-confidence, including believing that one will do well on class assignments/tests, being able to accurately assess areas of strength and weakness, not being easily discouraged by small setbacks, viewing criticism or mistakes as learning opportunities rather than being devastated by them, taking responsibility for one's behavior rather than making excuses, not being afraid to seek help from professors or other campus resources, taking risks, actively participating in class without being afraid of giving the wrong answer, and not needing to compare oneself to other students to feel better about one's performance.

4. Ask students the following: What impedes academic self-confidence? Supplement their answers if necessary.
   - Previous negative academic experiences
   - Lack of familiarity with the academic culture (e.g., different expectations in high school and college, deference to the professor and listening during class rather than expressing one's opinion might be the norm in other cultures)
   - Limited experience with the subject matter
   - Poor study skills
   - Too many competing demands—not enough study time
   - Avoidance/procrastination
   - Negative self-talk/cognitive distortions
   - Anxiety, depression, or substance abuse (including abuse of caffeine and nicotine)

5. Note that students may be confident in one academic subject but lack confidence in another. Like being a star athlete, being able to accurately assess their strengths and weaknesses and develop confidence in their academic ability takes practice. Until they have had a lot of experience in a course or subject, they should err on the side of more practice rather than less. Mention Svanum & Bigatti's (2006) study about students with lower cumulative GPAs predicting course grades less accurately.

6. Help students to identify and challenge negative self-talk/cognitive distortions (e.g., Beck, 1976; Burns, 1980; McKay & Fanning, 1992). Explain what negative self-talk is and state that people are often unaware of it. Self-talk may take some time to recognize and change. Cognitive distortions include
   - *Overgeneralization*—Making a general, universal rule from one isolated incident. Example: "I failed once, I'll always fail."
   - *Filtering*—Selectively paying attention to the negative and disregarding the positive. Example: You couldn't find a parking spot on campus, so your entire day seems to go badly.
   - *Labeling*—Using pejorative or stereotypical labels to describe oneself or others rather than accurately describing one's qualities. Example: "I am a loser, a failure, a pig, stupid, etc."

- *Jumping to conclusions*—Making assumptions about others (mind reading) or attempting to predict the future without any real evidence (fortune telling). Example: You're sure you'll get a low test grade even though you studied a lot.
- *Personalization and blame*—Feeling guilty and taking responsibility for a negative event even though there is no reason to do so. A person sees it as his or her fault or due to his or her inadequacy. Example: A friend says she is bored, and you assume that means she is bored with you.
- *Control fallacies*—Feeling totally responsible for everyone and everything or feeling like a victim with no control over anything. Example: "It won't matter how much I study for a test, the professor makes the tests too hard."
- *Emotional reasoning*—Assuming things are the way one feels about them. Example: You feel worthless, so you are worthless.
- *Shoulds*—Using "should" or "must" statements to try motivating oneself or others. Instead, however, one ends up feeling apathy or negative emotions such as frustration, guilt, or shame. Example: "I should be able to take 15 credits per semester, work 30 hours per week, and graduate in 4 years."
- *All-or-nothing thinking*—Lumping things into absolute, black-and-white categories with no middle ground. Example: "If I don't get a perfect score on this test, I'm a failure."
- *Catastrophizing or minimizing*—Exaggerating things (e.g., a relationship breakup is the end of the world) or shrinking them (e.g., the award you earned is no big deal).

7. Ask participants for examples of the preceding cognitive distortions. Ask what the purpose of their negative self-talk is. Whose voice do they hear?
8. Help students to practice effective study strategies:
   - Attend class regularly.
   - Review their class notes and assigned readings often—if material is covered in both places, it's more likely to be on the test.
   - Find a quiet place to study. Study in short blocks of time over several days rather than trying to study everything right before the test.
   - Before the test day, find out as much as they can about the test format (number and types of questions, how long they will have to take it, how much it will count toward their final grade).
   - Work with the course material as much as they can (read it, recopy their notes, make flashcards, study with classmates and see how well they can explain the material to one another).
9. Identify helpful test-taking strategies:
   - Get a good night's rest before the test and eat nutritious meals the day of the test.
   - Allow plenty of time to get to the test and select their preferred seat.

- If they get anxious about test taking, they should avoid being around anxious people cramming right before the test. These people might increase their anxiety.
- Preview the test so they know what's expected of them and can budget their time accordingly. Answer questions that are easiest first, then those with the highest point value. Save the most difficult or time-consuming questions, or those worth the least amount of points, for last.
- If they feel anxious during the test, they should take some deep breaths and try to relax. They should counter negative thoughts such as "I'm so nervous I'm not going to do well on this test!" with positive self-statements such as "I have time, I don't need to rush" or "I can do well on this test. I know the material."
- For multiple-choice questions, they should start by eliminating answers they know are wrong. If there is no penalty for guessing or they can eliminate options, they should pick the answer they think is best. It is recommended that they *do not* guess if there is no basis for their guess and they will be penalized for guessing.
- For true/false questions, they should be wary of absolutes such as "all," "none," "always," and "never." If any part of the question is false, it's all false.
- For essay questions, they should jot down ideas they want to include, then determine the order in which they want to present them. When writing an essay, they should get to the point! They should start by giving an overview of the topic, then discuss key points in more detail. Students should use specific information from readings and lectures to support the point(s) they want to make.
- For short-answer and fill-in-the-blank questions, they should look for answer clues in the language and structure of the question. Sometimes the number of blanks can provide a clue. Professors usually are looking for key words or phrases from lectures or assigned reading. If students don't know the specific answer, they should give a more general answer and write as much detail as they can remember. They might get partial credit.
- Students should use any leftover time to review their answers and correct any errors.

10. Ask students to share any other study or test-taking strategies that work for them. (For more strategies, see Kesselman-Turkel & Peterson, 1981; O'Brien, 2005.)

11. Advise students to develop a network of people who support their academic goals. If they know someone who has the academic self-confidence and skills they desire, they should find out how that person developed those skills and work on developing them themselves. Tell students not to be afraid to say "no" to unreasonable demands from others that interfere with their academic goals.

12. Review campus resources:
    - Counseling center
    - Tutoring center
    - Writing center
    - Student disability services
    - Other campus-specific resources (You may want to provide a handout of locations and contact information for resources on your campus.)
13. Ask for any questions and review the session.

References

Bandura, A. (1986). *Social foundations of thought and action.* Englewood Cliffs, NJ: Prentice Hall.

Bandura, A. (1995). *Self-efficacy in changing societies.* Cambridge, England: Cambridge University Press.

Bandura, A. (1997). Self-efficacy. *Harvard Mental Health Letter, 13*(9), 4–5.

Beck, A. T. (1976). *Cognitive therapy and the emotional disorders.* New York, NY: International Universities Press.

Burns, D. (1980). *Feeling good: The new mood therapy.* New York, NY: New American Library.

Kesselman-Turkel, J., & Peterson, F. (1981). *Test-taking strategies.* Lincolnwood, IL: Contemporary Books.

Klassen, R. M. (2004). Optimism and realism: A review of self-efficacy from a cross-cultural perspective. *International Journal of Psychology, 39*(3), 205–230.

McKay, M., & Fanning, P. (1992). *Self-esteem.* Oakland, CA: New Harbinger.

O'Brien, L. (2005). *How to get good grades in college.* Dayton, OH: Woodburn Press.

Robbins, S. B., Lauver, K., Le, H., Davis, D., Langley, R., & Carlstrom, A. (2004). Do psychological and study skill factors predict college outcomes? A meta-analysis. *Psychological Bulletin, 130,* 261–288.

Svanum, S., & Bigatti, S. (2006). Grade expectations: Informed or uninformed optimism, or both? *Teaching of Psychology, 33*(1), 14–18.

Weisberg, N. C., Owen, D. R., Jenkins, A. H., & Harburg, E. (2003). The incremental variance problem: Enhancing the predictability of academic success in an urban, commuter institution. *Genetic, Social, and General Psychology Monographs, 129*(2), 153–180.

Planning Your Career Path

Chester Robinson

Consider this: An individual only has one career. Super (1990) described a *career* as "the life course of a person encountering a series of developmental tasks and attempting to handle them in such a way as to become the kind of person he or she wants to become" (pp. 225–226). Thus, individuals are not tasked with choosing a career but instead planning one. As with any plan, preparation prior to implementation is essential. Arguments have been made that preparation involves the following: self-knowledge (Dawis, 2002; Holland, 1997; Lent, Brown, & Hackett, 1994, 2002; Parsons, 1909; Peterson, Sampson, Lenz, & Reardon, 2002; Roe & Lunneborg, 1990; Super, 1990), work environment knowledge (Dawis, 2002; Mitchell & Krumboltz, 1996; Peterson et al., 2002), specific occupational knowledge (Dawis, 2002; Holland, 1997; Parsons, 1909; Peterson et al., 2002; Super, 1990), barrier awareness (Gottfredson, 1981, 1996, 2002; Lent et al., 1994, 2002), and decision-making skills (Gelatt, 1973; Janis & Mann, 1977; Katz, 1993; Klein, 2002; Peterson et al., 2002; Super, 1990; Tiedeman & Miller-Tiedeman, 1975; Tiedeman & O'Hara, 1963). A brief examination of each of these components is warranted.

Self-knowledge includes, of course, the Big 3: interests, capacities or aptitudes or abilities, and values. Some career scholars (Cochran, 1998; Gottfredson, 1981, 1996, 2002; Mitchell & Krumboltz, 1996; Savickas, 2002; Super, 1990; Young, Valach, & Collin, 2002) include personal history within the self-knowledge paradigm. Interests long have been the primary focus of counselors who have adopted trait-and-factor or person–environment congruence approaches to career counseling. However, Spokane, Meir, and Catalano (2000) found that person–environment congruence accounts for only approximately 5% of the variance in employee satisfaction in the workplace. Aptitudes have long been considered central to vocational success. Super was among the first to suggest that values play an important role in job satisfaction. Later, Brown (2002) offered a career choice theory based solely on values. Values also play a central role in an individual's personal history. The notion of personal history is considered differently by different theorists. Gottfredson's (1981, 1996) initial research was stimulated by her observation "why do children seem to recreate the social inequalities among their elders long before they themselves experience any barriers to pursuing their dreams?" (1996, p. 179). Mitchell and Krumboltz referred to genetic influences, environmental events and conditions, and learning histories, all of which include personal history as a component. Super also noted that career development occurs within an environment and is shaped by one's personal experiences. Individuals' past experiences comprise a portion of the context discussed by Young et al. However, Cochran considered personal history as having the most influence in his narrative approach. Regardless, career development does not occur in a vacuum. Individuals' life experiences seem to influence their career plans, directions, choices, and decisions.

Work environment knowledge may also be referred to as *world-of-work knowledge*. With the exception of Peterson et al. (2002), researchers seem to pay little attention to this factor, but individuals who lack this general work environment knowledge are doomed to failure. Work environment knowledge includes knowing how to communicate effectively in the workplace with peers, superiors, and subordinates. Also included are capacities for time management and scheduling, task persistence, activity planning, and task valuing (ordering tasks with regard to immediacy and importance) and personal work behaviors such as arriving punctually, giving one's best efforts, and being able to value tasks and assignments in relation to extramural responsibilities and diversions. Knowing how to access the world of work also falls within this factor. Job searching, résumé and cover letter writing, and interviewing skills and etiquette all are important components of work environment knowledge.

The goal of the program described here is for participants to learn what they need to do in order to have a career plan upon graduation. The actual activities participants will undertake "post-outreach" will vary with their development "pre-outreach." A somewhat broad programmatic approach is described here with the note that counselors can adapt it to the needs of a particular group of participants. Program goals, objectives, and information are highlighted. Specific activity choices are the responsibility of the presenter.

Group Outreach Plan

1. Review how to gain understanding and how to gain self-knowledge. Discuss the use of formal assessments and how they can be paper and pencil, computer assisted, computerized, or Internet based. Interest inventories abound, with most being based on Holland's (1997)

person–environment congruence theory. Fewer values inventories are available. Aptitude inventories tend toward the general (e.g., mathematical, verbal, spatial, manual dexterity, comprehension, processing speed, mechanical), but some measures of specific aptitudes are available (e.g., music, accounting, office skills, computer programming, nursing, sales). Abilities inventories focus primarily on cognitive abilities such as reading, learning, and reasoning. List a few specific assessments in each category and show students where they can go to take them.

2. Encourage the use of personal interviews conducted by knowledgeable, skilled counselors who can elicit responses from the students that will help them to identify their interests, values, aptitudes/abilities, and personal histories. Holland (1997) contended that expressed interests are better indicators of individuals' true interests than assessed interests. Assessing abilities and aptitudes through interviews typically generates clients' self-efficacies regarding their abilities and aptitudes, perhaps accurate, perhaps not. Interviewing to ascertain clients' values includes identifying values that are central to the clients, then helping them prioritize these values. Provide information on where to receive career counseling services.

3. Use guided imagery to ascertain general self-knowledge. Heppner, O'Brien, Hinkelman, and Humphrey (1994) suggested that guided imagery has wide applicability in helping students explore occupational options. Depending upon the prompts used, interests, values, preferred work settings, and other characteristics can be identified. In an earlier study, Wilson and John (1982) contended that personal values, attitudes, and beliefs can be similarly identified. Give a specific example of guided imagery.

4. Review world-of-work knowledge and discuss the following:
   - Résumé and cover letter preparation
   - Job search skills
   - Interview skills
   - Dressing for interviews and work
   - Relating to coworkers, superiors, and subordinates
   - Time and task management
   - Workplace politics

5. Review where and how to obtain specific occupational knowledge. Obtaining specific occupational knowledge is all about career-related information. The most readily available resource is the Internet. Students can conduct Internet searches using an occupation as a search term. O*Net, the occupational database created for the U.S. Department of Labor by the National Center for O*Net Development, provides specific occupational data for approximately 1,000 occupations. Another convenient option for obtaining specific occupational knowledge is to talk to campus faculty who teach in majors related to the occupation under consideration. A final option for obtaining

specific occupational knowledge is to interview individuals employed in the occupational field.

6. Discuss what kinds of barriers students might encounter as they prepare to enter the world of work. Are these real or merely perceived barriers? Occupational/educational barriers most often identified include perceived access to either educational opportunities or occupational opportunities followed by familial concerns. Talking about overcoming barriers with students is much easier than students actually overcoming them. Helping students develop barrier awareness is as simple as discussing with them various possible barriers.

7. Many students will readily acknowledge financial barriers, such as the cost of continuing their college education, pursuing advanced academic or occupational training, or even moving to and living somewhere else. These are valid concerns, but solutions abound. Most students are aware of various forms of financial aid.

8. Discuss the fact that although grants and scholarships and even work-study programs are good sources of funding for education, subsidized and unsubsidized loans can become a burden much later in students' lives.

9. Loans are viable resources that enable students to continue their education through whatever level of education they choose to pursue. However, students should consider their postgraduation earning potential as they apply for and accept such loans. For example, it is not unusual for students pursuing an MD to graduate from medical school with debt in excess of $100,000. But given their potential income (2008 median annual income: $161,490; Bureau of Labor Statistics, 2010), they will be able to retire this debt easily within a few years. However, students pursuing a counseling degree would be challenged to retire such a debt in a reasonable amount of time given their postgraduation earning potential (2008 median annual income: $42,240; Bureau of Labor Statistics, 2010). Students should be made aware of student loan forgiveness programs. In essence, students choosing certain occupations and agreeing to work in specified geographic areas may have a portion or all of their student loans forgiven based on the amount of time they work in this occupational/ geographic area.

10. Review the less discussed and seldom acknowledged issues of geographic and familial barriers. Both of these often relate to ancestral roots. Many students, like their adult parents, refuse to relocate to another geographic region for the sake of work or education.

11. As students become aware of barriers, they may need assistance in examining and, possibly, overcoming them. Career counselors should assess their personal counseling skills and be prepared either to work with students on these issues or make a referral to a personal counselor, on campus or off, who can help students successfully address these barriers. Counselors must be cognizant that the successful

resolution of barrier issues can mean that students stop, drop out, stay put, persist, or move. Success must be defined in the students' terms.

12. Review campus resources, because students need to know where they can go for assistance and what kind of assistance they can expect to receive there. Does your campus have a dedicated career services center or office? Are career-related services provided through a counseling center or some other student services center or office? What services are available? Explore the following services:
    - Interest/values/aptitude/personal preferences assessment
    - Internship placement, mentor matching, job shadowing placement
    - Résumé/cover letter preparation and/or review, interview skills training
    - On-campus interviews
    - Occupational placement

    Merely making an announcement about the availability of these services is inadequate. Students must be invited to take advantage of them.

13. Help students learn at least one decision-making model. Several decision-making models have been presented over the past several decades (Gelatt, 1973; Janis & Mann, 1977; Katz, 1993; Klein, 2002; Peterson et al., 2002; Tiedeman & Miller-Tiedeman, 1975; Tiedeman & O'Hara, 1963).

References

Brown, D. (2002). The role of work values and cultural values in occupational choice, satisfaction, and success: A theoretical statement. *Journal of Counseling & Development, 80,* 48–56.

Bureau of Labor Statistics. (2010). *May 2008 occupational employment and wage estimates.* Retrieved from http://www.bls.gov/oes/2008/may/oes_nat.htm#b19-0000

Cochran, L. (1998). *Career counseling: A narrative approach.* Newbury Park, CA: Sage.

Dawis, R. V. (2002). Person–environment correspondence theory. In D. Brown & Associates (Eds.), *Career choice and development* (4th ed., pp. 427–464). San Francisco, CA: Jossey-Bass.

Gelatt, H. B. (1973). *Decisions and outcomes.* New York, NY: College Entrance Examination Board.

Gottfredson, L. S. (1981). Circumscription and compromise: A developmental theory of vocational aspirations. *Journal of Counseling Psychology, 28,* 545–579.

Gottfredson, L. S. (1996). Gottfredson's theory of circumscription and compromise. In D. Brown, L. Brooks, & Associates (Eds.), *Career choice and development* (3rd ed., pp. 179–232). San Francisco, CA: Jossey-Bass.

Gottfredson, L. S. (2002). Gottfredson's theory of circumscription, compromise, and self-creation. In D. Brown & Associates (Eds.), *Career choice and development* (4th ed., pp. 85–148). San Francisco, CA: Jossey-Bass.

Heppner, M. J., O'Brien, K. M., Hinkelman, J. M., & Humphrey, C. F. (1994). Shifting the paradigm: The use of creativity in career counseling. *Journal of Career Development, 21*, 77–96.

Holland, J. L. (1997). *Making vocational choices: A theory of vocational personalities and work environments* (3rd ed.). Lutz, FL: PAR.

Janis, I. L., & Mann, L. (1977). *Decision making*. New York, NY: Free Press.

Katz, M. R. (1993). *Computer-assisted career decision making: The guide in the machine*. Hillsdale, NJ: Erlbaum.

Klein, G. (2002). *Intuition at work: Developing your gut instincts will make you better at what you do*. New York, NY: Currency Doubleday.

Lent, R. W., Brown, S. D., & Hackett, G. (1994). Toward a unifying social cognitive theory of career and academic interest, choice, and performance. *Journal of Vocational Behavior, 45*, 79–122.

Lent, R. W., Brown, S. D., & Hackett, G. (2002). Social cognitive career theory. In D. Brown & Associates (Eds.), *Career choice and development* (4th ed., pp. 255–311). San Francisco, CA: Jossey-Bass.

Mitchell, L. K., & Krumboltz, J. D. (1996). Krumboltz's learning theory of career choice and counseling. In D. Brown, L. Brooks, & Associates (Eds.), *Career choice and development* (3rd ed., pp. 233–280). San Francisco, CA: Jossey-Bass.

Parsons, F. (1909). *Choosing a vocation*. Boston, MA: Houghton Mifflin.

Peterson, G. W., Sampson, J. P., Jr., Lenz, J. G., & Reardon, R. C. (2002). A cognitive information processing approach to career problem solving and decision making. In D. Brown & Associates (Eds.), *Career choice and development* (4th ed., pp. 312–372). San Francisco, CA: Jossey-Bass.

Roe, A., & Lunneborg, P. W. (1990). Personality development and career choice. In D. Brown, L. Brooks, & Associates (Eds.), *Career choice and development: Applying contemporary theories to practice* (2nd ed., pp. 68–101). San Francisco, CA: Jossey-Bass.

Savickas, M. L. (2002). Career construction: A developmental theory of vocational behavior. In D. Brown & Associates (Eds.), *Career choice and development* (4th ed., pp. 149–205). San Francisco, CA: Jossey-Bass.

Spokane, A. R., Meir, I. E., & Catalano, M. (2000). Person–environment congruence and Holland's theory: A review and reconsideration. *Journal of Vocational Behavior, 57*, 137–187.

Super, D. E. (1990). A life-span, life-space approach to career development. In D. Brown, L. Brooks, & Associates (Eds.), *Career choice and development: Applying contemporary theories to practice* (2nd ed., pp. 197–261). San Francisco, CA: Jossey-Bass.

Tiedeman, D. V., & Miller-Tiedeman, A. (1975). Choice and decision processes and careers. In A. M. Mitchell, W. R. Unruh, & G. B. Jones (Eds.), *Technical report of a conference on career decision making* (pp. 60–113). Palo Alto, CA: American Institutes for Research.

Tiedeman, D., & O'Hara, R. (1963). *Choice and decision processes and careers.* DeKalb, IL: ERIC Clearinghouse in Career Education.

Wilson, W. C., & John, E. (1982). Guided imagery in career awareness. *Rehabilitation Counseling Bulletin, 25,* 291–295.

Young, R. A., Valach, L., & Collin, A. (2002). A contextualist explanation of career. In D. Brown & Associates (Eds.), *Career choice and development* (4th ed., pp. 206–252). San Francisco, CA: Jossey-Bass.

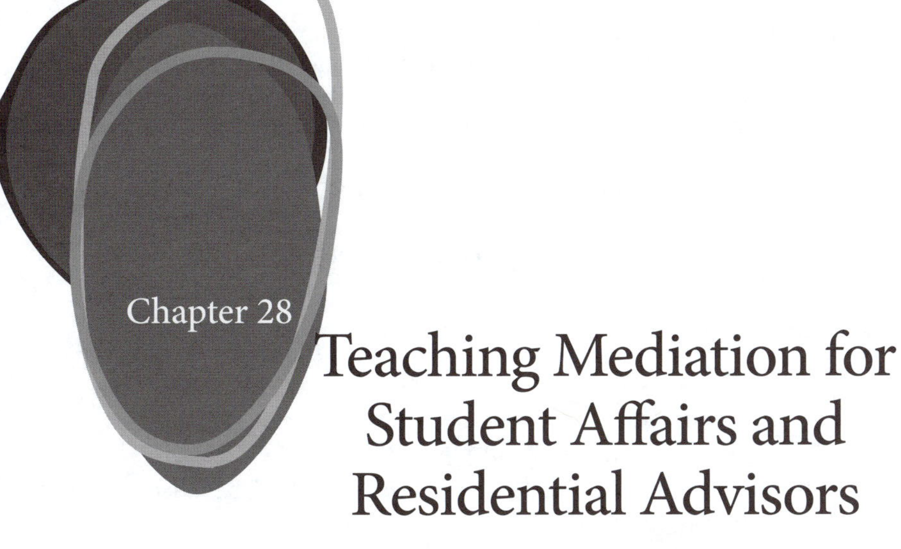

Teaching Mediation for Student Affairs and Residential Advisors

Jennifer L. Marshall

This outreach program is designed to provide student affairs and residential advisors (RAs) with an overview of mediation training and guidelines for effectively using mediation with students. *Mediation* is a way to resolve a variety of problems, such as roommate and relationship issues, money disputes, and everyday conflicts. A *mediator* is an individual who is in a position to help others resolve their issues in an unbiased manner. Mediation should give control and power to all parties in need of a resolution. Good mediators are nonjudgmental, willing to listen, and open to what they hear; they should also make sure that all parties can share their thoughts and feelings in a safe climate. The role of the mediator is to help empower the parties to come to a mutual resolution on their own terms by asking the correct questions and restating the obvious. Mediation uses several counseling microskills, such as active listening, reframing, paraphrasing, and summarizing, to help individuals come to a mutually agreeable outcome. Usually mediation occurs in one to two sessions (Moore, 2003).

Mediation has been used for several years within educational institutions to help junior high and high school students resolve their own issues peacefully (Casella, 2000). College campuses also use mediation to handle conflict resolution in light of the increased diversity of student populations (Gerzon, 2006). This resolution is an educational service in which students learn constructive ways to handle disputes without resorting to more belligerent methods (Makdad, 2002; Warters, 1999). Most issues can be solved student to student with a third party (e.g., an RA) present.

The mediator needs to be sensitive to regional and ethnic differences and might want to address any issues that the individuals involved might have in dealing with these differences (Bresnahan, Guan, Shearman, & Donohue, 2009). Several factors contribute to the effectiveness of mediation in an educational setting. All parties involved must agree to mediation. There must also be a training period for the mediator as well as resources he or she can consult if necessary. Mediation needs to be marketed as an accessible, confidential means of resolving issues (Theberge & Orv, 2004).

Group Outreach Plan

1. Define *mediation* as a process in which an impartial person helps two or more parties come to a mutual resolution. Review the benefits of mediation.
   - It is cost effective.
   - It can save a lot of time and hassle.
   - It can be empowering to the parties involved because they are resolving their own issues.
   - It is a practical solution.
   - It allows individuals to talk about important issues in a safe environment.
2. Discuss when parties should use mediation.
   - Mediation should be used when parties are unable to come to an agreement on a particular topic.
   - All parties need to agree to be part of the mediation process.
3. Discuss the process of mediation. (Below you will find a 16-point mediation script to use with students during role plays.)
   - Talk to each individual separately to see what the issues are.
   - Make sure that both individuals agree on mediation.
   - Set rules for the mediation session (e.g., no interrupting; no name calling; be willing to listen to the other person; people do not have to agree with the other party, just listen to them).
   - Ask the first individual to share his or her thoughts and feelings about the issue.
   - Make sure to keep this sharing to 3–5 minutes so that the other individual does not get overwhelmed.
   - Ask the second individual to repeat what the first individual said. Please make sure that he or she knows that he or she does not have to agree with what was said but does need to have heard it.
   - After the second individual has repeated what was said, ask the first individual whether this synopsis was correct. If it was not, then have the first individual repeat himself or herself again.
   - The goal is for each individual to feel that he or she has been heard.
   - If you and the individuals feel that they have been heard, then repeat these steps with the second individual.
   - After each individual feels that he or she has been heard, then summarize their arguments.

- Have each individual come up with possible solutions to the problem. See if they will agree on any of the solutions; if not, then have them keep coming up with solutions until they agree on one.
- Check back later with both individuals to see how they are handling the issue.

4. Review the following mediation script. This script can be made into colorful cards or printed on an index card so RAs can keep it handy for use in the dorm.

Mediation Script

(A = first person; B = second person)

1. Ask A & B, "Do either of you need a cooling off period?"
2. Ask A & B, "Do you want to mediate?"
3. Tell A & B that there are rules to the mediation: (a) no interrupting and (b) no name calling. Set rules you think are appropriate for the individuals.
4. Ask A, "What is going on?" (Set a time limit of 3–4 minutes)
5. Ask B, "What did A just say?" (Emphasize that B does not have to agree with what was said, he or she just has to have heard it.)
6. Ask A, "Is that what you said?"(If A agrees, then move on to Step 7; if he or she disagrees, go back to Step 4.)
7. Ask B, "What is going on?" (Set a time limit of 3–4 minutes)
8. Ask A, "What did B just say?" (Emphasize that A does not have to agree with what was said, he or she just has to have heard it.)
9. Ask B, "Is that what you said?" (If B agrees, then move on to Step 10; if he or she disagrees, go back to Step 7.)
10. Summarize what both A & B have said.
11. Ask A & B if they agree with your summary.
12. Ask A for three possible solutions.
13. Ask B for three possible solutions.
14. Evaluate the options and how realistic they are.
15. Have A & B pick a common solution and try it. (If no common solutions are reached after each person suggests three, have them keep giving solutions until a common one is reached.)
16. Check back with A & B in about 1–2 week(s) and see if there is still a problem.

5. Use the following role play scenario to practice mediation skills. Allow the group to process the first example in discussion and then role play the following examples.

You are an RA in one of the residence halls. You have just been informed that a resident in Room 3 needs to speak to you. The resident tells you that she absolutely can't live with her roommate because of her "nasty" habits. The roommate, she claims, is messy, is not friendly, and ignores the student's requests to clean up. You then hear from the roommate later that day that the student is too organized, selfish, and outspoken. What do you do? Solve this conflict.

Roommate 1 (Role play)

You are a resident in Room 3. You approach your RA and tell her you absolutely can't live with your roommate because of her "nasty" habits. She is messy, is not friendly, and ignores your requests to clean up. What do you want done? Solve this conflict.

Roommate 2 (Role play)

You are a resident in Room 3. You approach your RA and inform her that you absolutely can't live with your roommate because she is too anal. She is too organized, selfish, and too outspoken. What do you want done? Solve this conflict.

6. Discuss the results of the role play sessions. Ask what worked well, and what challenges did the RAs face? Encourage them to practice independently after the session.

References

Bresnahan, M. J., Guan, X., Shearman, S. M., & Donohue, W. A. (2009). Roommate conflict: Does race matter? *Howard Journal of Communications, 20,* 394–412.

Casella, R. (2000). The benefits of peer mediation in the context of urban conflict and program status. *Urban Education, 35,* 324–355.

Gerzon, M. (2006). *Leading through conflict: How successful leaders transform differences into opportunities.* Cambridge, MA: Harvard Business School Press.

Makdad, N. (2002). 10 challenges facing campus mediation programs. *Conflict Management in Higher Education, 2,* 1–7.

Moore, C. W. (2003). *The mediation process: An interdisciplinary approach to service-learning and mediation assistance.* Albany: NY: Government Law Center of Albany Law School.

Theberge, S. K., & Orv, K. C. (2004). Six factors inhibiting the use of peer mediation in a junior high school. *Professional School Counseling, 7*(4), 283–290.

Warters, W. C. (1999). *Mediation in the campus community: Designing and managing effective programs.* San Francisco, CA: Jossey-Bass.

Chapter 29

Life Gets Overwhelming! Tips for Overcoming

Carolyn W. Kern and Sheila Soslow

Students attending graduate school experience many challenges. Along with the rigor of graduate academic coursework, juggling family, employment, and finances can add additional burdens. Graduate students make an effort to deal with these pressures in several ways: Some effectively manage stress through healthy strategies, whereas others could benefit from learning additional coping strategies. Significant relationships may suffer during graduate school because of the demands put upon students. Time once spent with family and friends is needed to study. Students who are unable to cope effectively with both internal and external pressures often develop unhealthy practices that could result in physical, psychological, mental, and/or emotional harm (McGrath, 2006).

Increasing pressures on college students combined with national reports of greater anxiety, depression, and suicidal ideation in student populations underscore the need to provide opportunities for students to learn healthy strategies to successfully navigate graduate school. College counselors have an opportunity to contribute by providing students with necessary skills and opportunities. The American College Health Association (2008) asked 26,685 college students about their stress levels in the past year. A total of 87% reported feeling overwhelmed by all they had to accomplish; just under half affirmed feeling overwhelming anxiety at times, and 41% rated their stress levels as above average. Moreover, 27% reported that stress had disrupted academic performance, and almost half said that stress levels resulted in feelings of hopelessness. Just more than 5% reported intentional self-injury, and 6% said they felt so depressed they had considered suicide.

Gallagher (2009) reported that students are coming to campus with greater levels of anxiety and depression than ever before. Graduate students face greater academic pressures and have higher levels of internal stress with greater expectations for success. College counselors have an opportunity to help these students develop more effective coping strategies through workshop participation.

Group Description

Working with the university campus to promote workshops can help recruit participants. The graduate school can be a partner when it comes to advertising and coordinating participation. Students see the workshop as a graduate school activity and thus are often more ready to participate. Validation of graduate school as stressful helps to normalize students' experiences while encouraging their participation.

The workshop presented here is a one-time educational and experiential opportunity. Counselors can choose to develop groups from among students who may be seeking counseling or the broader campus community. This workshop can also lead to additional groups that develop out of participation in this workshop. Past participants in such a group have indicated an interest in developing educational support groups as well as interpersonal support groups. This workshop can be a way to promote groups as a strategy to help with stress.

Group Outreach Plan

1. Helping students identify areas that cause stress and find ways to overcome pressures related to those stressors can facilitate their success. Stressors come from cognitions (what we think about a stressor), which can result in stress or nonstress. Different people can have the same stressor and react very differently because of their individual cognitions.

2. Explain that personal stressors can include finances, family, relationships, physical health, home, and taking care of the home. How individuals think about life situations can add to feelings of discouragement and anxiety. Professional stressors in graduate school can include obtaining a degree, grade point average, scholarships and grants, tuition and fees, and postgraduate employment. By identifying stressors, participants are then able to develop strategies to reduce the effects of these pressures. Everyone has stress. There are two types of stress: *Good stress* motivates us to accomplish things; *dis-stress* can be unhealthy and needs to be effectively managed for one to stay both physically and emotionally healthy.

3. Individuals do not always realize how useful practical strategies can be for managing or reducing stress levels. The strategies identified in Handout 29.1 can bring a sense of calm to students' lives. Organizing and managing time provides a person with a sense of control. Also, managing finances and living expenses can be challenging. With

financial planning, budgeting, and money-saving strategies, graduate students can focus more on their studies and less on the economics of living. Universities that provide services to help students in these areas assist students in being successful.

4. Another area to discuss with students is setting boundaries in relationships. Nothing can be more challenging for some individuals than saying no. With the pressure of graduate studies, students can find it difficult to meet the needs of significant people in their lives. The beginning of graduate school can be especially challenging because students do not know how demanding it will be. A series of workshops that address specific areas in more detail would be an additional resource.

5. Another strategy to discuss is learning to overcome or prevent undue stress by planning and preparing for upcoming events. Discuss common triggers for stress, and ask group members to identify ways in which to respond when they anticipate stressful situations.

6. Diet and exercise play a significant role in how one feels and is able to deal with challenges. Having a purposeful plan for diet and exercise can reduce stress. An excellent idea is to have an exercise group within an academic area. Not only are the participants encouraged with exercise, but discussions around the academic area become natural. A final idea for reducing stress is to take a vacation. A student may not be able to take an extended vacation, but even a day or two to refresh the brain can energize and lead to creative thinking. Sometimes 5 minutes is all a person may have to relax. Using that time to take a mini-vacation can put the day back into perspective. People often forget how energizing anticipation can be. When we look forward to something in the future, often the present becomes bearable. Have students think about a positive upcoming event. After discussing these strategies, review some other ideas as time allows.

7. Review the fact that when stress levels are high, it is important to be proactive and avoid stressors and people who are stressful. Students should surround themselves with positive people. They should work on strategies to resolve conflict in their lives. They should determine what makes them angry and learn anger management skills, or participate in assertiveness training to learn appropriate ways to say no to people in their lives. Effective communication skills are also a key component to healthy relationships throughout life.

8. It is important for individuals to identify what helps them de-stress. The following activity provides directions to consider. Have students list what they like to do. Also have them list what has worked in the past to help them de-stress. Then have them prioritize these in order of availability/success and pick the easiest one to focus on. Ask them, "What is one thing you can do next week to start putting your de-stressor plan into action? Write it down." It is important that students make a doable plan to set themselves up for success.

9. Participants are looking for ideas and encouragement. The following suggestions can stimulate ideas: take care of yourself, get plenty of rest, exercise, accomplish one thing, do something you enjoy, relax, love yourself, and love someone else. Have students identify something they would be willing to do. Finally, ask, "What is *one* thing you can do today?"
10. Encourage students to use campus resources, including the counseling center, which may have a number of free sessions during the school year. Additional resources include the Office of Money Management, the Student Counseling Center, student activities/organizations, recreational sports, graduate student organizations, and volunteer opportunities.

References

American College Health Association. (2008). *American College Health Association—National College Health Assessment: Reference group executive summary fall 2008.* Retrieved from http://www.acha-ncha.org/docs/ACHA-NCHA_Reference_Group_ExecutiveSummary_Fall2008.pdf

Gallagher, R. (2009). *National survey of counseling center directors.* Retrieved from the International Association of Counseling Services website: http://www.iacsinc.org/2009%20National%20Survey.pdf

McGrath, R. (2006). Stress. In P. A. Grayson & P. W. Meilman (Eds.), *College mental health practice* (pp. 135–151). New York, NY: Routledge.

Handout 29.1

Stress Reduction Activities

Each of the following activities can be done in a workshop. The amount of time allocated for the workshop will determine which activities to include. The scripts included here have been found to be effective in leading the experiential components. Activities may be spread throughout different parts of the workshop as well.

Oxygenizing Your Brain and Body

Our brains need oxygen to function. Sitting at a computer, reading, sitting on the couch and watching television, and even standing can cause poor posture. We hunch over and compress our lungs, which compromises our breathing. Most people use only half their lung capacity. Practice deep breathing: Put one arm across your stomach and the other arm across your chest, resting your hand on your shoulder. Breathe in through your nose, filling first your lower lungs (your abdomen will rise) and then your upper lungs (your chest will rise). Now exhale through your mouth, reversing the process (your chest will lower first, then your stomach). Sometimes increases in oxygen can cause lightheadedness, so it is helpful the first time you practice deep breathing to sit in a chair with your feet firmly on the ground and your eyes open.

Other Breathing Exercises

- *Balloon exercise.* Blow up a balloon while imagining you are filling it with things that are stressing you.
- *Blowing bubbles.* Say what you are stressed about and then blow a bubble, imagine your stressor is floating away inside the bubble.
- *Laughing.* Belly laughs relax your whole body, including your face and muscles.
- *Relaxing.* Watch an infant breathe and notice his or her belly moving. Then try it: Lie on the floor on your back, place an object on your stomach, and try to breathe in deeply enough to make the object move up and down.

Deep Breathing With Key Words

- Practice inhaling and exhaling using the deep-breathing process. As you inhale through your nose, think of a positive word, such as *peace.*
- As you exhale through your mouth, think of another positive word, such as *relax.* Inhale to a slow count of 10, and exhale to a slow count of 10.
- Repeat this cycle at least four times.

Progressive Relaxation

Lie on your back on the floor, or sit in a chair. Close your eyes if you like, and get in a comfortable position. Tense your body: Beginning with one arm, tense it up, make your hand into a fist, stretch it up to the ceiling, and release, letting your arm relax. Roll your arm from side to side and forget about it. Repeat for the other parts of your body, including your face. Next mentally go through each part of your body, making sure it is relaxed. Start by saying or thinking, "Relax toes," "Relax ankles," "Relax back," and so on, ending with the individual parts of your face. Then exhale while thinking "Relax." Bring your attention to your mind and thoughts, but don't attach yourself to any one thought. Allow 3–5 minutes of quiet relaxation. Do three deep-breathing cycles, then slowly wake up your body by wiggling your fingers and toes, roll your head gently side to side, and open your eyes. Do about 3–5 minutes of this relaxation exercise the first time. Slowly increase the time until the entire process takes 15 minutes to complete. This exercise works well while soft relaxation music is playing.

Relaxation Bags

The following items can be given to workshop participants in small brown paper bags to encourage relaxation during and after the workshop: a small bottle of bubbles, a balloon, a piece of bubblegum, a squishy or squeeze toy, a mini-Slinky, and a small jar of play dough. Facilitators can include any other items they believe would be effective.

Chapter 30

Beating Stress

*Brian Van Brunt, Courtney Clippert,
and Rodney Martin*

"Quick! I need someone to do a program to help my students manage their stress!" is probably the most common request made to college counselors in terms of outreach programs. These programs are offered during student orientation events; as preventive measures to reduce stress during final exams and midterms; prior to holidays and school breaks; for athletes and students involved with Greek life who have programming requirements; and for students with specific majors (e.g., nursing, pre-med) or students in first-year writing courses, who typically experience increased stress.

Stress programs are typically an hour in length but should have an "accordion feature" built in to shrink them down to 15-minute quick lectures or out to 2-hour discussion, question-and-answer programs. Stress reduction programs can be taught directly to students in classroom and residence hall settings or condensed into passive advertisements and handouts made available at orientation tables or in high-stress areas, like the library at finals time. In this chapter general ideas for conducting these programs are discussed. Please review other chapters of this book for specific program outlines.

Core Concepts of Stress Reduction

Rational Emotive Behavior Therapy

Most stress reduction programming works well with Albert Ellis's rational emotive behavior therapy (Ellis & Dryden, 2007). Ellis found this approach useful in assisting students to identify irrational thoughts that they had in reaction to activating events. The rational emotive behavior therapy approach can be described in terms of ABCs: *Activating* events, *Beliefs* about these events, and *Consequences* of these beliefs. Activating events

can be anything from having an argument, getting cut off in traffic, spilling coffee on a favorite shirt, or having a computer crash. These events cannot be prevented; they occur throughout life.

It is people's beliefs about the activating events that lead to aggressive actions and negative consequences. People cannot change the activating events in their lives, but they can change their beliefs about these events and the resulting consequences of their behavior.

Life in Balance

Any stress reduction programming should also include a discussion of how to live a life in balance (see Handout 30.1). College is a struggle to balance multiple tasks while keeping some semblance of sanity throughout the experience. Students learn how to balance aspects of their lives (e.g., peers, academics, physical or dating relationships, family) while they are away from home and moving toward adulthood. Stress reduction programming should include some discussion of how to learn to take a break and identify the signs of early stress and burnout.

William Glasser (1975, 2001), the founder of reality therapy, talked about the importance of living a life in balance. He argued that people must balance five essential needs in order to live a happy life: survival, love/belonging, power/achievement, freedom, and fun. It would be easy to imagine an entire program designed around helping college students identify these five key areas of their lives and how each area competes for time and energy.

Better Make It Fun

Many times students are required to attend stress reduction programming as a preventive step for combating any anxiety they may be experiencing. It is important then to understand that many who will be on the receiving end of an hour-long "How to Beat Stress" lecture may be required to attend the lecture. The workshop itself thus becomes a source of stress!

Teach Them How to Breathe

Staff should teach students the process of breathing or meditating to better control their stress and anxiety to prevent the development of a panic attack. There are many approaches to controlling breathing used by everyone from Navy SEALs in sniper training to yoga practitioners.

An approach called *cycle breathing* is useful for reducing the biological changes that overcome a person escalating toward crisis. This process involves breathing in to a slow count of 4, holding the breath for a slow count of 4, breathing out for a slow count of 4, and then repeating. This process lowers blood pressure and heart rate, allowing students to regain calm and regain their ability to think creatively and rationally about their stress.

Time Management

Often college students underestimate the importance of time management. They do not always understand that their increased stress is a direct result of a lack of effort in organizing their schedule or planning for tests, homework, and assignments.

College students struggle with responsibilities that are more pressing than those they encountered while in high school. It is important to teach students ways in which they can cope when their perceived demands exceed their perceived resources. Staff should teach students that time management is about prioritizing, and thus students should ask themselves three questions: "Do I work best with a full or empty schedule?" "Am I a morning or an evening person?" "Can I tune out distractions easily?" (Nichols, 2004). One important component in the time management equation is to anticipate and plan. It is beneficial for students to have a tool that helps them keep track of things that they need to do (e.g., a planner, a calendar, to-do lists). Also, staff should teach students the dangers of procrastination. Some ways to avoid procrastination include identifying things that lead to procrastination, breaking tasks into manageable parts, trying to do the first draft of a paper in advance, and changing the study environment (Nichols, 2004).

Creative Ideas for Stress Programming

There are many ways to run a creative and fun program for students to teach the benefits of dealing with stress and how to tackle anxiety. Here we discuss some common approaches to stress reduction programming and how they can be interesting and useful to students.

Give Away Items

Many students who attend programming on stress reduction are required to do so as part of an academic class, club, or organization. Thus, anything that can be done to help these students walk away with exciting reminders or fun items to highlight their experience will help reduce their boredom and encourage them to make use of referrals to counseling and academic advising. Items are available through various Internet companies such as www.branders.com. It typically makes better fiscal sense to place large orders at the start of the year rather than smaller orders throughout the year. It may also be useful to have key departments like counseling and academic affairs put their logo on the items to encourage students to call and make an appointment.

Use Video Clips and Clipart

The best stress programs are those that keep the audience engaged. One way to accomplish this is to use creative, fun, and current movie clips and graphic images to draw students' attention and focus. If the staff who are offering the program are a bit out of touch with current movies, TV shows, and culture, consider involving graduate students who have a better understanding of what would captivate students.

Be Aware of Time and Location

Consider the importance of when the program will occur. Is it right before lunch? Is it the last of five lectures students will be hearing? Did students

just walk up a half-mile hill to get there? Is it at 8 a.m.? Understand why the students are coming to your program and what their expectations are in terms of how long it will last and how comfortable the environment will be. Although you cannot change some of these variables, it may help students feel more engaged if you share an understanding of how they feel about the program.

Make It Interactive

Programs can reach students in two main ways: through process and content. The *content* is the information the presenter has to share. The *process* is the way the information is shared. Look for ways to engage the audience and help students take an active role in listening to and understanding the information. This may involve passing out index cards at the start of the talk and asking the students to write questions down that they want answered but do not want to ask themselves. Another method may be to create a quiz show like *Jeopardy!* Or hand out candy to those who answer stress-related trivia questions correctly.

Consider Some Quotes

"Twenty years from now you will be more disappointed
by the things you didn't do than by the ones you did.
So throw off the bowlines. Sail away from the safe harbor.
Catch the trade winds in your sails.
Explore. Dream. Discover."

—Mark Twain

"What is there to be afraid of? The worst thing that can
happen is you fail. So what? I failed at a lot of things.
My first record was horrible."

—John Mellencamp

"I am an optimist. It does not seem too much use being
anything else."

—Winston Churchill

References

Ellis, A., & Dryden, W. (2007). *The practice of rational emotive behavior therapy* (2nd ed.). New York, NY: Springer.

Glasser, A. (1975). *Reality therapy: A new approach to psychiatry.* New York, NY: Harper & Row.

Glasser, A. (2001). *Counseling with choice theory: The new reality therapy.* New York, NY: HarperCollins.

Nichols, J. (2004). Get TIME on your side. *Careers & Colleges, 24,* 25–29.

Handout 30.1

Stress Management

- Prepare for the morning the evening before. Choose breakfast, make plans for lunch, put out the clothes you plan to wear, and so on.
- Don't rely on your memory. Write down appointment times, when to do the laundry, when library books are due, when papers need to be turned in.
- Do nothing that, after being done, leads you to tell a lie.
- Be prepared to wait. A paperback can make a wait in a post office line almost pleasant.
- Procrastination is stressful. Whatever you want to do tomorrow, do today; whatever you want to do today, do it now.
- Don't put up with something that doesn't work right. If your alarm clock, wallet, shoelaces, windshield wipers—whatever—is a constant aggravation, get it fixed or get a new one.
- Eliminate (or restrict) the amount of caffeine in your diet.
- Always set up contingency plans just in case (e.g., "If for some reason either of us is delayed, here's what we'll do . . ." or "If we get split up in the shopping center, here's where we'll meet").
- Say "No!" Saying no to extra projects, social activities, and invitations you know you don't have the time or energy for takes practice, self-respect, and a belief that everyone, every day, needs quiet time to relax and be alone.
- Allow yourself time—every day—for privacy, quiet, and introspection.
- Turn off your phone. Want to take a long bath, meditate, sleep, or read without interruption? Drum up the courage to temporarily disconnect. (The possibility of there being a terrible emergency in the next hour or so is almost nil.) Or let calls go to voicemail.
- Make friends with nonworriers. Nothing can get you into the habit of worrying faster than associating with chronic worrywarts.
- Create order out of chaos. Organize your home and workspace so that you always know exactly where things are. Put things away where they belong, and you won't have to go through the stress of losing things.
- Writing your thoughts and feelings down (in a journal, or on paper to be thrown away) can help you clarify things and can give you a renewed perspective.
- When the stress of having to get a job done gets in the way of getting the job done, diversion—a voluntary change in activity and/or environment—may be just what you need.
- Talk it out. Discussing your problems with a trusted friend can help clear your mind of confusion so you can concentrate on problem solving.

- Do one thing at a time. When you are with someone, be with that person and with no one or nothing else. When you are busy with a project, concentrate on doing that project and forget about everything else you have to do.
- If an especially unpleasant task faces you, do it early in the day and get it over with. Then the rest of your day will be free of anxiety.
- Have an optimistic view of the world. Believe that most people are doing the best they can.

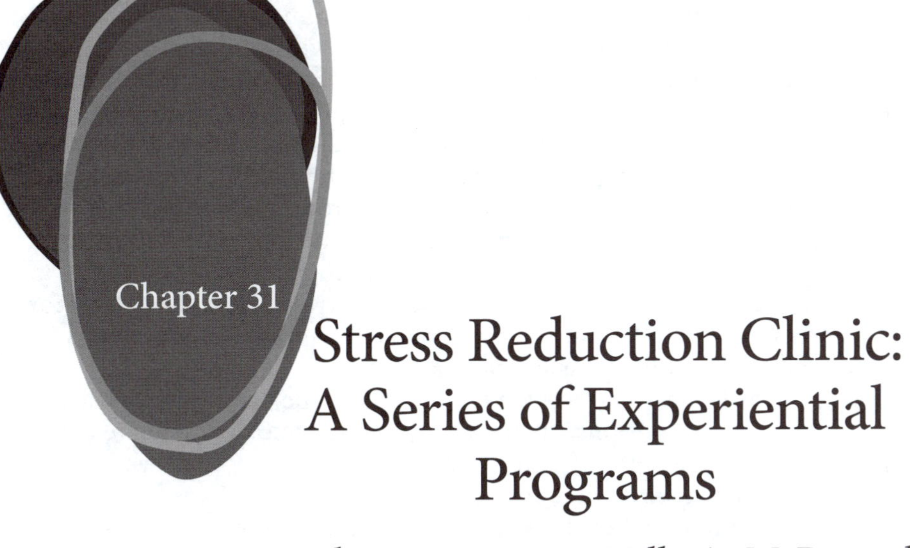

Stress Reduction Clinic: A Series of Experiential Programs

Mark W. St. Martin, Kelly A. McDonnell, and Elaine L. Phillips

Beyond the apparent stress associated with the academic demands and pressures of college, students face challenges in terms of intrapersonal and interpersonal development, the forging of one's personal identity, seeking out fulfilling relationships, the shaping of career aspirations, transition and adjustment, conflicts with roommates, loneliness, and finances (Amada, 2005). Students may also be confronted by a disparity between the values and expectations of their family of origin and the "cultural milieu of the university" (Amada, 2005, p. 71). International and minority students are at particular risk for discrimination, a sense of displacement, language differences, and an unfamiliar culture. Tragic events on university campuses, such as those at Virginia Tech and Northern Illinois University, add to the stress and help create feelings of vulnerability and insecurity. Prolonged and intense exposure to these and other stressors place college students at risk for psychological and physical health problems, which can serve to negatively impact academic performance. About a third of the student respondents to the American College Health Association–National College Health Assessment (American College Health Association, 2008) indicated that stress has affected their academic performance, about 35% reported taking medication for depression, and approximately 10% indicated that they had seriously considered attempting suicide on at least one occasion in the previous 12 months. Owens and Rodolfa (2009) pointed out the key role that counseling centers play in providing preventive mental health services for students. They highlighted the fact that drop-in groups, similar to the one described in this chapter, that address such issues as stress, relaxation training, and mindfulness provide meaningful information and social support and represent a point of contact with students.

The Stress Reduction Clinic is an example of a response to the call for more nontraditional preventive and skills-training-type programs aimed at stress reduction, social support, and self-care (Owens & Rodolfa, 2009; Pinkerton, Talley, & Cooper, 2009; Stone & Archer, 1990). It incorporates several self-contained, independent outreach programs that together represent a set of complementary activities. The clinic operates on a drop-in basis, so it is not an appropriate referral for students who are currently in crisis, even if that crisis is related to anxiety or stress. It may be helpful for those wishing to implement such programs to have an informed consent document that outlines possible contraindications (e.g., seizure disorder, thought disorder) associated with taking part in the programs. In each of the experiential programs, the facilitating counselor participates with the students in the activity. This allows the counselor to serve as a visual model of how to engage in the exercise and also serves to decrease any anxiety participants might have regarding the counselor staring at them during the program. The counselor should, however, periodically look around the room to determine whether participants seem comfortable and able to participate. If someone appears to be having difficulty, the counselor might adjust the instructions accordingly and/ or consider referring that participant to other more appropriate services. Although the Stress Reduction Clinic contains multiple experiential and psychoeducational components, because of space limitations just a few are described here.

Group Outreach Plan

Activity 1: Meditation

1. When introducing yourself for any of the outreach programs, state your name, role or position, and credentials. Provide an overview of what will be covered during the session. Include information regarding the benefits of the specific program (i.e., meditation, body scanning, muscle relaxation, or mindfulness) and a brief description of the procedures. Ask students to turn off cell phones and other electronic devices. The introduction should be 5 minutes or less.

2. Encourage participants to find a comfortable position in their chairs with both feet on the floor or, if they are comfortable doing so, have them sit with their legs crossed in the chair (modified lotus position). It is recommended that you model this by settling comfortably in a chair and preparing to meditate with the participants. Ask participants to choose a word to focus on during the meditation. Common words include *calm, one, peace,* or *serenity.*

3. Invite participants to close their eyes or, if they prefer, find a spot straight ahead of them on the wall to look at. Invite all participants

to participate in the manner that is most comfortable for them (eyes open or closed; feet on the floor or in the lotus position).

4. Once all participants are settled and quiet, begin the meditation with a focus on slowing the breath. Ask participants to focus on long, slow inhalations and long, slow exhalations. Encourage everyone to focus on releasing any tension in the body and becoming more comfortable and relaxed in their chosen position. While continuing to breathe slowly, ask participants to focus on inhaling and exhaling; on the exhalation participants are to silently say the chosen word. State that when the mind wanders, participants should gently bring it back by silently repeating the chosen word. This focus on the breath and the chosen word should continue in silence for approximately 20 minutes.

5. At the end of the session, ask participants to slowly open their eyes and bring their awareness back to the room when they are ready. Ask participants whether they would like to share how they feel or comment on anything that they noticed during the meditation. Discussion occurs if participants wish. At the end of the discussion, thank participants for attending the session and invite them to return again as often as they wish. Encourage them to practice at home for maximum benefits.

Helpful resources:
- A transcript and video example of meditation can be found at http://www.mayoclinic.com/health/meditation/MM00623 (Mayo Clinic, 2010).

Activity 2: Progressive Muscle Relaxation and Body Scanning

1. For the introduction, refer to the general introductions for the previous activity. Tell participants that these techniques are sometimes used to facilitate sleep, and if they fall asleep during the session, this is fine.

2. Invite participants to close their eyes or, if they prefer, to find a spot straight ahead of them on the wall or ceiling (depending on whether they are lying down or seated) to look at. Ask all participants to participate in the manner that is most comfortable for them.

3. Once all participants are settled and quiet, begin the training session with a focus on slowing the breath. Ask participants to focus on long, slow inhalations and long, slow exhalations. Continue by asking everyone to inhale slowly for a count of 4 and exhale slowly for a count of 4. You may model and facilitate this by counting aloud for several inhalations and exhalations.

4. Instruct the participants to gently tighten and relax each of the voluntary muscle groups of the body starting with the toes. Tightening should not be to the point of pain but rather to the point at which tension is felt in that area. Ask participants to gently tighten each muscle group and hold for a count of 4 and then relax for a count of 4.

5. Encourage participants to focus on the sensation of tensing and relaxing each muscle group and to gently bring awareness back to the body if the mind begins to wander. The tightening and relaxing of each muscle group moves up the body with breaks at various points during which you again focus on slowed breath, counting slowly to 4 during inhalations and 4 during exhalations, then moving smoothly back to tightening and relaxing various muscle groups.

6. For body scanning, instruct the participants to focus on various voluntary muscle groups starting at the toes and moving up the body. Ask participants to notice any feelings, sensations, thoughts, and emotions that arise while they are focused on that area of the body. Encourage participants to gently bring awareness back to that area of the body if the mind wanders. Have participants imagine on inhalation that the breath is moving through the body to the area of focus. Have them imagine on exhalation that the breath is releasing the tension, thoughts, and emotions associated with this area. (Note that this is different from the progressive muscle relaxation exercise in that the muscles are not tightened and relaxed physically. Relaxation occurs through awareness and use of the breath.)

7. At the end of each training, ask participants to slowly open their eyes and bring their awareness back to the room when they are ready. Then ask them to bring their hands above their heads and stretch for a few minutes before getting up from the floor or chair, as this exercise lowers the heart rate and getting up abruptly can result in feeling dizzy. Ask participants how they feel and where they notice particular tension in the body. Discussion occurs if participants wish. Thank them for attending the session and invite them to return again as often as they wish and to practice at home for maximum relaxation benefits.

Helpful resources:
- A good example of an abbreviated progressive muscle relaxation and body scanning exercise can be found at Simon Fraser University's website: http://students.sfu.ca/health/healthpromotion/yourhealth-videoandaudio.html (Trudeau & Horwitz, 2011).
- A transcript of a progressive muscle relaxation exercise can be found in Davis, Eshelman, and McKay (2008).
- A transcript and audio example of a body scanning exercise can be found in Williams, Teasdale, Segal, and Kabat-Zinn (2007).

Activity 3: Mindfulness Training

1. Encourage participants to find a good area where they can stretch out and get comfortable. Provide a brief introduction similar to that of the first activity.
2. During the first 5 minutes after the introduction, help participants begin taking deep belly breaths. Have them notice that with deep breathing their stomach will go up and down rather than just their chest.

3. Once participants are breathing deeply, begin the mindfulness exercises by encouraging them to count to 5 as they breathe in as well as when they breathe out. Once participants appear to have established a rhythm with their breathing, state that you want them to focus on the breath as the air moves through their nostrils.

4. Have them focus on the breath as it goes down the back of their throat. Gradually continue to have them focus on different bodily sensations that the breathing elicits. The main purpose of this exercise is to help participants become very focused on the present and here-and-now sensations.

5. Direct participants to become aware of any sensations in their body where they are feeling tension or tightness. Encourage them to breathe into that spot (e.g., shoulder or knee). Allow participants to be in that experience for a while by having them feel the breath going up their spine or to the top of their head. Have them then return to focusing exclusively on their breathing rather than other bodily sensations.

6. Allow them to be in silence for 5 minutes as they continue focusing on their breaths. Gently state that some of them may find that thoughts or images intrude, and guide them to practice letting these thoughts or images go by again focusing on breathing. If they are having physical sensations they can practice breathing into those points on their body. During this time, pay attention to the participants and incorporate what you see into the training. For example, if you notice clenched muscles, gently encourage participants to breathe into those points and release the tension.

7. During the final 15 minutes, gently bring participants back to a state of alertness. Ask them about their experience. This can help them develop a way of speaking to themselves so that they can use mindfulness in the future. State that they can use this activity to stay in the present. However, emphasize that it is important to practice every day so that they can use the techniques effectively in times of stress or anxiety or when they experience intrusive thoughts or images. Encourage them to practice daily for 5 minutes in the morning and 5 minutes in the evening.

Helpful resource:
*   *Calming Your Anxious Mind* (Brantley, 2007).

References

Amada, G. (2005). Book review: College of the overwhelmed: The campus mental health crisis and what to do about it. *Journal of College Student Psychotherapy, 19*(4), 71–77.

American College Health Association. (2008). American College Health Association–National College Health Assessment spring 2007 reference group data report (abridged). *Journal of American College Health, 56,* 469–479.

Brantley, J. (2007). *Calming your anxious mind: How mindfulness and compassion can free you from anxiety, fear, and panic.* Oakland, CA: New Harbinger.

Davis, M., Eshelman, E. R., & McKay, M. (2008). *The relaxation and stress reduction workbook* (6th ed.). Oakland, CA: New Harbinger.

Mayo Clinic. (2010). *Video: Need to relax? Take a break to meditate.* Retrieved from http://www.mayoclinic.com/health/meditation/MM00623

Owens, J., & Rodolfa, E. (2009). Prevention through connection: Creating a campus climate of care. *Planning for Higher Education, 37*(2), 26–33.

Pinkerton, R., Talley, J. E., & Cooper, S. L. (2009). Reflections on individual psychotherapy with university students: What seems to work. *Journal of College Student Psychotherapy, 23,* 153–171.

Stone, G., & Archer, J. (1990). College and university counseling centers in the 1990s: Challenges and limits. *The Counseling Psychologist, 18,* 539–607.

Trudeau, C., & Horwitz, E. (2011). *Your health: Video and audio* [Audio recording]. Retrieved from http://students.sfu.ca/health/healthpromotion/yourhealth-videoandaudio.html

Williams, M., Teasdale, J., Segal, Z., & Kabat-Zinn, J. (2007). *The mindful way through depression: Freeing yourself from chronic unhappiness.* New York, NY: Guilford Press.

Chapter 32

Ayeli:
A Native American–Based Group Centering Technique for College Students

Michael Tlanusta Garrett, Michael D. Brubaker, Edil Torres Rivera, Dennis E. Gregory, and Cyrus R. Williams

"The center of the universe is everywhere."
—Black Elk, Oglala Lakota
medicine man

• • •

Many helping professionals use centering practices to promote healing, focus, and even physical performance. Often these involve meditative techniques in conjunction with breathing techniques to enable a person to become more mindful (Shapiro, Rucker, & Robitshek, 2006). Cole (2003) recognized centering as one of the five primary healing principles used in ritual therapy. In her model, centering is practiced by eliminating distracting forces so that one may focus on the divine or supernatural forces to promote healing. Sport psychologists have also recognized the benefits of centering and have promoted centering techniques for improving mental focus and physical balance among athletes (Rogerson & Hrycaiko, 2002).

Other centering practices are less meditative and more relational in nature, as they promote awareness and a sense of being grounded. Garrett and Garrett (2002) adapted the Native American principle of Ayeli as a centering technique to help an individual "orient, reorient, and honor one's relation to things" (p. 154) to increase wellness in his or her everyday life. *Wellness*, according to Hatfield and Hatfield (1992), is "a process that involves . . . striving for balance and integration in one's life, adding and refining skills, [and] rethinking previous beliefs and stances toward issues as appropriate" (p. 164). In Native American terms, this means walking the path of Good Medicine (living a good way of life) in harmony and balance (through the harmonious interaction of mind, body, spirit, and natural environment) with all our relations (with all living beings with whom we are connected; Garrett & Garrett, 1996, 2002).

Group Outreach Plan

After obtaining consensus for the need for the Ayeli technique and establishing the groundwork, take the following steps to implement the intervention:

1. Clear the way. Initiate the technique by letting the group know that it involves freedom of movement and so a space will need to be cleared. This might mean needing to rearrange chairs or any other objects to create an open, clear space in the room in the form of a circle where participants can move freely. This is also an opportunity for the group to claim the space as sacred. You may suggest that members use the act of clearing space as a way to clear their minds in order to be present with their inner selves and those around them. You may state that this space is not designed to be religious; rather, it is to be sacred, or set aside for an intentional purpose. Have the students engage in an imagining of the circle that they are preparing to enter, and have them locate this imagined space where they are safe and surrounded by those who support them.
2. Once the space is clear, invite the group members to reflect inwardly and share outwardly if they wish concerning what creates balance and harmony in their lives. You may suggest that group members consider not only where they feel weak or find deficits but also where they are gifted or have strengths. Family support, determination, good friends, awareness, or a successful career are examples that may be identified as strengths. You may also suggest that, as in traditional Native American ceremonies, participants may wish to bring a medicine bag (imagined in this case) that contains a gift that can be offered to the group. Such gifts could be similar to the aforementioned strengths or could even be imagined objects that represent something important to the participant.
3. Invite the group members to join in a circle while standing, then identify and briefly describe the four directions discussed in Handout 32.1 (a compass can be helpful if the group is unsure of these points in relation to the actual space). If possible and desirable, the group may step outside to orient itself to the natural surroundings as would be done in a traditional Native way before returning to the setting in which the group actually resides—this also could serve as another way of clearing the mind, heart, and body, especially through a deep breath, prayer, saying, quietness, or whatever else participants may want to do while there.

4. Based on the description of the directions and Handout 32.1, ask members to consider which direction is most salient for them in their lives currently and have them physically move to that direction:
   - *East (belonging—representing Spirit):* Where do you belong (or not belong)? Who is your family/clan/tribe/community?
   - *South (mastery—representing Natural Environment):* What do you do well? What do you enjoy doing?
   - *West (independence—representing Body):* What are (the sources of) your strengths? What limits you?
   - *North (generosity—representing Mind):* What do you have to offer? What do you need to receive?

5. Once members have moved to their direction and have had a chance to share with the group why they chose that direction, use the following additional questions to process:
   - How have you embraced or distanced yourself from this direction?
   - Who in your life represents the characteristics of this direction, and what is your relationship to them?
   - What images come to mind when you think about the meaning of this direction?
   - How has your relationship with this direction affected your connection to the other directions?

6. Once group members have had a chance to process their individual directions, it could be helpful to explore the relationship of the directions to one another as represented by the issues and experiences described by members in those directions.

7. Ask who would like to go ahead and move to the center of the circle as a way of beginning to explore his or her experience with finding balance between the four directions in his or her own life journey. This then serves as centering. As with the traditional way, it could be mentioned that to ask permission of the group to enter the circle would be considered respectful of the group and one's surroundings. Any one member of the circle may be invited to the center to give voice to their experience.

8. Guide the volunteer around the circle to respond to the questions read by each of the four directions. Ask the group member closest to that direction to read the question associated with that circle point found on Handout 32.1.

9. Once the center participant has responded to these questions, ask him or her to return to the center, to face north, and to reflect on where he or she is currently in his or her life. Then ask this member to visualize the axis between east and west (based on the symbolic meaning of those directions and the answers that the participant provided to specific questions for those directions) and to physically shift left to right along that axis to a place that represents his or her current state of balance between those two directions. Then ask the member to face east and shift himself or herself on the north–south

axis. The resulting spot in the circle now represents where the center is currently in the person's life.

10. Ask the student to repeat Steps 7–9, focusing on where he or she would like to be—that is, the ideal center. Now that the member has a physical and symbolic representation of his or her current center and ideal center with the resulting space in between, a natural next step for both the individual and the group is to explore ways for that individual to "get from here to there," so to speak. A final step in this process is to offer thankfulness, in whatever way the group chooses, for one another, for any helpers (seen or unseen), for the many connections that make members who they are, and for the gift of life itself.

11. As the student explores his or her plan of movement to center, you may encourage him or her to engage the group. For example, using the group as a resource, he or she can think through what kinds of things are possible given the ideal center that he or she is seeking and the kinds of choices that he or she would need to make to be able to move to that ideal center.

12. As a part of the closing of the group, encourage students to reflect on what gift they brought with them into the circle and what new gift they have found in their imagined medicine bag that they may be taking away from the circle to share with others in a positive, healing way. Of course, some gifts are not realized until after students leave the group. You should also remind the students that the circle is representative of the Circle of Life and that this circle is present wherever they go. You should help the members be aware that the centeredness that they seek is always within them and can be accessed at any time they choose; they should not be afraid to ask for the support and guidance they may need from trusted persons in various contexts of their lives.

Note: A word on *respectful implementation*. For non-Native group counselors, the choice to use Ayeli should be based on the intent to use a technique that provides healing for group participants in very universal ways, drawing upon cultural practices or beliefs of Native people. It should not be based on the intent to represent themselves as "healers" in a Native tradition, to conduct Native ceremonies, or to make Indians out of group participants. Thus, intention is the key to respectful implementation.

References

Cole, V. L. (2003). Healing principles: A model for the use of ritual in psychotherapy. *Counseling and Values, 47,* 184–194.

Garrett, J. T., & Garrett, M. T. (1996). *Medicine of the Cherokee: The way of right relationship.* Santa Fe, NM: Bear.

Garrett, J. T., & Garrett, M. T. (2002). *The Cherokee full circle: A practical guide to ceremonies and traditions.* Rochester, VT: Bear.

Hatfield, T., & Hatfield, S. R. (1992). As if your life depended on it: Promoting cognitive development to promote wellness. *Journal of Counseling & Development, 71,* 164–167.

Rogerson, L. J., & Hrycaiko, D. W. (2002). Enhancing competitive performance of ice hockey goaltenders using centering and self-talk. *Journal of Applied Sport Psychology, 14,* 14–26.

Shapiro, J., Rucker, L., & Robitshek, D. (2006). Teaching the art of doctoring: An innovative medical student elective. *Medical Teacher, 28,* 30–35.

Handout 32.1

Medicine Circle Representing the Four Directions

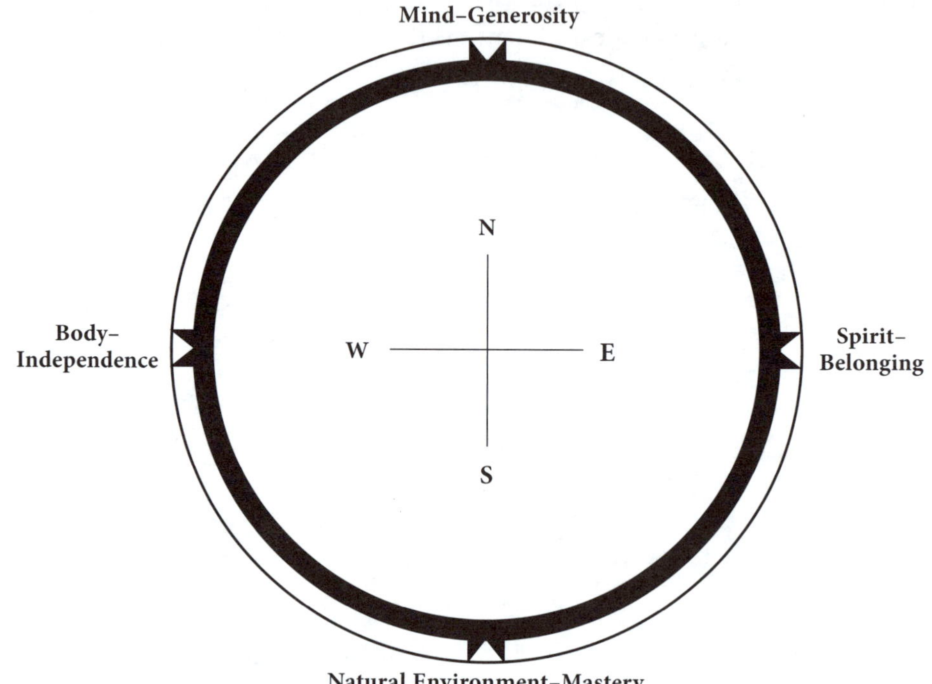

East (belonging—representing Spirit):
Where do you belong (or not belong)?
Who is your family/clan/tribe/community?

South (mastery—representing Natural Environment):
What do you do well? What do you enjoy doing?

West (independence—representing Body):
What are (the sources of) your strengths? What limits you?

North (generosity—representing Mind):
What do you have to offer? What do you need to receive?

Chapter 33

Overview of Psychological Disorders for Faculty and Staff Development

Jennifer L. Marshall and Trey Fitch

Success in college has been linked to both cognitive and noncognitive factors (Chickering & Reisser, 1993). Most college faculty members feel comfortable with the intellectual components but are confused or apprehensive when faced with student mental health concerns. For example, a normally conscientious student misses a test while receiving treatment for problems such as depression or panic attacks. How does the faculty member balance the need for support with the desire to hold all students accountable to the same expectations? In addition, many students seek help from faculty in times of distress. How do teachers give support without becoming counselors? The outreach program described here is designed to educate college faculty about the mental health concerns of their students. Faculty will learn about various disorders, treatment, and reacting to students in distress.

College counselors can help faculty by providing training in mental health disorders and the nature of treatment in the college setting. Counselors also can inform teachers about how to support students in distress while maintaining appropriate boundaries. This training reviews disorders in the *Diagnostic and Statistical Manual of Mental Disorders, Fourth Edition, Text Revision* (*DSM–IV–TR;* American Psychiatric Association, 2000), reports from college counselors on the problems they treat (Stone, Vespia, & Kanz, 2000), the nature of treatment, and ways for reacting to students. The presentation engages the audience by using discussion questions, examples, and vignettes and by reserving time for questions and answers. The format is designed for a one-time 60-minute outreach program, but it can be broken down into two or three shorter sessions. It could also be adapted for a brown bag format or exhibit table.

Group Outreach Plan

1. When you introduce yourself, provide your educational and counseling background and related professional licenses. In one sentence express the purpose of this outreach program, and tell participants the topics you will address and the objectives of the program. After the introduction, provide a personal example of how faculty have to work with student mental health issues (e.g., a student comes to class intoxicated or has a panic attack during a classroom presentation).

2. Provide information about the location of the counseling center, its hours, staff qualifications, and any related fees (if applicable). Tell the faculty about other outreach programs that are available and how to schedule them. Counseling services will be discussed in detail later in this program.

3. Review the nature of assessment and the components of the initial counseling meeting. Explain to the faculty how the *DSM–IV–TR* (American Psychiatric Association, 2000) is used to classify and organize mental disorders. If possible, bring a copy for faculty to view and clarify that diagnosis can only be done by a licensed mental health professional. Give a brief description of the five-axis diagnosis. Provide a sample five-axis diagnosis. Although faculty do not need a working knowledge of assessment, it is helpful if they understand the process from the counselor's perspective.

4. Highlight the multimethod approach to assessment in counseling. Summarize the importance of the diagnostic interview, screening tools (depression and anxiety inventories), and the symptoms checklist. Provide an example of a depressed student who is interviewed about the history of the problem, completes a depression inventory, and then outlines his or her symptoms of depression (using a checklist or the *DSM–IV–TR*).

5. Review common symptoms that students exhibit. These include both physical and emotional components (see Handout 33.1). Discuss with the faculty that mental health disorders are classified into general categories. For example, mood disorders include major depression, bipolar disorders, and dysthymia, which will be discussed later. For each disorder, provide a clinical example or ask the participants for an example they have seen from a student.

6. Discuss the fact that in a study of university counseling centers, 97% reported that they treat adjustment disorders (Stone et al., 2000). Many students who come into the counseling center are dealing with adjustment issues. These issues might revolve around, for example, social, academic, and/or family issues. Students with adjustment issues might show some symptoms of anxiety and depression; however, these symptoms are related to a change within their lives.

7. Discuss the fact that in a study of university counseling centers, 90% reported that they treat anxiety disorders (Stone et al., 2000). These

include generalized anxiety disorder, which is free-floating anxiety; panic disorder, which includes panic attacks; and phobias, which include test anxiety or speech anxiety. Discuss the fact that 87% of counseling centers reported treating mood disorders (Stone et al., 2000). Mood disorders include major depressive disorder, which includes hopelessness/helplessness, chronic sadness, and suicidal ideation; dysthymia, which includes more minor symptoms of major depression that tend to be more long lasting in nature; and bipolar disorders, which include dramatic shifts in mood from mania to depression.

8. Explain to participants that eating issues range from stress-induced eating to starvation and/or purging. Highlight the fact that anorexia and bulimia nervosa can be life-threatening disorders and may require specialized care.

9. Review the differences between substance abuse and dependence, and provide some examples of stimulants, depressants, opiates, and hallucinogens. Stress that treatment often occurs in many cycles and that these problems often overlap with other mental health disorders such as depression and anxiety.

10. Communicate to the participants that creating an identity is a major psychological task for teenagers and young adults, and many college students have concerns about gender identity and gay/lesbian/bisexual/ transgender issues. Note that gay/lesbian/bisexual/transgender students have an elevated risk of depression and suicidal ideation (Russell & Joyner, 2001). Relate information about any support groups that are available on your campus.

11. Summarize personality disorders as rigid and inflexible characteristics that are chronic and pervasive throughout every aspect of the individual's life. Describe borderline personality disorder, highlighting emotional volatility, self-injurious behaviors, self-hatred, and risk-taking behaviors.

12. Relate to the participants that although schizophrenia is rare (1% of the general population is affected; American Psychiatric Association, 2000), it is probably the most debilitating mental illness. Report the symptoms of poor concentration, delusions, hallucinations, and bizarre behaviors. Highlight the fact that schizophrenia often begins in late adolescence or young adulthood. Emphasize the importance of antipsychotic medication and taking such medication as prescribed.

13. Emphasize that most research suggests that most therapy models are equally effective (Prochaska & Norcross, 2003). Factors such as client motivation and type of disorder are strong predictors of treatment success.

14. Explain how counselors help students identify and change destructive thinking and behavior patterns. Discuss the interdependence between thoughts and behaviors and how counselors try to identify the underlying meaning of the thought.

15. Explain that brief therapy helps students break patterns and identify strengths. Give the example of someone who has lost his or her keys

walking back and forth through the house looking in the same places over and over again. Remind them that the definition of *insanity* is doing the same thing but expecting different results. For example, sometimes therapy can be effective simply because it helps break harmful patterns.

16. Tell the participants that many counselors believe that if students understand why they are having a problem, then many symptoms will start to be relieved. Regardless of whether it is insight into the unconscious or insight for self-awareness, the common theme is understanding and internal change.

17. Emphasize to the faculty that they may be the first to become aware that a student is dealing with an issue, and if they can be open, patient, and willing to listen to the student, this can open the door for referrals.

18. Discuss boundary setting. Note that participants are not counselors and that they are not trained to handle mental health issues, but they can help by listening and referring.

19. Review services provided by the counseling center:
    - Individual therapy
    - Group therapy
    - Assessment
    - Crisis management
    - Consultation
    - Referral

References

American Psychiatric Association. (2000). *Diagnostic and statistical manual of mental disorders* (4th ed., text rev.). Washington, DC: Author.

Chickering, A. W., & Reisser, L. (1993). *Education and identity* (2nd ed.). San Francisco, CA: Jossey-Bass.

Prochaska, J., & Norcross, J. (2003). *Systems of psychotherapy: A transtheoretical analysis* (5th ed.). Pacific Grove, CA: Thompson.

Russell, S. T., & Joyner, K. (2001). Adolescent sexual orientation and suicide risk: Evidence from a national study. *American Journal of Public Health, 91,* 1276–1281.

Stone, G. L., Vespia, K. M., & Kanz, J. E. (2000). How good is mental health care on college campuses? *Journal of Counseling Psychology, 47,* 498–510.

Handout 33.1

Overview of Psychological Disorders for Faculty and Staff Development

Introduction

- Counseling center overview
- Location
- Hours
- Eligibility for services and fees, if applicable
- Contact information for referrals and consultation

Physical and Cognitive Signs

- Complaints about sleep or sleeping through class
- More frequent illnesses
- Disruptive behaviors, such as harassing other students or faculty
- Changes in concentration
- Abrupt change in grades or attendance

Emotional Signs

- Agitation, such as frequent arguing and complaining
- Low tolerance for stress
- Frequent crying
- Becoming too emotionally attached to, or totally detached from, teachers
- Extreme nervousness about performance

What Happens When a Student Seeks Counseling?

- Counseling begins with an interview to assess the problem.
- The student will be asked about symptoms, history, and overall functioning.
- A book called the *DSM–IV–TR* is often used to categorize problems.
- Counselors also might use screening tools to measure different disorders such as depression.

Types of Disorders

- More than 90% of counseling centers work with adjustment problems and anxiety problems (Stone, Vespia, & Kanz, 2000).
- 87% work with mood disorders (Stone et al., 2000).
- Only 28% work with schizophrenia and psychosis (Stone et al., 2000).
- Adjustment disorders involve reactions to changes in life, such as a breakup, loss of friend, and so on.
- Anxiety disorders include generalized anxiety disorder (free-floating anxiety), panic disorder (panic attacks), phobias (test anxiety), and others.

- Mood disorders include major depressive disorder, bipolar disorders, and dysthymia.
- More than half of centers report working with eating disorders, substance abuse, personality, and gender issues (Stone et al., 2000).

Student Examples

- Julio is a high-achieving and thoughtful student. Late in the quarter he disappears for several days. He says he took a 72-hour road trip and planned on staying up 2 days straight to catch up on classes. What disorder does this seem like, and how would you react?
- Wendi is very inconsistent with her school performance, wavering from As to Fs within a quarter. Some days she is very active, and other days (often Mondays) she is very withdrawn and fatigued. What disorder does this resemble, and how would you react? Be specific.

Therapies

- Brief therapy: focuses on finding immediate solutions using student strengths
- Cognitive behavior therapy: develops awareness of negative thinking and reactions to situations
- Insight therapies: students gain deeper awareness of underlying issues and improve self-concept

What Can You Do?

- Observe changes in personality or performance.
- State your concern directly, saying, "I am worried because . . ."
- Provide support without becoming a counselor.
- Provide a reference: Role play five ways to word this as a group.

What Can We Do?

- Assess the issue and refer, if necessary.
- Provide brief individual counseling services.
- Provide group counseling, if appropriate.
- Respond to crisis.
- Consult with you about student issues.
- Provide training.

References

Stone, G. L., Vespia, K. M., & Kanz, J. E. (2000). How good is mental health care on college campuses? *Journal of Counseling Psychology, 47,* 498–510.

Chapter 34

Outreach for College Students Related to Mood and Anxiety Management

*Janice Delucia-Waack, Deepti Athalye,
Kelly Floyd, Mandy Howard, and
Sarah Kuszczak*

College students experience more distress than the general population (Stewart-Brown et al., 2000). College students have to adapt to academic demands, prepare for their careers, and adjust to and balance new social roles (Bayram & Bilgel, 2008; Vaez & Laflamme, 2008). These challenges and demands may increase pressure, which places students at risk for developing anxiety symptoms. Successful coping with stress and anxiety is essential for college students' mental health.

One manifestation of ongoing stress and anxiety is rumination (Trapnell & Campbell, 1999), which predicts depression (Nolen-Hoeksema & Morrow, 1991) and social dysfunction (Morrison & O'Connor, 2005) in college students. Therefore, helping students to reduce their ruminations may help decrease their social problems and reduce the likelihood of depression, which may in turn reduce suicidal ideation and suicide attempts.

Perfectionism can be a positive attribute if individuals set realistic standards for themselves, derive pleasure from their efforts, and are capable of choosing to be less precise in some instances; however, perfectionism can also be problematic when individuals set excessively high standards of performance, find their efforts to be unsatisfactory, and are unable to relax their standards (Hamachek, 1978). Hewitt and Flett (1991) identified three types of perfectionism: self-oriented, socially prescribed, and other oriented. Self-oriented perfectionists possess a strong motivation to be perfect, set unrealistic standards for themselves, and focus on their flaws. Socially prescribed perfectionists and other-oriented perfectionists, in contrast, focus on interpersonal dimensions. For example, socially pre-scribed perfectionists believe others hold unrealistic standards for them, fear negative social evaluation, and have a strong need for social approval; other-oriented perfectionists hold unrealistically high standards for others.

Perfectionism has also been described in terms of adaptive and maladaptive features (Slaney, Rice, Mobley, Trippi, & Ashby, 2001). Adaptive features associated with perfectionism include higher self-esteem, resourcefulness, and enthusiasm (Flett, Hewitt, Blankstein, & Koledin, 1991; Hart, Gilner, Handal, & Gfeller, 1998). Perfectionistic objectives, however, become self-defeating or maladaptive when individuals are unable to differentially apply standards and accept being less than perfect (Lundh, 2004). Maladaptive perfectionism relates to low self-esteem and depression in college students (Ashby & Rice, 2002).

In college students, coping styles such as active coping, planning, and positive reinterpretation and growth are correlated with optimism and high self-esteem. These coping styles also correlate with hardiness, which diminishes the adverse effects of stress (Carver, Scheier, & Weintraub, 1989). Hardy individuals are active copers and tend not to engage in denial and avoidance. Coping styles such as denial, behavioral disengagement, and mental disengagement are negatively correlated with optimism and self-esteem. Denial and behavioral disengagement are negatively correlated with hardiness but positively correlated with anxiety. Gil (2005) found that risky sexual behavior in college students was significantly correlated with an avoidant coping style, which is a maladaptive style of coping.

The purpose of the chapter is to describe an outreach program that emphasizes coping skills to manage stress and reduce anxiety focusing on maladaptive thoughts (perfectionism and rumination). A cognitive be-havioral model is used, as it focuses on the identification of behaviors and cognitions that are helpful in alleviating negative mood and anxiety. Based on this model, alternative cognitive strategies and behaviors are suggested.

Group Outreach Plan

This outreach program is designed to be implemented in one or two time blocks totaling 3 hours. An outline follows of the major topics and inter-ventions, with details provided in the handouts.

Group Plan: One 3-Hour Session or Two 1½-Hour Sessions

1. Provide group introductions and key concepts using the outline below. Introduce yourself and your professional background. (10–15 minutes)

    Review ground rules for the session:
    - Be honest with yourself.
    - Share when you feel comfortable.
    - Please don't share outside of this session what other students have shared.

Identify general goals for this outreach session:
- To identify strengths and areas to work on to improve mood and decrease anxiety and stress.
- To teach coping strategies and intervention strategies.

Briefly introduce members:
- Ask members to say their name and a feeling word that describes how they are feeling right now that also starts with the first letter of their last name.

2. Briefly assess areas to focus on. (20 minutes)
   - Explain to the group members that they will take a few minutes to assess their strengths and areas to potentially develop.
   - *Rumination.* Ask students to use the 10-item self-report Response Styles Questionnaire (Handout 34.1; Davis & Nolen-Hoeksema, 2000) and discuss their tendency to ruminate and the types of rumination they use as reviewed in "Reflection" and/or "Brooding" (Handout 34.2).
   - *Perfectionism.* Have students go to the following website (http://www.bbc.co.uk/science/humanbody/mind/surveys/perfectionism/) and complete the questions or use a similar online assessment of perfectionism.
   - *Anxiety/stress.* Have students use a stress scale such as the Perceived Stress Scale (Cohen, Kamarck, & Mermelstein, 1983) to determine the general amount of stress they have been experiencing lately. A copy is available at http://www.mindgarden.com/products/pss.htm.
   - *Coping styles.* Coping styles may be identified using the Brief COPE (Carver, 1997; see http://www.psy.miami.edu/faculty/ccarver/sclBrCOPE.html). The Brief COPE is a 28-item self-report inventory that includes 14 different coping styles: self-distraction, active coping, denial, substance use, use of emotional support, use of instrumental support, behavioral disengagement, venting, positive reframing, planning, humor, acceptance, religion, and self-blame.

3. Facilitate a discussion of the assessment results and then set goals for this session. State that the students have 3 hours: What do they most want to get out of this? What do they want to learn and change? Ask members to briefly share goals based on where they scored on these scales relative to mean scores. Help them to be specific and concrete.

4. Lead the group through the following interventions. (30 minutes)
   - *Seated meditation (Nhat Hanh, 2003).* Sit with your spine relatively straight but comfortable. Eyes may remain open or closed, but the gaze should be at about a 45° angle toward the floor. Sit quietly noticing your breath, not trying to change or alter it in any way. As you notice thoughts, don't try to push them away or engage in them; rather, just notice the thoughts and return to focusing on your breathing. The mind is very active, and thoughts will recur. Again, just notice that you are having a thought

and gently return your focus to your breath. Do this exercise for 10 minutes. As you develop a meditation practice, you will find yourself more able to notice and let go of thoughts. The important element is to practice this skill daily.

- *Mindfulness exercise.* Sit with your spine relatively straight but comfortable. Eyes may remain open or closed, but the gaze should be at a 45° angle toward the floor. Clench one hand into a fist; keep the other hand relaxed. Draw your attention first to your relaxed hand. Notice what it feels like, and notice any thoughts or feelings that you associate with that hand. Then turn your attention to your clenched hand. Again, notice what it feels like and any thoughts or feelings that you associate with that hand. Alternate your focus from hand to hand, noticing the sensations, thoughts, and feelings associated with each for about 5 minutes. This exercise helps individuals learn that they can be in a state of relaxation and tension simultaneously and often are much of the time.

5. Review the benefits and problems of perfectionism using the following points. (30 minutes)
   - Give definitions of perfectionism, and discuss when it is adaptive and when it is maladaptive (Handout 34.3).
   - Interventions: Use the Perfectionism and Self-Talk activity outlined in Handout 34.4.
   - Other possible strategies (Handout 34.5).

6. Discuss how to reduce anxiety using the following information. (30 minutes)
   - Self-care—eating right, getting enough sleep and exercise.
   - Ask, "What are the roadblocks to effective self-care? What can you do about these?"
   - Time management—put study/work schedules on a calendar, keep track of assignments.
   - Break long and complex assignments or tasks down into smaller, more manageable ones.
   - Relaxation techniques—do a few of them in the session (see Handout 34.6).
   - Some ways to relieve stress and anxiety do not work for everybody. Ask students to share how they have tried to reduce stress, what has worked, and what has not.

7. Review coping styles using the following information.
   - Definitions (see Handout 34.7).
   - Interventions (see Handout 34.8).

8. Summarize and integrate the information. Ask members what they have learned. For example, "We have discussed a lot of possible strategies today. What are three things you heard that might be helpful or sounded interesting?" Ask whether members can identify silently or out loud how they might use one of these strategies. (30 minutes)

- *What was most helpful today?* Say, for example, "It is helpful for us as group facilitators to know what is most helpful for you so as we do these workshops we can make sure we include certain topics and interventions. In addition, different people learn differently and utilize different strategies, so it is useful for you to take a minute and identify what has been most helpful for you. Please share out loud or in writing what has been helpful. Thanks."

References

Ashby, J. S., & Rice, K. G. (2002). Perfectionism, dysfunctional attitudes, and self-esteem: A structural equations analysis. *Journal of Counseling & Development, 80,* 197–203.

Bayram, N., & Bilgel, N. (2008). The prevalence and socio-demographic correlations of depression, anxiety and stress among a group of university students. *Social Psychiatry and Psychiatric Epidemiology, 43,* 667–672.

Carver, C. S. (1997). You want to measure coping but your protocol's too long: Consider the Brief COPE. *International Journal of Behavioral Medicine, 4,* 92–100.

Carver, C. S., Scheier, M. F., & Weintraub, J. K. (1989). Assessing coping strategies: A theoretically based approach. *Journal of Personality and Social Psychology, 56,* 267–283.

Cohen, S., Kamarck, T., & Mermelstein, R. (1983). A global measure of perceived stress. *Journal of Health and Social Behavior, 24,* 385–396.

Davis, R. N., & Nolen-Hoeksema, S. (2000). Cognitive inflexibility among ruminators and nonruminators. *Cognitive Therapy and Research, 24,* 699–711.

Flett, G. L., Hewitt, P. L., Blankstein, K. R., & Koledin, S. (1991). Dimensions of perfectionism and irrational thinking. *Journal of Rational-Emotive & Cognitive Behavior Therapy, 9,* 185–201.

Gil, S. (2005). Personality traits and coping styles as mediators in risky sexual behavior: A comparison of male and female undergraduate students. *Social Behavior and Personality, 33*(2), 149–158.

Hamachek, D. E. (1978). Psychodynamics of normal and neurotic perfectionism. *Psychology, 15,* 27–33.

Hart, B. A., Gilner, F. H., Handal, P. J., & Gfeller, J. D. (1998). The relationship between perfectionism and self-efficacy. *Personality and Individual Differences, 24,* 109–113.

Hewitt, P., & Flett, G. (1991). Dimensions of perfectionism in unipolar depression. *Journal of Abnormal Psychology, 100,* 98–101.

Lundh, L. (2004). Perfectionism and acceptance. *Journal of Rational-Emotive & Cognitive Behavior Therapy, 22,* 255–269.

Morrison, R., &. O'Connor, R. C. (2005). Predicting psychological distress in college students: The role of rumination and stress. *Journal of Clinical Psychology, 61,* 447–460.

Nhat Hanh, T. (2003). *Creating true peace: Ending violence in yourself, your family, your community, and the world.* New York, NY: Free Press.

Nolen-Hoeksema, S., & Morrow, J. (1991). A prospective study of depression and posttraumatic stress symptoms after a natural disaster: The 1989 Loma Prieta earthquake. *Journal of Personality & Social Psychology, 61,* 115–121.

Slaney, R., Rice, K., Mobley, M., Trippi, J., & Ashby, J. (2001). The revised almost perfect scale. *Measurement and Evaluation in Counseling and Development, 34,* 130–145.

Stewart-Brown, S., Patterson, J., Petersen, S., Doll, H., Balding, J., & Regis, D. (2000). The health of students in institutes of higher education: An important and neglected public health problem? *Journal of Public Health Medicine, 22,* 492–499.

Trapnell, P. D., & Campbell, J. D. (1999). Private self-consciousness and the 5-factor model of personality: Distinguishing rumination from reflection. *Journal of Personality & Social Psychology, 76,* 284–304.

Vaez, M., & Laflamme, L. (2008). Experienced stress, psychological symptoms, self-rated health and academic achievement: A longitudinal study of Swedish university students. *Social Behavior & Personality, 36,* 183–196.

Handout 34.1

Response Styles Questionnaire

People think and do many different things when they feel depressed. Please read each of the items below and indicate whether you almost never, sometimes, often, or almost always think or do each one when you feel down, sad, or depressed. Please indicate what you generally do, not what you think you should do.

		1 *almost never*	2 *sometimes*	3 *often*	4 *almost always*
1.	I think "What am I doing to deserve this?"	1	2	3	4
2.	I analyze recent events to try to understand why I am depressed.	1	2	3	4
3.	I think "Why do I always react this way?"	1	2	3	4
4.	I go away by myself and think about why I feel this way.	1	2	3	4
5.	I write down what I am thinking about and analyze it.	1	2	3	4
6.	I think about a recent situation, wishing it had gone better.	1	2	3	4
7.	I think "Why do I have problems other people don't have?"				
8.	I think "Why can't I handle things better?"	1	2	3	4
9.	I analyze my personality to try to understand why I am depressed.	1	2	3	4
10.	I go someplace alone to think about my feelings.	1	2	3	4

Scoring

Reflection = sum of Items 2, 4, 5, 9, and 10
Brooding = sum of Items 1, 3, 6, 7, and 8

Reflection captures the contemplative and coping aspects of rumination. Brooding captures anxious and pessimistic recurrent thoughts.

Higher scores indicate more recurrent thinking of the rumination type reflected by that subscale. Mean scores within a healthy sample were 10 for both Reflection and Brooding (Treynor, Gonzalez, & Nolen-Hoeksema, 2003).

References

Treynor, W., Gonzalez, R., & Nolen-Hoeksema, S. (2003). Rumination reconsidered: A psychometric analysis. *Cognitive Therapy & Research, 22,* 247–259.

Handout 34.2

Definitions of Rumination

- *Rumination* is conscious and recurrent thinking that has an instrumental theme and that occurs without being triggered by an environmental cue. Rumination is also easily triggered because of its connection to goals that are important to the individual (Martin & Tesser, 1996). Most clinicians tend to think of rumination as maladaptive in that people focus on negative emotions and their meaning without resolving their problem or decreasing their anxiety (Michael & Snyder, 2005). Several types of rumination have been identified (Treynor, Gonzalez, & Nolen-Hoeksema, 2003), including the following:
  - *Reflection*—Contemplation that is neutrally valenced and engaged in as an attempt to solve problems. An example is analyzing recent events to try to understand why you are depressed.
  - *Brooding*—Anxious or pessimistic "moody pondering." An example is thinking thoughts such as "Why do I have problems other people don't have?" or "Why can't I handle things better?"
  - *Depressive rumination*—Recurrent depression-related thoughts. An example is thinking about how sad you feel.
  - *Reflection* is thought to be more instrumental and related to more successful problem solving. Both brooding and depressive rumination are associated with depression and maladaptive thoughts and behaviors (Treynor et al., 2003).

References

Martin, L. L., & Tesser, A. (1996). Some ruminative thoughts. In R. S. Wyer (Ed.), *Ruminative thoughts: Advances in social cognition* (Vol. 9, pp. 1–47). Hillsdale, NJ: Erlbaum.

Michael, S. T., & Snyder, C. R. (2005). Getting unstuck: The roles of hope, finding meaning, and rumination in the adjustment to bereavement among college students. *Death Studies, 29,* 435–458.

Treynor, W., Gonzalez, R., & Nolen-Hoeksema, S. (2003). Rumination reconsidered: A psychometric analysis. *Cognitive Therapy & Research, 22,* 247–259.

Handout 34.3

Perfectionism—Adaptive or Maladaptive

Adaptive Perfectionists

Adaptive perfectionists derive satisfaction from achievements resulting from intense efforts but also tolerate imperfection without resorting to the harsh self-criticism characteristic of maladaptive perfectionists (Hamachek, 1978).

Maladaptive Perfectionists

Maladaptive perfectionists never seem to evaluate achievement as good enough and always believe that they should do better (Hamachek, 1978). Stoltz and Ashby (2007) suggested that maladaptive perfectionists

- view the environment as competitive and approach relationships with a more aggressive demeanor;
- perceive a need to control the environment and develop negative attitudes when events do not match their plans;
- experience heightened sensitivity for environmental feedback; and
- perceive the environment as unpredictable, unfair, or dangerous.

References

Hamachek, D. E. (1978). Psychodynamics of normal and neurotic perfectionism. *Psychology, 15,* 27–33.

Stoltz, K., & Ashby, J. S. (2007). Perfectionism and lifestyle: Personality differences among adaptive perfectionists, maladaptive perfectionists, and nonperfectionists. *Journal of Individual Psychology, 63,* 414–423.

Handout 34.4

Perfectionism and Self-Talk

1. **Self-Talk:** My paper must be perfect.

    a. Cognitive Distortion: (What happens if my paper is not perfect?)

    b. Restructured Thought:

2. **Self-Talk:** I have to appear perfect in the eyes of my friends.

    a. Cognitive Distortion: (What if my friends see my imperfections?)

    b. Restructured Thought:

3. **Self-Talk:** I cannot answer the professor's question incorrectly in class.

    a. Cognitive Distortion: (What will happen if you are wrong?)

    b. Restructured Thought:

4. **Self-Talk:** I have to do well on this exam.

    a. Cognitive Distortion: (What if you do not do well on the exam?)

    b. Restructured Thought:

What other negative self-talk and cognitive distortions do you possess?

1.

2.

3.

How can you restructure these thoughts?

1.

2.

3.

Handout 34.5

Strategies for Overcoming Perfectionism

Do not procrastinate

Problem: Believing every detail must be perfect can result in procrastination, which can make a task seem even more overwhelming.

Remedy: Break large tasks down into smaller assignments. Concentrate initially on producing ideas, and later focus on refining the specifics.

Show your weaknesses

Problem: No one is perfect, and pretending to be so only masks who you truly are and prevents you from connecting with others.

Remedy: Revealing your imperfections demonstrates your authenticity, results in better interpersonal connections, and decreases anxiety. Imagine you are very nervous about an important interview, and another applicant begins discussing her anxiety with you prior to a group interview. As a result, you may feel more connected to the person, and you both will probably feel less anxious about your interviewing skills.

Recognize the shades of gray

Problem: Exclusively viewing actions or answers in terms of black and white (right and wrong) increases anxiety; the truth is that there are usually multiple solutions to most problems.

Remedy: Accept the ambiguity inherent in most tasks. If you wanted to do your job perfectly, you could choose a monotonous job that provides little stimulation. Instead, you challenge yourself by stepping outside your comfort zone. View this as an accomplishment in itself!

View mistakes as an opportunity for learning

Problem: Successful people did not begin their careers at the top.

Remedy: Making mistakes results in learning. Admired doctors, for example, become well known because they accumulate a lot of knowledge through seeing what has not worked with patients in the past. Being afraid to make mistakes will only prevent you from accomplishing your goals, whereas embracing the learning that results from mistakes can improve your competence.

Broaden the ways in which you evaluate yourself

Problem: Putting conditions of worth on performance results in greater anxiety, which can stifle creativity in work and negatively impact relationships.

Remedy: Identify what you value most about yourself. Then list the characteristics of the people in your life whom you admire and compare the two lists. Generally speaking, we admire others for qualities we rarely acknowledge or appreciate in ourselves.

Handout 34.6

Short Relaxation Techniques

Great for when you only have a few minutes!

REMEMBER: Preventing stress is as important as stopping it. Practice these techniques as often as possible, even when you are not stressed.

Correct Breathing: Learn to always breathe using the diaphragm. Let the breath reach the bottom of the lungs, and let the chest and shoulders relax. High, shallow chest breathing is stressful and gives messages of stress to the brain.

Three-Part Breathing: Take a deep diaphragmatic breath and imagine the lungs divided into three parts. Visualize the lowest part of the lungs filling with air; the chest should remain relatively still. Imagine the middle part of the lungs filling; visualize the rib cage expanding. Visualize the upper part filling with air as your shoulders rise slightly and move backward. Exhale fully and completely; drop your shoulders, feel your rib cage contract, and force every last bit of air from the bottom of the lungs. Repeat.

Stretching: Gently roll your head and shoulders many times a day. Also, gently stretch other areas of the body that may need it.

Tense–Relax Muscles: Tighten the muscles you want to relax and *feel the tension.* Let the muscles become loose and limp and *feel the relaxation.*

Body Scan: With your mind, briefly scan every muscle in your body from your toes to the top of your head. Release any tension with a relaxing diaphragmatic breath. Correct your posture and relax all the muscles that are not being used.

Jaw Drop: Be aware of any tightness in your jaw. Allow your jaw to loosen by separating your teeth.

Heaviness and Warmth in Hands and Arms: Relax your body and consciously feel heaviness in your arms and hands. *Imagine warmth flowing into them.* Imagine and experience your shoulders, arms, and hands becoming heavy, relaxed, and warm.

Mind-Quieting Meditation: Begin by focusing on your breathing. Use a special phrase that helps you focus on relaxation, and quiet your mind.

Attitudes and Perceptions: Pay attention to your perceptions and attitudes. Allow yourself to put a stress-reducing "frame" around the stressor. Remember, stress affects the body based on your perceptions of the outside world. *Do not see a snake when it is only a garden hose.*

Handout 34.7

Coping Styles

Carver, Scheier, and Weintraub (1989) outlined a variety of positive and negative strategies for coping. These strategies include

- Active coping
- Planning
- Suppression of competing activities
- Restraint coping (waiting for the right moment to react)
- Seeking social support
- Focusing on and venting emotions
- Mental disengagement (a negative reaction using distractions and avoidance activities)
- Positive reinterpretation and growth
- Denial
- Acceptance
- Religious coping

Rate yourself in each area on a scale of 1 to 10, where 10 means that you use that method frequently.

References

Carver, C. S., Scheier, M. F., & Weintraub, J. K. (1989). Assessing coping strategies: A theoretically based approach. *Journal of Personality and Social Psychology, 56,* 267–283.

Handout 34.8

Coping Skills Activity

Seeking Instrumental and Emotional Support

- Form groups of three or four individuals.
- Each group member comes up with a hypothetical or experienced stressful situation.
- Talk to your group members and find out how each of them would deal with the situation.
- Share your emotions and fears with other group members, and provide feedback to others.
- Combine the strategies of all of the members to come up with the best way of handling the stressor: The strategy should involve behavior, emotion, and thinking that may be adaptive in the situation.

Positive Reinterpretation

Initial Negative Emotional Reactions to Stress	Initial Negative Thoughts and Fears	*Evidence Seeking:* How threatening is this situation? What's the worst that can happen?	New Positive View of the Situation

Responding to a Death on Campus

Brian Van Brunt, Ron Rountree,
Debra Crisp, and Perry Francis

"Healing or grief is a journey, not a destination.
The journey into our healing asks us to weave our losses into
the fabric of our lives."

—Author unknown

• • •

One of the more unpleasant tasks facing college counselors is responding to a campus death or tragedy. Cintron, Weathers, and Garlough (2007) suggested that university administrators, faculty, and students do not anticipate facing death on campus, although Iserson and Bollet (1999) estimated that between 6,000 and 22,000 students die every year on campuses. Responding to a student death involves a variety of tasks, including providing compassion to those who are grieving, supporting administrative efforts to contact families and the community, normalizing the feelings of those left behind, and facilitating the remembrance of those who have died.

A wide range of grief and emotions can follow a death. Any response to a student death on campus should start with the assumption that everyone has his or her own grieving process. Some students want to talk. Others want to avoid contact. Some avoid class and work. Others find the distractions helpful. Attention should also be paid to the fact that the death of a student often violates the assumptions that students hold. David Elkind (1976), in his extension of Piaget's model of cognitive development, wrote about the personal fable. The personal fable points to the uniqueness and invincibility of those in adolescence through much of early adulthood (Schwartz, Maynard, & Uzelac, 2008). A death on campus may awaken thoughts of mortality in a group that had no such awareness before this crisis. As a result, the university's response needs to be flexible. This flexibility may include providing information to professors and other professionals who do not deal with such intense emotion and existential angst on a daily basis.

In times of crisis, offices may isolate themselves, limit communication with other offices, and develop separate reactions based on their respective expertise (e.g., counseling services may offer a support group, the dean's office may draft a campus-wide e-mail, the public relations office may address the press, and resident assistants may hold floor meetings). These are all important functions; however, it is also important to have a coordinated response among the departments of student affairs and academic affairs and various other departments that become involved. The motto "We can accomplish more working together than working alone" should be the central theme when responding to loss and grieving. Not only does this approach gather needed resources (such as fiscal budgets and staff/faculty time), it also allows for community members to become involved in the response process and allows friends of the deceased to feel that something is being done campus-wide to signal the importance of the event. These are all important parts of the grieving process.

Group Outreach Plan

1. Introduce yourself and explain the goals of the program. Say to the group, "Start with yourself. Are you ready to help students? Why are you helping? (Is it for you or them?)" Explain that if a counselor is experiencing intense grief as well, he or she may not be ready to help students. Above all else, do no harm.
2. Review the following tips for helping those who are grieving (see Handout 35.1).
   - History shows us that people can cope and people can suffer.
   - Talk less, say more (listening is doing).
   - People need repetition (this lets the information sink in and become real).
   - Moderate eye contact (sometimes constant direct eye contact can be overwhelming).
   - Maintain a reasonable space between yourself and the person.
   - Avoid using "I," "We," or "They" . . . focus on "You."
   - Talk less, say more—yes, again!
   - Stimulate talking with repeating and agreeing.
   - Avoid reassurances, promises, and other lies.
   - Expect and allow all emotions.
   - Avoid the temptation to find a rational reason or solution—some things won't be explained.
3. Know the signs of depression and grieving.
   - Assess students for signs of depression, such as intense sadness, crying, guilt, sleep problems, irritability, and isolation.

- Know how to refer and when to refer; review the campus process for referrals.
- The only way out is through; you can't skip over, can't rush it
4. Discuss negative patterns of helping.
    - Review these negative patterns of helping:
        - *The teller:* "Here is what you are going through . . ."
        - *The thinker:* "Let me give you a rational analysis of why you feel bad . . ."
        - *The feeler:* "Let me cry on you and tell you how bad I feel."
        - *The stealer:* "Look how sensitive I am, I am helping you."
        - *The cheerleader:* "I am so afraid of pain I will not let you hurt. Let's go to Wal-Mart."
        - *The martyr:* "I will be strong for you; I will do everything for you so you can heal."
    - Ask the group how they think students will react to these statements.
5. Note that as helpers, counselors should educate students on the following themes:
    - *Normalization.* People's bodies and minds become overwhelmed in certain traumatic incidents. Individuals react differently to trauma, and treatment needs to provide general information and unique individual interventions. Likewise, appropriate treatment should focus first on students, faculty, and staff being empowered to help one another. Counseling and professional support should be focused on education and passing abilities, not attempting to conduct therapy on those affected.
    - *Information.* In times of crisis, a central location, person, or building should be identified as a safe place to obtain information and to gather to reflect and receive support. Multiple media channels should be used (e-mail, voicemail, intercampus mail, on-campus meetings and services, classroom talks, support groups, memorial events) to reach the maximum number of students. Efforts should be made to include those people important in students' lives. These may include parents, professors, religious figures, staff, and coaches.
    - *Follow-up.* Perhaps the most important piece of crisis response is the establishment of follow-up services and aftercare. As with the 9/11 tragedy, an outpouring of services almost always immediately follows a tragic event. Yet many times symptoms develop weeks and months after the tragedy. Education, support, and communication with those directly affected by the event is an essential part of the crisis response.
6. Review these basic needs that students have when grieving (see Handout 35.1).
    - *A need to talk about it.* A person's first need after a tragedy is information. Unfortunately, during a crisis there is limited information and many rumors. People instinctively share what

they do know with others in an attempt to gather information and try to make sense of it.

- *Concerns about safety.* Students naturally want to distance themselves from a tragic occurrence. This may be difficult to accomplish, as they often see the similarities between themselves and the victims. When a traumatic event such as a fatal car accident occurs, it is natural for students to wonder about their own safety and to be concerned about a similar incident affecting them or their loved ones.
- *Worries and fears.* Students pay closer attention to the news. Most will be much more vigilant about the possible dangers in their community. Some may become apprehensive going about their daily lives. Hypervigilance is stressful and tiring.

7. Keep these key concepts in mind when offering help.
   - *Give students an opportunity to process the experience.* Give your students time to deal with these experiences. Find a balance between acknowledging the obvious tragedy and returning to a sense of normalcy. If you set aside time for students to describe their reactions and to discuss the aftermath of the tragedy, they will be better able to turn to the work at hand. There are many ways to grieve—try to avoid expectations of a pattern.
   - *Be a good example.* Be especially calm, show your concern, and emphasize the positive by offering appropriate reassurances and reminders of safety. By your manner, you will be setting a powerful example of how students can manage their reactions in a productive way.
   - *Notice students who might be struggling.* If your students have had serious losses, such as the death of a loved one or a trauma of their own, or if they are a survivor of a school shooting, they may need more help. Refer them to a professional if they are having extreme reactions to the shooting, such as repeated nightmares, flashbacks, crying spells, behavior problems, and panic reactions.

References

Cintron, R., Weathers, E., & Garlough, K. (2007). *College student death: Guidance for a caring campus.* Lanham, MD: University Press of America.

Elkind, D. (1976). *Child development and education: A Piagetian perspective.* Oxford, England: Oxford University Press.

Iserson, K., & Bollet, A. J. (1999). *Grave words: Notifying survivors about sudden, unexpected deaths.* Tucson, AR: Galen Press.

Schwartz, P., Maynard, A., & Uzelac, S. (2008). Adolescent egocentrism: A contemporary view. *Journal of Adolescence, 43,* 441–448.

Handout 35.1

Grief and College Campuses

While processing grief, you will likely

- Experience a higher susceptibility to illness
- Experience the "zombie effect," in which feelings shut down your body's natural coping mechanism
- Have difficulty thinking clearly or remembering things, as if your brain is "scrambled"
- Experience continuous crying or an overflow of emotions
- Hold on to emotions, being unable to cry and instead bottling things up (they will come out years later)
- Stay extremely busy to avoid time to think
- Drink too much alcohol or take drugs
- Have difficulty falling or staying asleep
- Sigh and daydream
- Talk about the death over and over
- Lose interest in work, home life, or physical appearance
- Engage in self-criticism
- Feel as if there is a huge hole in your soul
- Think you will never recover from your loss
- Suffer from severe depression (external feelings of sadness or anger)
- See no reason to exist or carry on with daily tasks
- Have problems coming to terms with the reality of what has happened

Grief is . . .

- anything and everything you feel, think, and do following a loss
- a normal and healthy process that your body, gut, or heart knows how to do but your mind may try to fight
- individual and situational; it is not the same for everyone, only you can define why you grieve and how you grieve
- a process that will scare you, anger you, sadden you, numb you, excite you, and heal you
- something none of us knows how to do on our own

Grieving . . .

- will not hurt you, make things worse, or make you crazy
- means not fearing what you feel, but deciding what you will do with your feelings
- takes as long as it takes

Rules for grieving

- Make a point to eat and sleep even if you are not hungry or tired.

- Keep up your daily routine as much as possible.
- Don't compare yourself to others; this is your grief.
- Take time to be by yourself if you need it, but don't isolate yourself.
- Don't think alcohol, drugs, food, sex, or spending money will help.
- Decide how you will remember the person you have lost; begin to write the story you will tell about him or her to others.

How to cope with grief

- Talk to family and friends
- Read poetry or books
- Seek spiritual support
- Join a support group
- Be patient with yourself
- Engage in social activities
- Exercise
- Eat good foods
- Seek counseling
- Listen to music
- Let yourself feel the grief
- Take time to relax
- Seek time with pets (Calvin and Hobbes "fuzz" therapy)
- Reconnect with friends and loved ones

How to support others with grief

- Ask about their feelings
- Just sit with them and be a good listener
- Ask about their loss
- Make telephone calls
- Let them feel sad
- Do not minimize their grief
- Share your feelings
- Remember the loss
- Acknowledge the pain
- Be available when you can

Chapter 36

Suicide on College Campuses

Suzanne L. Dunn

The transition period through adolescence to young adulthood can be a very tumultuous time. Young people experience physical changes as well as mental and emotional changes. Striking a balance between individuating versus maintaining family connectedness creates stress. Belongingness becomes an issue when students matriculate out of high school and into college, leaving behind childhood friends and classmates. Finding new cohorts and meeting intimacy versus isolation needs are at the forefront for many students. These along with the stressors of meeting new academic requirements, working, and living independently create a challenge for the average college student.

Some students find this to be a very difficult time in their lives and may not be able to handle the stressors. For them, thoughts of suicide may be present, especially if there have been losses in their lives due to the death of a family member or the suicide of a family member or another contact (Pirelli & Jeglic, 2009). Suicide ranks as the number three cause of death among 15- to 24-year-olds (Brener, Hassan, & Barrios, 1999; Garlow et al., 2008). Given the lower rate of violent deaths among college-age students, suicide is the number two cause of death for this population (behind motor vehicle accidents; Drum, Brownson, Denmark, & Smith, 2009). The death rate from suicide increased from 5.6 per 100,000 college students in 1980 to 9.9 per 100,000 in 2006 (Westefeld et al., 2006). The highest rates of 9.1 and 11.6 per 100,000, respectively, occur among female and male graduate students older than 25 (Drum et al., 2009). Although most students want to be at college and making the necessary maturational moves, there is increased stress and subsequent depression if students are attending college to meet someone else's expectations and not their own (e.g., if the student is in college because of a family requirement, if the school was selected as part of a family tradition, if the student has an undetermined life purpose, or if college is serving as a place for experimentation; Westefeld et al., 2006).

Group Outreach Plan

1. Have the audience take the Suicide Among College Students pretest (Handout 36.1) and discuss their responses.
2. Explain that the transition period through adolescence to young adulthood can be a very tumultuous time. Review the following factors that relate to stress for young adults.
   - Physical changes
   - Mental and emotional changes
   - Striking a balance between individuating versus maintaining family connectedness
   - Leaving behind childhood friends and classmates
   - Finding new cohorts
   - Intimacy versus isolation needs
   - New academic requirements
   - Working and living independently
3. Summarize and discuss the nature of suicide in college campuses.
   - Stress causes thoughts of suicide, especially if there have been losses in students' lives due to death of a family member or the suicide of a family member or another contact (Pirelli & Jeglic, 2009).
   - Suicide ranks as the number three cause of death among 15- to 24-year-olds (Brener et al., 1999; Garlow et al., 2008; Manza & Sher, 2008).
   - The following are common risk factors for suicide (Furr, Westefeld, McConnell, & Jenkins, 2001; Schwartz & Friedman, 2009; Westefeld et al., 2006):
     - A history of suicide attempts
     - A pattern of substance use or abuse
     - A history of physical or sexual abuse
     - Feelings of helplessness or hopelessness
     - A history or diagnosis of depression
     - A highly creative nature
     - Financial difficulties
     - Loneliness
     - Relationship problems or a lack of support
4. The following factors that help students adapt to changing circumstances are also helpful in protecting them from engaging in suicidal behaviors:
   - Reason for living
   - Feelings of responsibility
   - Future plans
   - Religious or moral objections
   - Social supports from family or the college

- Extracurricular activities (Westefeld et al., 2006)
- Participation in sororities, fraternities, and team sports (Miller & Hoffman, 2009)

5. Summarize and discuss multicultural factors that relate to suicide on college campuses, and highlight the role of the campus in addressing issues of isolation, discrimination, and stress.
   - Latino and Hispanic students deal with acculturation issues as well as the transition from family and community to college. Acculturative stress contributes to risks of suicide in African, Asian, and Latin American international students (Walker, Wingate, Obasi, & Joiner, 2008).
   - The risk factors for suicide identified for Euro-Americans do not hold for African Americans. Most suicides among African Americans occur when the individuals are younger and are less predictable (Walker et al., 2008).
   - Native Americans have a suicide rate 1.9 times the national average (Muehlenkamp, Marrone, Gray, & Brown, 2009).
   - "Historical trauma" is a risk factor for suicide. It includes intergenerational distressors such as group genocide, torture, and cultural marginalization (Muehlenkamp et al., 2009).
   - Students who have worked to preserve their connections to their cultural heritage have a decreased risk of suicide (Muehlenkamp et al., 2009).

6. Review ideas for supporting students and identifying at-risk students. Emphasize the role that the entire campus community plays in prevention and intervention. Tell the group the following:
   - Introduce the counseling support provided on campus to all students. Specify where the student counseling center is located, what it offers, and how to access the center. (Teachers can do this in class, student affairs professionals during orientation, and others through conversations with students.)
   - If you notice warning signs but there seems to be no immediate risk, make a referral to the counseling center by giving the student the phone number of and directions to the counseling center. (Role play specific ways to give a referral as a group.)
   - If the student is in crisis, stay with him or her until help arrives.
   - Never leave someone alone if he or she appears suicidal. For example, do not leave the person alone to go get help. Have him or her come with you, or call for assistance.
   - Contact the security office and/or the counseling center.
   - Help connect the student with a support person, friend or family, to provide social support during the crisis.
   - Keep brochures and posters in common areas that describe the warning signs of depression and suicide.
   - Even though in most cases there is no attempt, take all suicidal remarks seriously.

References

Brener, N. D., Hassan, S. S., & Barrios, L. C. (1999). Suicidal ideation among college students in the United States. *Journal of Consulting and Clinical Psychology, 67,* 1004–1008.

Drum, D. J., Brownson, C., Denmark, A. B., & Smith, S. E. (2009). New data on the nature of suicidal crises in college students: Shifting the paradigm. *Professional Psychology: Research and Practice, 40,* 213–222.

Furr, S. R., Westefeld, J. S., McConnell, G. N., & Jenkins, J. M. (2001). Suicide and depression among college students: A decade later. *Professional Psychology: Research and Practice, 32,* 97–100.

Garlow, S. J., Rosenberg, J., Moore, J. D., Haas, A. P., Koestner, B., Hendin, H., & Nemeroff, C. B. (2008). Depression, desperation, and suicidal ideation in college students: Results from the American Foundation for Suicide Prevention college screening project at Emory University. *Depression and Anxiety, 25,* 482–488.

Manza, N., & Sher, L. (2008). Preventing alcohol abuse and suicidal behavior among college students. *The Royal Australian and New Zealand College of Psychiatrists, 42,* 746–747.

Miller, K. E., & Hoffman, J. H. (2009). Mental well-being and sport-related identities in college students. *Sociology of Sport Journal, 26,* 335–356.

Muehlenkamp, J. L., Marrone, S., Gray, J. S., & Brown, D. L. (2009). A college suicide prevention model for American Indian studies. *Professional Psychology: Research and Practice, 40,* 134–140.

Pirelli, G., & Jeglic, E. L. (2009). The influence of death exposure on suicidal thoughts and behaviors. *Archives of Suicide Research, 13,* 136–146.

Schwartz, L. J., & Friedman, H. A. (2009). College student suicide. *Journal of College Student Psychotherapy, 23,* 78–102.

Walker, R. L., Wingate, L. R., Obasi, E. M., & Joiner, T. E., Jr. (2008). An empirical investigation of acculturative stress and ethnic identity as moderators for depression and suicidal ideation in college students. *Cultural Diversity and Ethnic Minority Psychology, 14*(1), 75–62.

Westefeld, J. S., Button, C., Haley, J. T., Kettmann, J. J., Macconnell, J., Sandil, R., & Tallman, B. (2006). College student suicide: A call to action. *Death Studies, 30,* 931–956.

Handout 36.1

Pretest: Suicide Among College Students

Mark each statement below as *true* (T) or *false* (F).

☐ T ☐ F 1. More women than men commit suicide.

☐ T ☐ F 2. Suicide is the number three killer of adolescents and young adults.

☐ T ☐ F 3. African Americans have the second highest incidence of suicide.

☐ T ☐ F 4. "Historical trauma" has been identified as a risk factor for Native Americans.

☐ T ☐ F 5. College-age youth experiencing transition from adolescence to adulthood have few stressors.

☐ T ☐ F 6. Suicide rates among young adults have decreased steadily over the past decade.

☐ T ☐ F 7. College is the time when age-related psychological illnesses or disorders may appear.

☐ T ☐ F 8. Attending a major university is more stressful than attending community college.

☐ T ☐ F 9. Normalizing students' use of mental health facilities assists in facilitating their access.

☐ T ☐ F 10. All faculty and staff should be aware of the need for suicide prevention.

☐ T ☐ F 11. Acculturative stress contributes to the risk of suicide in African, Asian, and Latin American international students.

☐ T ☐ F 12. Native Americans have a suicide rate 1.9 times the national average.

☐ T ☐ F 13. Locating the student counseling center in an easily accessible and visible area is not helpful in normalizing its presence or its use by students.

☐ T ☐ F 14. Students who have a history of suicide attempts, who have or develop a pattern of substance use or abuse, who have a history of physical or sexual abuse, or who have feelings of helplessness or hopelessness may be at risk for suicide.